TRACKS and TRAILCRAFT

TRACKS and TRAILCRAFT

A Fully Illustrated Guide to the Identification of Animal
Tracks in Forest and Field, Barnyard and Backyard

Ellsworth Jaeger

The Lyons Press
Guilford, Connecticut
An imprint of Globe Pequot Press

Special contents of the first Lyons Press edition
copyright © 2001, 2002

Originally published by the Macmillan Company, an imprint of
Simon & Schuster Inc., copyright © 1948.

The Lyons Press is an imprint of Globe Pequot Press.

Library of Congress Cataloging-in-Publication Data
is available on file.

ISBN 978-1-59921-804-5

Printed in the United States of America

10 9 8 7 6 5 4 3 2 1

ACKNOWLEDGMENTS

I am much indebted to the various zoos and circuses throughout the country, especially the Bronx Zoo, the Washington Zoo, the St. Louis Zoo, the Philadelphia Zoo, the Buffalo Zoological Gardens, Ringling Brothers Circus, Karl Hagenbeck Shows, Barnum and Bailey Circus and others, some of whom were unaware that the autobiographies of their various animals would some day appear in this volume.

I am especially indebted to the late Ernest Thompson Seton, the foremost authority on tracks and tracking, for his interest and help in this collection of tracks, as well as to R. Marlin Perkins, Director of the Lincoln Park Zoo, Chicago whose help and cooperation made it possible to secure a number of tracks illustrated in this volume.

I am deeply appreciative of the interest and aid of Prof. Albert R. Shadle, Head of the Department of Zoology of the University of Buffalo and of the cooperation of Prof. Ralph T. King and Prof. William M. Harlow of the New York State College of Forestry, Syracuse, New York.

To Dr. Carlos E. Cummings, Director of the Buffalo Museum and to Prof. William Prindle Alexander, Curator Emeritus of Adult Education of the above Museum, I am most grateful for their interest, inspiration and suggestions.

And to Dr. Clark Wissler, Curator of Anthropology, American Museum of Natural History, New York City, whose helpful letters and suggestions greatly aided in planning the chapter on "The Indian and His Tracking," I give my thanks.

The paleontological collections of the American Museum of Natural History, New York City, the Buffalo Museum of Science, the National Museum of Washington, D. C., and the kindly interest of Irving G. Reimann, Paleontologist and Prefect of Exhibits of the University of Michigan Museums, Ann Arbor have been of great help in preparing the chapter on "Fossil Tracks."

I am deeply appreciative of the aid on research given me by Miss Ruth A. Sparrow, Librarian, and Miss Clara K. Risch, Assistant Librarian of the Buffalo Museum of Science.

And last but not least, I am greatly indebted to the numerous birds, mammals, insects, reptiles and other wild folk who so helpfully made the tracks which made this book possible.

ELLSWORTH JAEGER
Buffalo Museum of Science
Buffalo, New York

INTRODUCTION

We are all acquainted with the work of the "G" men and their clever use of fingerprinting, but Nature too has a way of fingerprinting her children, be they beetles or elephants. Long before Scotland Yard or the F.B.I., Nature fingerprinted her numerous family wherever they went. She took their prints in sand, dust, mud and snow. Often the mud prints hardened into rock and thus Nature's records become permanent and on file, sometimes for millions of years. And so today scientists find print records of that "Public Enemy Number One" of the Mesozoic, the dinosaur.

But Nature's records go back even farther than that. In the Coal or Carboniferous Age, some three hundred million years ago, Nature took prints of the ferns and other vegetation of that period in the steaming swamp muds, and these we find today when we delve into Nature's coal files.

And buried deeper still in the earth's petrified pages are earlier tracks, not of living things but of raindrops, of mud cracks made by the blistering primeval sun and wave marks of a primordial sea, that disappeared perhaps long before life appeared upon the earth. Thus Nature's tracks may take us back to the earth's beginnings or give us a complete autobiography of a living animal as we follow its fresh trail from day to day.

CONTENTS

TRACKS and TRAILCRAFT

FOSSIL TRACKS

1

While the fresh track of a living animal is interesting, it is most fascinating to backtrack through the centuries for a million years or more and follow the trail of some giant dinosaur as he made his earth-shaking way. Fossil trails may even lead us to the earth's beginnings, when the simpler forms of living things existed and left imperishable tracks in primordial mud.

Backtracking Nature's Autographs. Sometimes these tracks and trails formed beautiful designs such as the flowerlike rosette made by some Paleozoic worm as shown in (A), Plate I. This design was perhaps created by the worm projecting part of its body from its burrow in different directions and then drawing it back. This action is shown in (B).

In the Pennsylvanian sandstone of Texas, strange gastropod tracks are found (C). The common living gastropod *Littorina* makes a trail duplicating these ancient marks except that the ridges along the center are not so steep. Even Triassic insects have left their trails for our modern eyes to follow (D). In the Upper Cambrian, sluglike animals lived and crept through ooze and mud, making tracks as in (E).

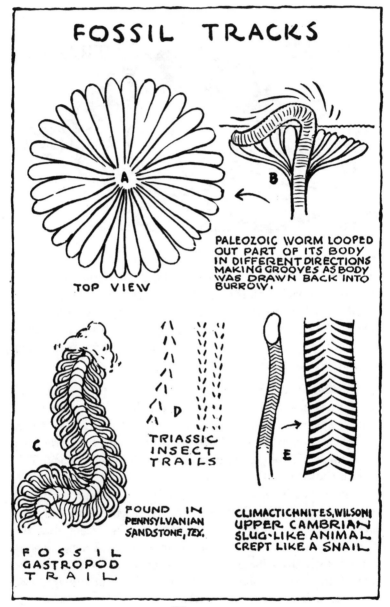

FOSSIL TRACKS

TOP VIEW

PALEOZOIC WORM LOOPED OUT PART OF ITS BODY IN DIFFERENT DIRECTIONS MAKING GROOVES AS BODY WAS DRAWN BACK INTO BURROW.

FOSSIL GASTROPOD TRAIL

FOUND IN PENNSYLVANIAN SANDSTONE, TEX.

TRIASSIC INSECT TRAILS

CLIMACTICHNITES, WILSONI UPPER CAMBRIAN SLUG-LIKE ANIMAL CREPT LIKE A SNAIL

Plate 1

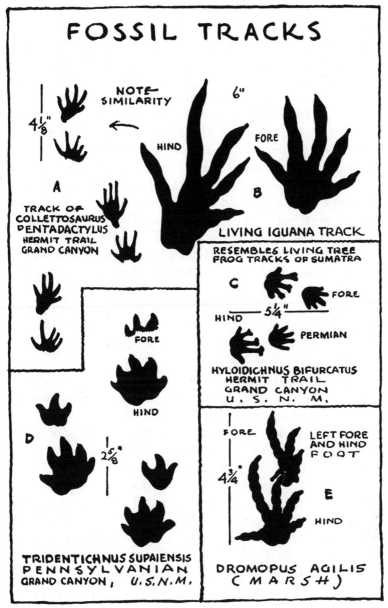

FOSSIL TRACKS

NOTE SIMILARITY

4⅛"

6"

HIND

FORE

A

TRACK OF COLLETTOSAURUS PENTADACTYLUS HERMIT TRAIL GRAND CANYON

B

LIVING IGUANA TRACK

RESEMBLES LIVING TREE FROG TRACKS OF SUMATRA

C

FORE

HIND

5¼"

PERMIAN

HYLOIDICHNUS BIFURCATUS HERMIT TRAIL GRAND CANYON U. S. N. M.

FORE

HIND

D

2⅝"

FORE

LEFT FORE AND HIND FOOT

4¾"

E

HIND

TRIDENTICHNUS SUPAIENSIS PENNSYLVANIAN GRAND CANYON, U.S.N.M.

DROMOPUS AGILIS (MARSH)

Plate 5

Those who have visited the Grand Canyon have no doubt seen the fossil tracks on Hermit and Bright Angel Trails. On the latter trail, for instance, strange tracks have been found, thought to be those of a Middle Cambrian trilobite. Hermit Trail in the Grand Canyon evidently served as a promenade for regular three-ring circuses and entire zoological gardens of animals in the fossil ages. There one can find the strangest collection of footprints perhaps ever assembled. Unfortunately there are no common names for many of these animals and it is difficult to say whether some were amphibians or reptiles. Some tracks like those of *Collettosaurus pentadactylus* (A), Plate 2, resemble the footprints of a living animal. In this case the similarity to the present living iguana (B) is so marked it would indicate that the fossil tracks might be those of a reptile. The drawings show a few of this strange collection of fossil autographs. One ancient stroller in the Permian muds was a batrachian of a walking type (C). Its strange bifurcated toes resemble those of a tree frog of Sumatra (*Rhacophorus maximus*). However, there is no relationship to the present-day frog. D and E on Plate 2 and the tracks (F to L) on Plate 3 also illustrate the footprints of creatures which disappeared countless ages ago.

As the Age of Reptiles came into its stride, the reptilian tracks of such as the dinosaurs and others increased in size until a single footprint sometimes measured a number of feet in width. The drawings show how the dinosaur tracks varied in shape. Recently on the Davenport Ranch in Bandera County, Texas, a whole runway was discovered showing numerous trails of that colossal creature, the brontosaurus, which often reached 70 feet in length and was thought to weigh some 30 tons. These trails are approximately 120 million years old. Since the brontosaurus frequented shallow water, marks left by his huge tail are seldom evident. At times only the tracks of the forefeet registered in the mud, indicating that the reptile was swimming (A) Plate 4.

Gradually the warm-blooded creatures began to attain su-

FOSSIL TRACKS

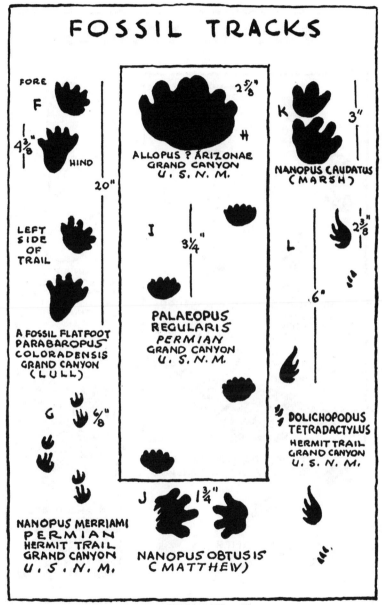

FORE
F

HIND

4⅜"

20"

ALLOPUS ? ARIZONAE
GRAND CANYON
U. S. N. M.

2⅝"

H

K

3"

NANOPUS CAUDATUS
(MARSH)

LEFT
SIDE
OF
TRAIL

I

3¼"

L

2⅜"

.6"

A FOSSIL FLATFOOT
PARABAROPUS
COLORADENSIS
GRAND CANYON
(LULL)

PALAEOPUS
REGULARIS
PERMIAN
GRAND CANYON
U. S. N. M.

G

⅝"

DOLICHOPODUS
TETRADACTYLUS
HERMIT TRAIL
GRAND CANYON
U. S. N. M.

NANOPUS MERRIAMI
PERMIAN
HERMIT TRAIL
GRAND CANYON
U. S. N. M.

J

1¾"

NANOPUS OBTUSIS
(MATTHEW)

Plate 3

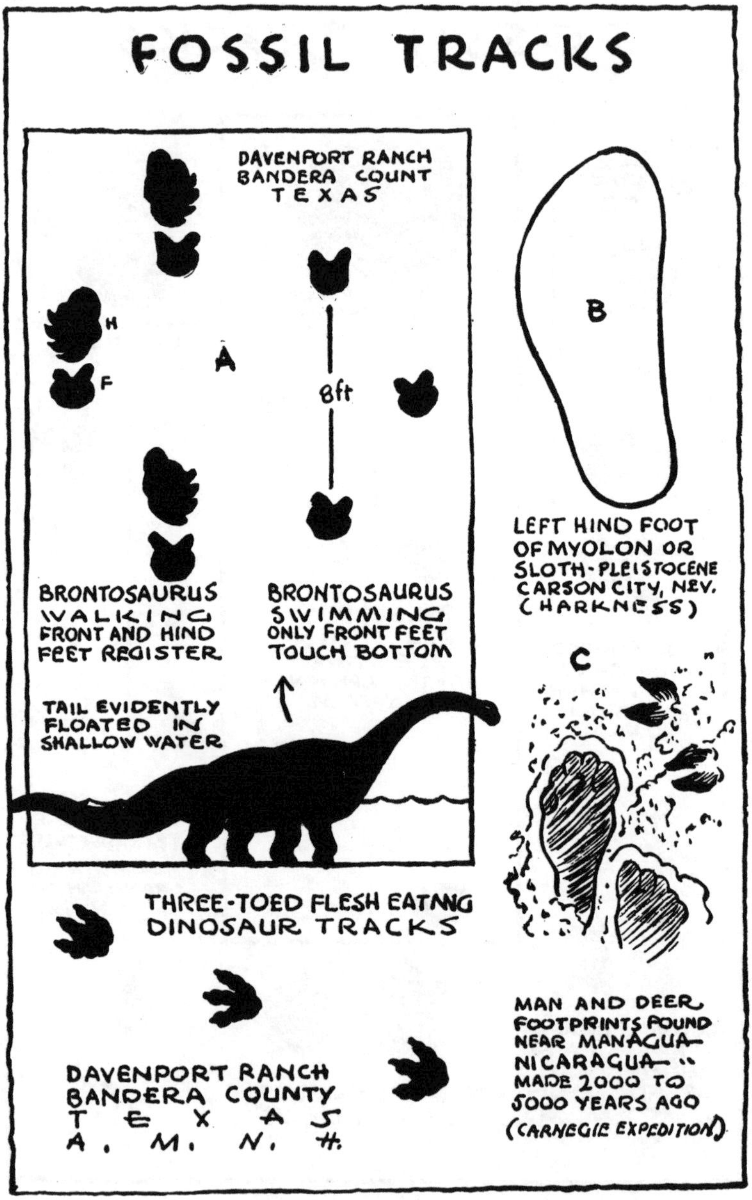

FOSSIL TRACKS

DAVENPORT RANCH
BANDERA COUNT
TEXAS

H
F
A
8ft

B

BRONTOSAURUS
WALKING
FRONT AND HIND
FEET REGISTER

BRONTOSAURUS
SWIMMING
ONLY FRONT FEET
TOUCH BOTTOM

LEFT HIND FOOT
OF MYOLON OR
SLOTH - PLEISTOCENE
CARSON CITY, NEV.
(HARKNESS)

TAIL EVIDENTLY
FLOATED IN
SHALLOW WATER

C

THREE-TOED FLESH EATING
DINOSAUR TRACKS

MAN AND DEER
FOOTPRINTS FOUND
NEAR MANAGUA-
NICARAGUA- "
MADE 2000 TO
5000 YEARS AGO
(CARNEGIE EXPEDITION)

DAVENPORT RANCH
BANDERA COUNTY
TEXAS
A. M. N. H.

Plate 4

premacy and their progress is indicated by their trails. Many of these wonder creatures lived and died leaving their footprints and their bones in the sands of time; the many-toed horse, the sabre-toothed tiger, the huge sloths and others. The sloth made strange tracks very like those of a huge moccasined foot as shown in the illustration (B).

One of the earliest evidences of human beings in Central America are the tracks of human feet together with some deer tracks found by the Carnegie expedition in Nicaragua at the outskirts of the city of Managua (C). These footprints are thought to be from 2000 to 5000 years old and were made in volcanic mud by men and deer fleeing some prehistoric eruption.

Thus a good tracker can follow Mother Nature's trail from the very beginning of time down through the ages.

THE INDIAN AND
HIS TRACKING
2

The Indian Tracker. Like Fenimore Cooper, numerous authors have pointed out and glorified the Indian's craft and lore, yet few have made an effort to describe this lore and pass it on. The Indian's expertness in trailing, for instance, is not a lost art of yesterday. Even today the woods Indians are past masters in this craft and follow the sometimes faint trail of their game through a hundred mystifying places. They can often tell at a glance what animal made the track, in which direction the animal went and how fresh is its trail. The signatures of hundreds of wood folk are easily identified by them, not by their tracks alone but by numerous other signs as well. The Indian tracker combines the acute senses of the animal together with the brain of man. He uses his eyes, his ears and even his nose, and when the trail disappears entirely, like Sherlock Holmes, he does some human detective work.

Trifling, unusual signs are spotted by the keen eyes of the Indian tracker. For instance, a dropping of dung, a rotten log ripped open, tuberous plants dug up, all read bear to a woods Indian.

In the shallows, where the underwater grasses are disturbed and plants are uprooted, these indicate moose to him, which may be verified by the large cloven hoof tracks in the mud of the shore. If the water is still muddied, the moose has left only recently.

Grey, matted, feltlike pellets with tiny particles of bone scattered in them tell of an owl's roosting place. Small, dark droppings of dung upon a log slanting into a stream or pond or a number of empty mussel shells are muskrat signs. Floating yellow pond lily roots marked by the teeth of a gnawing animal are beaver signs. Musky mud pies often tell the Indian tracker's nose of the beaver's presence when no other sign is near. Often fur or wool on trees or bushes reveal an animal's passing. Gnawed and gouged trees are bear trees, registering posts for all transient bears to sign. Strong smelling wallows in the autumn woods tell of the presence of an amorous bull moose.

These and hundreds of other trail signs are taught the woods Indian child from babyhood. The older men take the boys on numerous trips, calling attention to all the minute signs on the trail and to the strange ways of the wild. Thus through his formative years, the woods and trail become a part of the Indian youngster's life.

Trails Tell Tales. To the Indian tracker, the tracks and trails of both humans and animals are like an open book, revealing many details about the trailmaker unobserved by the average person. Age, sex, physical condition and many other facts are clearly registered in most trails.

The woods Indian and the white man of the city can easily be distinguished by their tracks. Our stiff leather shoes with heels and their extreme styles have in many instances deformed our feet and have altered our way of walking. We bring our heels down first and then rock forward to our toes. We also turn our feet outward. All of these combine in developing weak and fallen arches.

The Indian hunter must have strong nimble feet, which often feel their way along the trail. Indian moccasins allow the foot to retain its natural shape and fallen or deformed arches are seldom

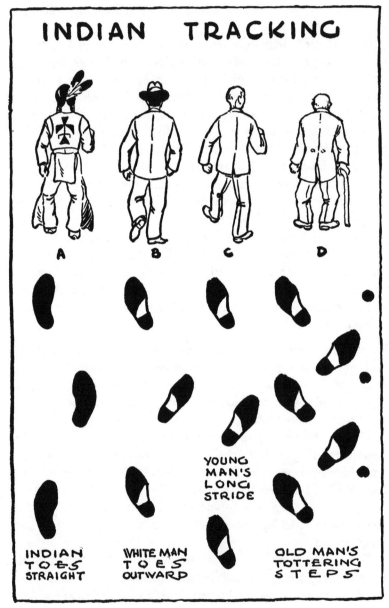

Plate 5

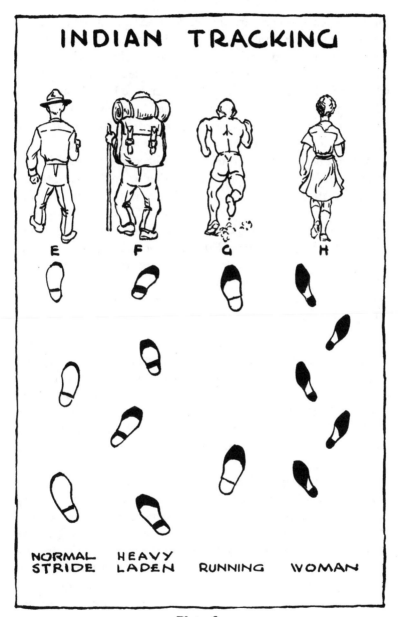

Plate 6

found. When you compare the track of an Indian with that of a white man, the straightforward stride of the Indian can be readily distinguished from the toeing-out so characteristic in the white man's track. The Indian stride is less fatiguing, covers more ground and also strengthens the arch. The moccasin literally keeps the Indian on his toes. The drawings (A) Plate 5, show the typical straightforward track of an Indian and the altered toeing-out track common to the white man (B).

Age can be detected in tracks. The purposeful long stride of a young man (C) can be easily distinguished from the short, tottering tracks of an old man (D). In ordinary walking, our heel and toe impression is almost of equal depth (E) Plate 6. A person carrying a heavy load makes a deep imprint and the right foot track at times is to the left of the left track (F), and vice-versa. The tracks of a running person are of course more widely spaced, form a straighter line and the toe prints are deeper (G). The slim, more delicate feminine footprint can easily be spotted whether it be shod or unshod (H).

Indian Tracking Tricks. In the old warlike days when many neighboring tribes were enemies, it was necessary to keep a vigilant watch at all times and to cover one's tracks. When actually pursued, utmost care was necessary so that no telltale tracks were left. Often false trails were made, such as running along stream banks and ending at the water's edge to lead pursuers to believe their quarry had jumped into the stream. The pursued then backtracked to hard ground.

In backtracking the Indian demonstrated his greatest skill, for a trained woodsman can tell tracks made by a person walking backward or forward. This is especially true in snow or soft earth, when great care must be taken so that the drag of the foot will not be in the wrong direction. Sometimes the Indians carried the feet of bear, wolves, horses, and used them to make tracks in the mud. The Catawba Indians were said by early explorers to be very clever at this. Some Indians in northern

INDIAN TRACKING

INDIAN
TRACKING
BOOTS

INDIANS OF
MANY TRIBES
WORE TRACKING
BOOTS MADE
FROM THE FEET
AND LEGS OF
LARGER ANIMALS

TARAHUMARA INDIAN TRACKING STICKS AND
BARK TRACKING SANDALS USED AS TOYS
WHICH FAMILIARIZED CHILDREN WITH THE
VARIOUS ANIMAL TRACKS AND TRAILS

Plate 7

Canada sometimes make a sort of moccasin boot of a bear's foot and leg (I) Plate 7.

In northern Mexico, the Tarahumara Indians, a large tribe north of Mexico City, have been little influenced by the Europeans. Living constantly in the out-of-doors and wandering over a wide area in search of food, pasturage and other living necessities, every track, dislodged pebble and every scratch is an important sign to them. They often hunt by persistent tracking and trailing until their wild game falls from exhaustion.

Tracking toys are made by these Indians to train their youngsters in the art of the trail. Hoofs of horses, burros, cattle and other animals are carved at the end of sticks which the children hold as they jump, making tracks in the soft earth (J) Plate 7. Sometimes sandals made of thick bark have animal tracks carved on the bottom of the soles. These too are used in making tracks in the earth or dust (K).

Indian Stalking. The purpose of an expert tracker is to get close to his game. In order to do this, a knowledge of stalking as well as tracking is necessary. The woods Indian is a past master in this art, since he has the infinite patience that is so necessary in dealing with the wilderness creatures. Many of the jungle fighters in the war, too, have learned some of the tricks employed in stalking.

When tracking animals, always test the wind to find its direction. Wild creatures depend upon the nose almost entirely to warn them of an enemy's approach. Hence it is necessary to come upon game in the direction where the wind is coming from the animal to you. At times it will be necessary to toss a bit of dust or a few grass blades in the air to discover the wind's direction (L) Plate 8. Again the air may be so quiet it will be necessary to wet a finger (M) and the wind's direction will be detected by the coolness.

Just as the animal's nose can detect a human's presence, so too can a tracking expert discover the doglike odor of a bear, the heavy smell of moose, a deer's musk or the reek of a fox. Most

Plate 8

animals give off trail odors. The deer and most of the cloven-hooved animals have scent glands located between the hooves. In addition the deer has quite a large scent gland located on each hind leg that exudes scent as the animal wanders through the brush and grass. These scent trails are touched upon in Chapter 3, however.

In stalking, be sure to keep out of sight of your game. However, where game is numerous and unafraid of man, many hunters casually walk close, being sure that the wind is in the right direction. In ordinary stalking, keep close to the earth (N) Plate 8. Never look over the top of a bush or a boulder. Get down in the undergrowth to one side of it. Beware of any movement of your shadow. Merge it with that of your cover. Wear clothing that blends with your background.

The Indians often wore the pelts of animals in stalking their enemies or game. Wolf skins were commonly worn by Plains Indian Scouts (O). Buffalo hunters often draped a buffalo robe over themselves and their horses (P) and allowed the horse to graze slowly toward the herd (see chapters on Stalking and Trailcraft in "Wildwood Wisdom," by the author). "Buffalo callers" wore heads and skins of buffalo and lured buffalo herds into traps with this disguise. Perhaps some form of scent lure was also used (Q). Many Indian tribes wore animal heads in stalking game. The Penobscots had a stalking hood with ears attached. The Pomo Indians of California wore a deer's head which was tied to the top of the head with tie straps. The Klamath of Oregon, too, used this disguise in stalking (R) Plate 8.

Indian Moccasin Tracks. Fenimore Cooper and others have romanticized the Indian's craft, and he and many other writers have described how Indians could tell at a glance at a moccasin track to what tribe the maker of the track belonged. While this statement may not be wholly true, nevertheless certain moccasin styles were so distinct as to be recognizable anywhere. For instance, the great Indian cultures of the woodland and plains were easily identified by their foot gear, for the former wore a soft sole moccasin (S) Plate 9, and the latter a hard sole (T), made of rawhide. Moccasins of the Apaches (U), Seminoles (V), and others also were easily recognized.

In a letter to me Clark Wissler, the noted Curator of Anthropology of the American Museum of Natural History, says, "I recall certain statements made to me by Indians to the effect that the identification of moccasin tracks was not due so much to the sole pattern as to secondary stylistic characteristics. One thing to look for was the presence or absence of a small trailer (or fringe) fastened to the heel of the moccasin. This might be a single piece, a pair of fringes or three or more. Such things were matters of style and would vary from year to year so that it was necessary to know the current style of a given tribe in order to identify its members by their tracks." The drawings show several moccasin types with the heel trailers or fringes attached. The Shoshone moccasin at one time had a broad flat "drag" (W) Plate 9. The Apache had numerous fringes all the way up the heel (X), while a Blackfoot moccasin shows only two heel fringes (Y) Plate 9.

Victor Tixier in his book "Voyage aux Prairies Osages Louisiane et Missouri, 1839–1840" says, "The Osage never tie the straps of their moccasins around their feet. This detail enables them to recognize the track of the Pawnee who pass this string under their feet."

However, the sole patterns too identified the tribe in some instances. Wissler called attention to the fact that the Commanche moccasin had a sole with a peculiarly straight inner side (Wissler, *op. cit.*, p. 150). See (Z) Plate 9 in drawing. The Osage moccasin on the other hand followed more closely the natural outline of the foot with characteristic curves of the sole. While the moccasins of many tribes varied only slightly in their shape, to the trained tracking eyes of the Indians these slight differences were very distinct. The drawings (XX) Plate 9 show several

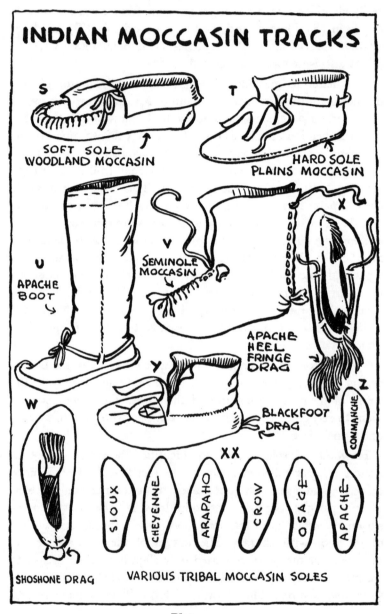

Plate 9

TRACKS IN INDIAN DESIGN

BUFFALO TRACK
A DEER TRACK
B ELK TRACK
OWL OR ROAD RUNNER
MOUND BUILDER BEAR TRACK
C COYOTE TRACK
SNAKE TRACKS D
TESUQUE LIZARD TRACK
E
GROUSE TRACKS
TURKEY TRACKS
BIRD TRACK
GROUSE TRACKS
CENTIPEDE TRACK
CROW TRACKS
WHITE MAN'S HORSE
HORSE TRACKS
HORSE TRACK
TRAVOIS TRAIL
TURTLE TRACK
PUEBLO HAND PRINT
KIOWA BEAR AND TRACKS
PLAINS INDIAN BEAR TRACKS
F
NAVAJO BEAR TRAIL

Plate 10

characteristic sole styles of a few tribes as drawn by various
Indians themselves.

Tracks in Indian Design. Since tracking was so important in the
life of the red man it is not surprising that it was used quite exten-
sively in his design and in turn in his rituals and ceremonies.
While the Indian sometimes drew the animal track as he saw it,
very often he made a conventionalized design of it to fit the
material he was working with. Many of the tracks were made
in straight lines, squares and angles to be used in porcupine quill
or beadwork. For instance the cloven hoof tracks of the deer,
buffalo and elk were made of two right angles opposed to each
other (A) Plate 10. The track of the road runner and that of
the owl were made in the shape of a St. Andrew's cross or the
letter X (B). The track of the coyote in the form of a cross (C)
was more conventionalized than the others. The four toe pads
are not at all in their natural position, yet to the Indian designer
this symbolized the coyote track.

Sometimes the Indian used curves and spirals in drawing
tracks. The curved and spiral snake tracks are typical (D). Another is the old Tesuque Pueblo pottery design of a lizard's trail
(E). The Indian used track designs upon his shields, clothing,
pottery, robes, dwellings, masks, musical instruments and among
the Navajo in Arizona as a motif for ceremonial sand paintings
(F) Plate 10.

Indian Trail Blazes. Although the Indian was numbered among
the world's best trackers, nevertheless he often blazed his trails to
make them more visible. Many of the old Indian trail signs still
remain, trail markers made before the white man came. The
drawings (A), Plate 11, show how these blazes look today.

Just as the present-day woodsman blazes his trail through new
country by bending saplings in the direction of his journey, so
too did the Indian of the past. The young trees that were not
broken grew into these deformed shapes and formed permanent

trail markers. At Highland Park, Illinois, seven of these ancient trail signs still mark the old Indian trail from the shores of Lake Michigan. Old marked trails may still be found throughout the Mississippi valley, in the Great Smoky Mountains, and in numerous other areas.

Trailmaking is not confined to man's activities alone, however. The first trails in the wilderness were made by the wild creatures themselves. Many animals make definite pathways, which they follow from year to year, sometimes for generations. This is especially true of the bears. The Alaskan brown bear makes a deeply rutted, double track trail worn into the earth by bear generations. Deer, buffalo and many of the smaller animals such as the meadow mouse make and use definite runways. Many of these game trails were well chosen routes from place to place and were later used by the Indians and whites alike for trails and roads.

Though you be an excellent woodsman, it is always a good idea to mark your trail when traveling through strange country. There are numerous traditional blazes used for years by wilderness travelers. A common trail sign, used whenever a marker is needed, which can be seen for miles, is the so-called "lop stick." This is a very prominent tree with its branches lopped off so as to create an unusual mark in the distant landscape. The "lop stick" is often used as a portage sign by the Indians.

The Ojibway, Penobscot and other woods Indians often mark the direction of their travel with a slanted stick stuck in the ground (B and C) Plate 11. Sometimes the stick is split at the top and a bit of moss or grass inserted to better attract the eye. Again a sharpened stick may be thrust through the bark of a tree at eye level to indicate direction (D). Indian canoeists often drive slanting poles into the stream to show direction (E, F, G and H) Plate 11.

Tree Blazes. Tree blazes commonly used in the woods today are shown in the drawing (I) Plate 11. In blazing a trail, the bark is chipped away on the tree trunk at about eye level revealing the

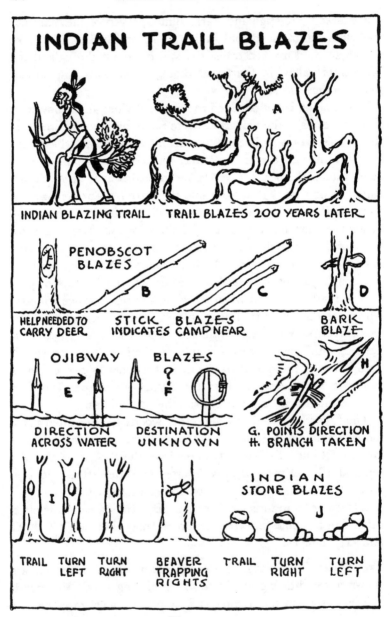

Plate 11

white wood beneath. The blaze should be made so that the trail can easily be followed when back trailing.

Bush Trail Signs. When traveling through bushy undergrowth, break the bushes as you go along. A series of broken bushes makes a trail easy to follow. When a broken branch with the butt end to the right is placed upon the ground, it indicates the trail turns right; one to the left indicates left. A split bush stem with a broken end resting in the crotch tells of a message at that spot.

Grass Trail Markers. Similar signs may be left in grassy areas by tying the grass into bunches. A knotted grass top pointing right tells that the trail is to the right. If it points left, the trail is to the left. Three knotted grass bunches tell of a message.

Rock Blazes. Rocks are used to blaze trails in deserts and rocky bad lands (J) Plate 11. A small rock on top of a larger one is used to mark a trail. If the trail is to the right, another rock is placed to the right of the rock marker; if to the left, the rock is placed on the left side. Three rocks, one on top of the other, indicates a message. (See Chapter 15 on Trailcraft, "Wildwood Wisdom," by the author.)

SCENT TRAILS
AND BLAZES

3

Scent Trails. Every pet dog knows how numerous are the inter-mingled scent trails in his neighborhood. Every living creature in passing gives off his own peculiar scent. This enables the dog to follow his master's trail through the maze of hundreds of others on a city street. Animals depend almost entirely upon invisible scent trails to inform them of the proximity of their friends and enemies. The visible tracks and trails mean nothing to the animal folk. Even humans sometimes take advantage of scent in tracking. Primitive trackers often smell the tracks to test their freshness.

Scent trails deteriorate, for the odor grows weaker as the trail becomes older. Scent trails too are stronger in certain kinds of weather. Scent will linger longer when the weather is warm and damp. Extremes in heat or cold lessen the clarity of track odors. The nerve endings in the nose too must have a certain amount of moisture to assimilate the scent particles. If there is too much moisture or mucous, as when one has a cold, or not enough, as in extremely hot weather, these nerve endings do not function properly. Some odors seem to evaporate.

To the animal's nose, track odors not only identify the species of animal, but also may indicate the state of mind and the physical condition of the animal. Emotions such as fear, hate, love

24

and others seem to be part of the scent messages given off in the tracks. Often a dog, seemingly at peace with the world, will suddenly display great anger on coming to a post where some other dog has previously registered. A snake at mating time makes a scent trail so others of its kind will know that it is matrimonially inclined.

Ernest Thompson Seton once told me of a scent trail adventure he had with a caribou. He had been watching a herd with the wind in the right direction. A lone cow came down the trail, but suddenly made a tremendous leap and fled when a shifting breeze told of his presence. A short time afterward several other caribou came down the trail. Since the wind now came from the direction of the animals, there was no chance of their scenting him, yet as they arrived at the exact spot where the first cow became frightened, each caribou leaped in fear, exactly as the first had done. This proved rather conclusively that fear had been left in the scent of the tracks.

Scent Glands. Scent is left on the trail in various ways. Deer and other members of that family, including the caribou, have what are known as interdigital glands located between the hooves (A) Plate 12. These give off a scent secretion as the animal wanders along the trail.

Deer also have another type of scent gland located on the lower part of the hind leg, known as the metatarsal gland (B) Plate 12. In shape it resembles a slit in the leg surrounded by pure white hair. The size of the gland varies with the kind of deer. In the whitetail or Virginia deer, the gland slit is only an inch long (C). In the coast blacktail it is 3 inches (D), while the mule deer has the longest of all, measuring 5 inches in length (E). These glands give off scent which adheres to the grass and brush as the deer moves about.

Some animals have scent glands located on their backs. The peccary, the little wild piglike animal found in our Southwest, has a musk gland on top of the rump about 8 inches from the

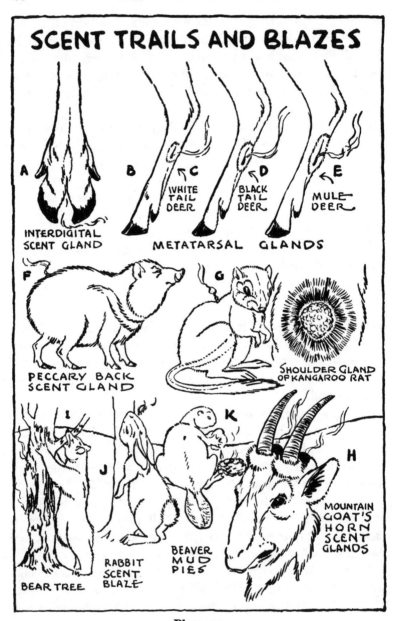

SCENT TRAILS AND BLAZES

A INTERDIGITAL SCENT GLAND

B C WHITE TAIL DEER D BLACK TAIL DEER E MULE DEER

METATARSAL GLANDS

F PECCARY BACK SCENT GLAND

G

SHOULDER GLAND OF KANGAROO RAT

I BEAR TREE

J RABBIT SCENT BLAZE

K BEAVER MUD PIES

H MOUNTAIN GOAT'S HORN SCENT GLANDS

Plate 12

tail (F) Plate 12. It looks like a deep fold in the skin and both sexes have it. The boars rub their backs on low brush, thus marking their range. The odor seems to be stronger when the animal is excited.

Both sexes of the kangaroo rat of the Southwest have a large scent gland on the back between the shoulders (G) Plate 12, which gives off a waxy matter of a peculiar odor. The gland seems to be more active during the breeding season, perhaps acting as trailside matrimonial publicity.

The mountain goat has a black rubbery gland at the base of each horn which is also especially active in the mating season (H) Plate 12. The goat blazes his scent trail by rubbing his horns on the underbrush as he wanders about.

Mountain sheep, commonly known as "bighorn," have a scent gland under each eye. This gives off a waxy substance with a peculiar sheep smell. These glands probably leave scent messages on the vegetation as the sheep graze.

Scent Blazes. While these animals and many others leave definite scent trails, others blaze signposts here and there. All members of the dog family including the wolf and the coyote are noted for their scented signposts. These seem to be sort of bulletin boards where each passing traveler registers his musky message.

Bears are well known tree blazers. Bear trees are often found along some well worn bear trail (I) Plate 12. The trunk is usually clawed and the bark scraped off in large areas, the wood gouged and splintered and marked with deep grooves, the marks of their teeth. A passing bear will stop and examine this signpost for several minutes, reading every scent message left by previous visitors. After he has all the news, he will rise on his hind legs and rip and tear the bark with his claws and teeth, even gnawing out chunks of living wood. Sometimes the tree is plastered with mud and hair.

Rabbits too are tree blazers. All buck rabbits seem to do it. They will stand upright on their heels and rub their chins upon the tree trunk as far as they can reach (J) Plate 12. These blazes may mark off their home range or they may serve as friendly messages or challenges to other bucks.

Just as many woodsmen blaze the trees about their cache to show ownership, so too do some of the animals with their scent. The wolverine especially is most liberal with his particularly obnoxious odor and he covers everything with it that appeals to his fancy. Once he blazes an object with his secretion, no one in the forest will ever want it again.

The beavers blaze trails of matrimonial adventure. They make mud pies and place a drop of beaver castoreum upon them as a hint to lady beavers of their matrimonial inclinations (K) Plate 12. So enamoured are the beaver with this odor, they frequently castorize their playgrounds. These spots are usually on dry ground near the beaver pond or stream.

Sky and Water Trails. Although no tracks are left by sky and water travelers, often their course in the heavens or in the waters identifies them. For instance, we are all familiar with the "V" trails made in the sky by migrating geese. The geese may be mere specks in the heavens yet their "V" shaped flight immediately labels them (A) Plate 13. The wavy flight of the black and gold goldfinch is a characteristic sky trail for this bird. It seems so filled with the joy of living it weaves an ecstatic wavy pattern in its flight (B). The red-winged blackbirds are sociable and often gather in numbers after nesting. When feasting together, their movement takes on a strange hooplike formation (C). This is due to their habit of alternately walking and flying. Those in the rear of the gathering are continually flying into the air over the feeding birds and alighting ahead of them. If you see this strange hoop rolling across the country, you will know it to be a gathering of blackbirds.

Beaver, otter and mink can be identified by their water trails. A beaver is a slow swimmer and swims in a straight course (D), Plate 13. He looks like a black arrowhead swimming. The otter and mink have sinuous bodies and quick movements and so their water trails zig-zag (E). This course may have been developed in hunting fish.

Migration and Spawning Trails. Perhaps the strangest of trails are the migration trails of birds and insects. With no trail markers and often no previous knowledge of the traditional migration routes to guide them, these creatures follow the same migration trails each year and have done so for countless generations.

Bird Sky Trails. The birds not only fly along the same sky courses each year but many of them come back to the same home locality to nest. The famous swallows of Capistrano are a good example. However, this is not uncommon, for most birds come back to the same nesting site annually.

There are a number of known bird migration routes. Some are extremely complicated. Each species follows a migration trail that has been perfected by trial and error through the centuries. Bird migration trails are generally thought of as north and south movements with lanes of greater concentration along the coasts, mountains and principal rivers. In general these bird sky trails do follow these topographical features when they are in the general direction of the travel routes. Bird migration trails may be narrow pathways that closely follow some valley, river or coastline, or they may be broad areas that follow landmarks only in a general way. The drawing, Plate 14, shows the location of the best known sky trails of the feathered folk.

Insect Migration Trails. Many insects too follow strange invisible air trails in spring and fall migrations. It is difficult to imagine such fragile beings as butterflies withstanding the buffetings of thousands of miles of air travel over land and sea. Yet a number of species of butterflies and other insects each year go upon distant journeys to other hemispheres and to other climes.

Like the birds, the butterflies seem to follow definite routes. The monarch or milkweed butterfly, for instance, journeys south

Plate 13

COMMON BIRD MIGRATION TRAILS

MIGRATION ROUTES PERFECTED
THROUGH CENTURIES OF SKY TRAVEL

Plate 14

each fall and north each spring. In their autumn journeys they seem to follow four great continental flight ways southward. Sometimes the monarch flight seems to be a single file air trail, again they form a great moving red cloud. At night they rest in swarms and cover large trees with living foliage (F) Plate 13. Their sky trails lead them as far as Mexico and sometimes farther. Their trek north every spring is not so noticeable as the fall migration, since they seem to return one by one at that time. Their travel northward is largely governed by the sprouting of milkweed. Since the caterpillars feed upon this plant, the monarch mothers follow it northward, laying their eggs upon it as it develops. One of the migration mysteries is how the next generation finds its way south in the fall, since none are among those who flew north in the spring.

Other butterflies too go on great migration flight trails. Some 250 different species make such long or short journeys during the brief span of their lives. Another famous butterfly traveler is the painted lady. Some years vast hordes of these butterflies travel in one huge company. In 1924 such a migration passed over southern California. The column was forty miles wide and for three whole days it streamed over the countryside. Certain of the sulphur butterflies travel in yellow clouds, often crossing hundreds of miles of open sea as far as Bermuda.

The September sunlight is sometimes aglitter with the movement of thousands of iridescent wings of the dragonflies on their migration trail. This is not a rare occurrence, but few folks seldom observe it. Some flies, such as *Helophilus fasciatus,* the flower fly, often move along their skyways by the thousands in late September.

Spawning Trails. In the waters of rivers and oceans great invisible spawning trails occur. There seem to be no guideposts for the human eye to see, yet each year various tribes of fish and eels follow definite routes along the ocean and rivers for hundreds of miles (G) Plate 13.

The eel is perhaps the most famous of these travelers of water trails. They depart in great crowds from their home rivers into the Atlantic and follow the ocean currents to the deep waters between Bermuda and the Leeward Islands. Here the spawning takes place. The young eels hatch and while still very young they backtrack along the route of their parents to old home rivers. No one knows how they find their way back (G) Plate 13.

During the May moon, smelts in great schools follow migration trails at flood tide upstream, where they lay their eggs. Some members of the herring family, too, crowd upstream, sometimes scrambling up falls and over rocks.

In the spring the salmon get the travel urge and follow invisible water trails upstream, leaping over rapids and falls, until they arrive at their traditional spawning ground in quiet fresh waters. When the eggs hatch the next spring, the young salmon grow strong in the fresh waters and then trail to the sea of their parents.

THE ANATOMY OF
ANIMAL TRACKS
4

Animal tracks are accurate records of everything an animal does or tries to do. Many creatures are most elusive and seldom allow themselves to be seen abroad and so their prints tell the secrets of their movements and of their peculiarities, which otherwise could not be learned. Each animal of course has its own individual characteristics and so too do its footprints, but each species also has general characteristics easily recognized.

Environment and Tracks. Environment has played an important role in the development of the animal and its tracks. For instance, animals who dwell in marshy places must spread their weight over greater areas of ground than those who frequent dry ground, otherwise they would sink deeply. Traveling over the soft muskeg and snow has created the broadly spreading hooves and clouts of the caribou (A) Plate 15. Snow walkers too have specialized feet. Both the lynx and snowshoe rabbit have large snowshoe feet for winter travel and this characteristic is emphasized in their tracks (B and C).

The speed that must be attained by dwellers of the uplands has influenced the antelope perhaps to shed his dew claws entirely (D) Plate 15, while the horse, who always shuns marshy ground,

34

ENVIRONMENT AND TRACKS

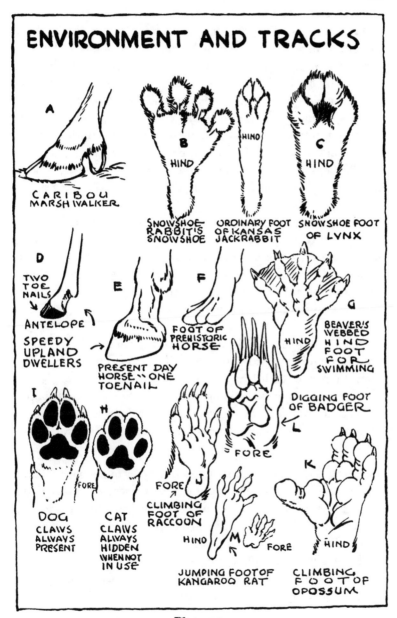

A — CARIBOU MARSH WALKER

B — SNOWSHOE RABBIT'S SNOWSHOE / HIND

ORDINARY FOOT OF KANSAS JACKRABBIT / HIND

C — SNOWSHOE FOOT OF LYNX / HIND

D — TWO TOE NAILS — ANTELOPE / SPEEDY UPLAND DWELLERS

E — FOOT OF PREHISTORIC HORSE / PRESENT DAY HORSE — ONE TOENAIL

F

G — BEAVER'S WEBBED HIND FOOT FOR SWIMMING / HIND

DIGGING FOOT OF BADGER / L

I — DOG CLAWS ALWAYS PRESENT / FORE

H — CAT CLAWS ALWAYS HIDDEN WHEN NOT IN USE

J — FORE / CLIMBING FOOT OF RACCOON / HIND

K — CLIMBING FOOT OF OPOSSUM / HIND

M — JUMPING FOOT OF KANGAROO RAT / HIND / FORE

FORE

Plate 15

has even cast away his extra toes and toenails, so that today he walks and runs upon one toenail only (E). Originally he is thought to have had five toes like many other animals (F).

Being a water animal, the beaver has evolved webs between the toes of his hind feet for swimming purposes. The webs, of course, appear in his characteristic track (G) Plate 15.

Cats, having great need of sharp claws in their hunting, have developed retractile claws which are sheathed until they are needed and so no sign of a claw appears in their tracks (H) Plate 15. The dogs on the other hand have little need for claws, depending more upon their fangs, and their claws always register in their tracks (I).

Tree climbers often have long claws. The raccoon is a good example of this type of animal development and his claws form an important part of his track (J) Plate 15. Another type of tree climber, the opossum, developed handlike feet with a thumb instead of long claws. In this case the thumbs are located on the hind feet and are the principal feature of his track identification (K).

Digging animals, like the badger and the mole, have specialized front feet equipped with long claws. These, of course, are a characteristic part of their tracks (L) Plate 15.

Some animals, like the kangaroo rat of the Southwest, hop or jump. Their forefeet, being of little use in locomotion, have become small so that only the hind feet register in their tracks (M) Plate 15.

The Four Tracking Groups. Joseph Brunner in his book "Tracks and Tracking" considers that the arrangement of tracks is due to the general anatomic make-up of the animal which made them and considers that four groups cover the mammals. (1) Plate 16. In the first group the length of body is correctly proportioned to the height of the animal and includes such mammals as deer, bear, dog, cat, etc. (2) Secondly those mammals whose hind legs are long in proportion to their front ones, as in the case of the

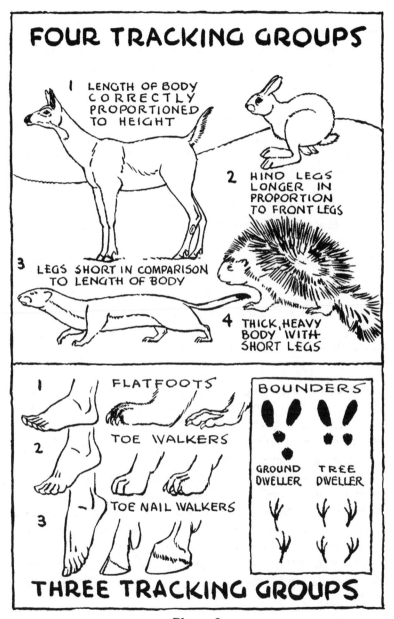

Plate 16

rabbit and squirrels. (3) This group includes animals whose legs are very short considering the length of their bodies, such as members of the weasel family. (4) Finally those animals who have thick heavy bodies with very short legs in contrast to their length. Porcupine, badger, etc., are among this group.

In tracking, animals too may be divided into three general groups—(1) Plate 16. "The Flatfoots" group includes a number of animals who walk upon the flat of their feet. Among these are the beaver, the porcupine, the skunk, the raccoon, the bear and even man himself. The hind feet of this group are longer than the forefeet, just as your tracks would show if you walked upon all fours. (2) The "Toe Walkers" group of animals might be eligible to join a Russian ballet, for they walk and dance upon their toes. In fact it can be rightly said that such animals as cats, dogs, wolves, foxes and coyotes are always "on their toes." (3) The "Toenail Walkers" group actually walk upon their toenails. Through the centuries they have developed these highly specialized feet, sometimes getting rid of three and even four toes in the process. All of the hooved animals are among this group and include deer, elk, caribou, moose, antelope, sheep, goats, cattle, horses, etc.

The Bounders may roughly be identified by their tracks as those who live upon the ground and those who climb trees. Animals with long hind legs, or bounders, can be readily identified as ground or tree dwellers. Such animals as rabbits squirrels and various mice and even birds are numbered among these. If they are ground dwellers, the forefeet are placed diagonally behind the tracks of the hind feet as in the track of the rabbit and hare. If they are tree dwellers, like the squirrels, the forefeet are paired behind the hind feet. A somewhat similar formation is also true among birds. Tree dwelling birds pair their feet and hop, as in the sparrow's track. Ground birds, such as the ruffed grouse, pheasant, chickens, etc., walk and place one foot ahead of the other (Plate 16).

BACK-YARD TRACKS
5

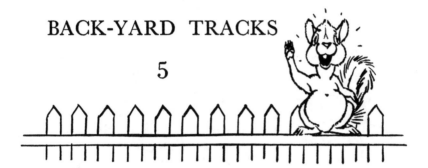

A good place to start hunting for tracks is in your own back yard. Two very common animal tracks found in the city are those of the cat and dog. Much has been said verbally and in print on how to tell a dog's track from that of the wolf's, but experienced woodsmen say it is next to impossible to distinguish them. A large dog's track will give you a very good idea of a wolf's footprint. You will then realize how close the wilderness is to your doorstep.

The Dog. The dog is a "toe walker" and makes prominent claw marks in his tracks. Unlike the cat family who have more important work for their daggerlike claws, the need for claws among canines is for occasional digging only. Although the dog has five toes only four register in both the fore and hind feet and like many animals the forefeet are wider than the hind (A) Plate 17.

A dog's trail is more direct in approaching an object of interest than that of a wolf's, since the dog lacks the suspicious and shy traits of his wild relative (Plate 18). He is not a perfect stalker like the cat and fox, and so his footprints often overlap. He frequently drags his toes, not at all in keeping with his wild relatives.

While many dogs have normal feet unchanged by centuries of domestication, some have feet deformed by intensive breeding. The Peterborough hound is a good example. The drawing (E)

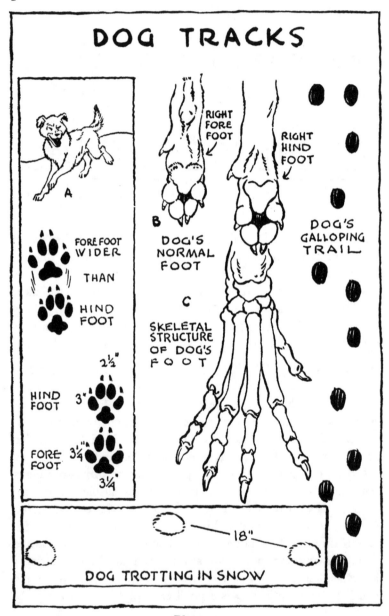

DOG TRACKS

A

FORE FOOT WIDER THAN HIND FOOT

HIND FOOT   2½"

HIND FOOT   3"

FORE FOOT   3¼"   3¼"

RIGHT FORE FOOT

RIGHT HIND FOOT

B
DOG'S NORMAL FOOT

C
SKELETAL STRUCTURE OF DOG'S FOOT

DOG'S GALLOPING TRAIL

18"

DOG TROTTING IN SNOW

Plate 17

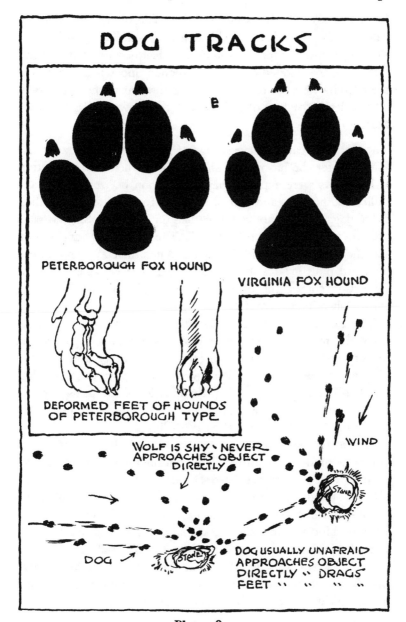

DOG TRACKS

PETERBOROUGH FOX HOUND

VIRGINIA FOX HOUND

DEFORMED FEET OF HOUNDS
OF PETERBOROUGH TYPE

WOLF IS SHY · NEVER
APPROACHES OBJECT
DIRECTLY

WIND

DOG

DOG USUALLY UNAFRAID
APPROACHES OBJECT
DIRECTLY ·· DRAGS
FEET ·· ·· ··

Plate 18

Plate 18 shows the track and the distortion of this hound's toes. There is also a tendency of this dog to toe-in. The drawing (B) Plate 17 shows the fore and hind right feet of a dog with normal feet. Note the padded toes and cushioned upper palm as well as the thumb, the print of which is never present in the dog's track. The skeletal structure of the dog's foot is shown in drawing (C) Plate 17.

The Cat. The cat has never a sign of her claws in her tracks (A) Plate 19, for she has use for sharp claws in her way of hunting. If her claws were exposed they would soon be worn down and dulled by the wear and tear of the trail. In order to protect these sharp daggers, they are kept sheathed until needed. She has what are known as "retractile claws." The claws are exposed or sheathed by two different ligaments. When the claw is not in use, one cord pulls it back into the sheath. However, when the time for action comes, the lower ligaments pull the claws forward, thus unsheathing them (B) Plate 19.

The cat is very careful to keep these weapons in good condition. She manicures her claws often by reaching high into an object and then pulling downward. This scrapes away surplus claw growth and polishes the claws into keen weapons (C) Plate 19. This habit, too, limbers up the muscles of the paws, keeping the toes flexible. The claws are not only weapons to aid in fighting or hunting but also enable the cat to climb.

Except for size, the cat's track could easily be that of any of her fierce predatory relatives. The lion, the tiger, leopard, jaguar, panther and lynx tracks all resemble those of pussy's. So after all, the jungle is little removed from our firesides. Being a "stalker," the cat is a perfect tracker. That is, she carefully steps with her hind feet into the tracks made by her forefeet. Thus she needs to find the right spot to place her feet only once, which makes for silent walking. She walks almost in a straight line with one footprint almost directly ahead of the other, a beautiful autograph in Nature's album (D) Plate 19.

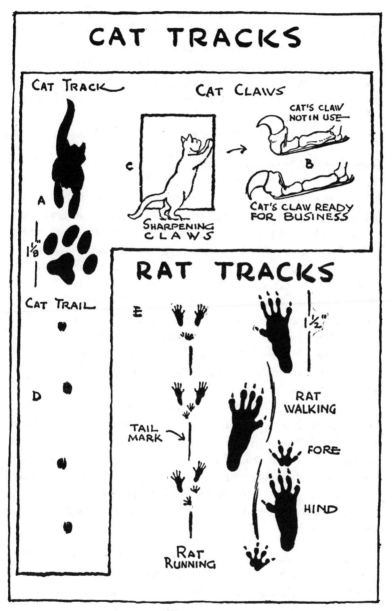

CAT TRACKS

Cat Track

Cat Claws

CAT'S CLAW NOT IN USE—

C

B

A

SHARPENING CLAWS

CAT'S CLAW READY FOR BUSINESS

1⅛"

Cat Trail

D

RAT TRACKS

E

1½"

RAT WALKING

TAIL MARK

FORE

HIND

Rat Running

Plate 19

Common Rat. A common track found in most of the back yards of our cities is that of the common rat. This rodent is a "flat foot," for it walks upon the flat of its feet like many of our animals. In studying the track we find that although a ground dweller, it often pairs its forefeet behind its hind feet like the tree climbers, indicating its climbing ability. The mark of the rat's tail is always a prominent feature of the trail. The drawing (E) Plate 19 shows tracks made by both walking and running.

Gray Squirrel. Another common rodent found in many cities is the beautiful gray squirred. This animal is a "bounder," that is it has longer hind legs than fore and, in running, pairs its forefeet behind its hind feet. The pairing of its forefeet indicates it is a tree climber (A) Plate 20. In walking, however, it alternates its hind and forefeet just as walking ground animals do (B).

Ordinarily the gray squirrel will take a half dozen or more hops and then takes time out for a look around (C) Plate 20. When hurrying, it can increase the distance between hops to five feet. This is perhaps the maximum distance it can cover in a bound. On closely examining the track you will note that five toes clearly register in the track of the hind foot, while only four show in the forefoot. The "thumb" has been lost in the course of the centuries.

A common sign of the gray squirrel's presence are its leafy dwellings high in the crotches of trees. These are leaf-thatched shelters built upon twig platforms which the squirrel uses temporarily (D) Plate 20. Most of our walnut groves of the past were results of the gray squirrel's planting. The walnut, in order to grow into a tree, must be planted in the earth. This job was neatly done by squirrels who were burying nuts for a rainy day (E) Plate 20.

English Sparrow. One of the common bird tracks of our back yards is that of the English sparrow, an emigrant from the Old World. Like the mammals, birds reveal their tree or ground

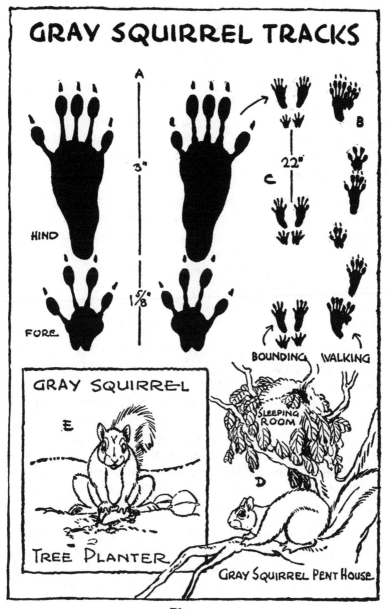

Plate 20

dwelling habits by their tracks. Just as the tree climbing mammal pairs its forefeet so too does the tree dwelling bird. The English sparrow's track shows its tree perching ability by this pairing of its feet as it hops (A) Plate 21.

The Robin. The robin, on the other hand, shows a combination of traits. The pairing of its feet as it hops identifies it as a perching bird, but when its tracks show one footprint ahead of the other, this indicates it is also at home on the ground. If you watch a robin you will see it take a number of hops and then it will run like any ground dwelling bird (B) Plate 21.

Pheasant. Sometimes in our vacant lots and city parks we find the walking track of the ring-necked pheasant. This bird was imported for hunting some years ago and has made itself at home in many areas in this country. The pheasant is a ground dwelling bird and in walking places one foot ahead of the other. Three toes in front with claws as well as a very small hind toe register in its track (E) Plate 21. This bird points its feet straight ahead as it walks, the middle toe forming almost a straight line.

Flicker. If you find a paired track that looks as if some one has imprinted two "K's" facing each other in the dust, you will know that you have "high hole," the flicker, for a neighbor (C) Plate 21. Although it is more at home as a lineman propping itself on a telegraph pole, it also frequents anthills. There it protrudes its sticky tongue until it has it covered with ants, when it quickly draws it into its bill and swallows the protesting insects (D) Plate 21. The pairing of its feet shows that it is a perching bird and the "K"-like construction of the feet tells of its ability to hang on to vertical surfaces.

Slug. One of the garden's inhabitants, which gardeners detest, is the slimy slug. It is responsible for damage to some plants, and its silvery trails can often be found upon our sidewalks in the morning (A) Plate 22. The slug, like the snail, has only one foot

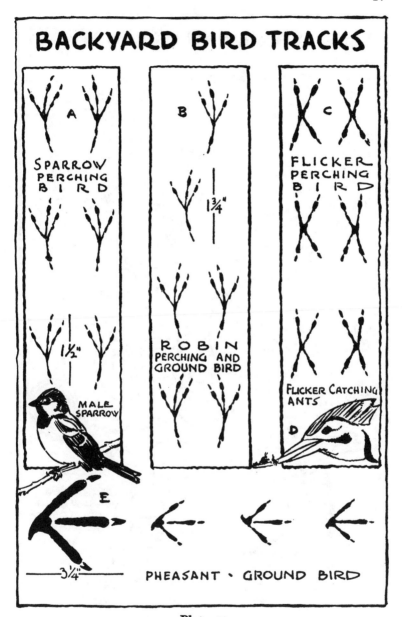

BACKYARD BIRD TRACKS

A — SPARROW PERCHING BIRD

MALE SPARROW — 1½"

B — ROBIN PERCHING AND GROUND BIRD — 1¾"

C — FLICKER PERCHING BIRD

D — FLICKER CATCHING ANTS

E — PHEASANT · GROUND BIRD — 3¼"

Plate 21

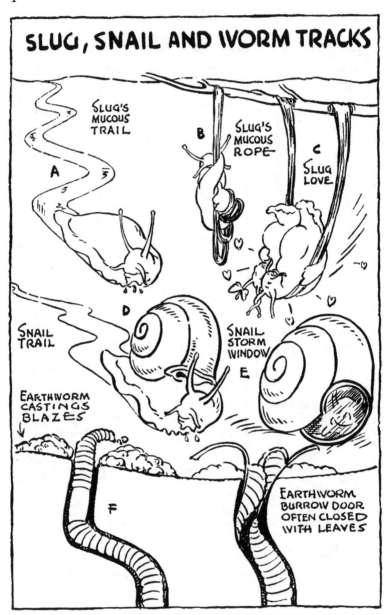

SLUG, SNAIL AND WORM TRACKS

A — Slug's Mucous Trail
B — Slug's Mucous Rope
C — Slug Love
D — Snail Trail
E — Snail Storm Window
F — Earthworm Castings Blazes — Earthworm Burrow Door Often Closed With Leaves

Plate 22

and, to travel, it makes its own sticky macadam road everywhere it goes. This road material is a slimy substance which enables it to get a foothold with its lone foot. Later, however, this material dries into the beautiful trail of silver. Slugs also use this slimy material as ropes to descend and ascend (B). Often, too, it forms a swing for cupid, for in mating slugs suspend themselves head down, swinging back and forth in cupid's arms (C). Thus the slug's silver trails often lead to romance.

Garden Snail. Another silver trail in our back yards is that of the common garden snail. Like the slug, it excretes a slimy substance to enable its one foot to travel (D) Plate 22. Without this special roadway the snail could not cover the ground even at a snail's pace. Like a pioneer and his covered wagon, the snail travels with his shelter. At any time it can withdraw from the world into its shell. In times of drought or in winter, the snail covers its entrance with this slime which hardens into a "storm window," keeping the snail snug in its shelter (E).

Earthworm. Another interesting neighbor is that dual personality the earthworm, who combines both sexes in one being and if cut in half can form two separate living creatures. The blazes of its underground trails are the little round entrances and the worm's castings, the small piles of digested earth the earthworm leaves at the trail entrance (F) Plate 22. The casting blazes are important to our welfare, for the millions of worms thus work for us in renewing the fertility of the soil.

BARNYARD TRACKS

The barnyard is a wonderful place in which to study the footprints of our domestic animals, once the wild creatures of the forests and plains of Europe and Asia. The pig, the cow, the horse and the sheep have been so long a part of men's lives, it is difficult to realize that they too were as wild at one time as the deer of our forests today. However, when you see the free, wild horses in the West, it is easy to visualize in their unshod hoof tracks the footprints of their wild ancestors of thousands of years ago.

Horse. The horse, like all of us, has had many amazing ancestors, one of the earliest being a strange creature about the size of a fox. This early dawn horse (*Eohippus*) had no hoofs but it did have four toes and a splint of a fifth on the forefoot and three toes and a splint of a fourth on the hind foot (A) Plate 23. However, the horse of today is a large beautiful animal which has lost all but one toe in its gamble with its environment having sacrificed its other toes to speed. The horse is a "toenail walker" for its hoof is really the nail at the end of its middle toe (B). The hoofs of its front feet are wider and rounder than those of its hind feet (C). The greater size and roundness distinguish horse tracks from those of asses and mules. When a horse is shod, the toe calks register deeply in the tracks. Without shoes, the hoof shows an unbroken front edge. Some horses walk in correct register, that is, they place their hind feet exactly into the tracks made by the front feet. Others do not. Mules, however, are more exact in track register than horses. The drawing (D) shows the underside of the right fore hoof of a horse. (C) and (E) show tracks made by shod and unshod hoofs. The horse's dung, about the size of tennis balls, is also a sign of this animal's proximity.

Donkey. Donkey, burro and ass are common names for this animal (F) Plate 23. The true wild ass is found in northern Africa and it is thought that it was domesticated on the shores of the Mediterranean and distributed to all parts of the world in the course of centuries.

The donkey is patient, gentle and able to thrive on very meager pasturage. Although small in size, it often carries unbelievable loads. The donkey or burro is frequently used in arid regions in pack trains and its diminutive hoofprints are commonly seen on desert trails. The hoof in this case is much smaller and less round than that of the horse (G), Plate 23, and is concave with sharp rims, especially made for rough, stony, precipitous trails.

Mule. The mule is a hybrid, the result of mating a jack or male donkey with a mare or female horse. This union produces the mule, which, strange to say, cannot reproduce its kind. Although it can do almost the same work as the horse in many fields of employment, it requires less food and is more free from lameness and disease. Then too, the mule is less nervous than the horse and may even have a longer life span. Although many characteristics of the horse are retained by the mule, it also has the long ears, the peculiar tail and the oval shaped hoof of the donkey (G) Plate 23. Mules are careful walkers and their track register is more exact than that of horses.

Cow. The domestic cow of our barnyard is also a "toenail walker." She, however, has cloven hoofs (A), Plate 24, that is, the nails of

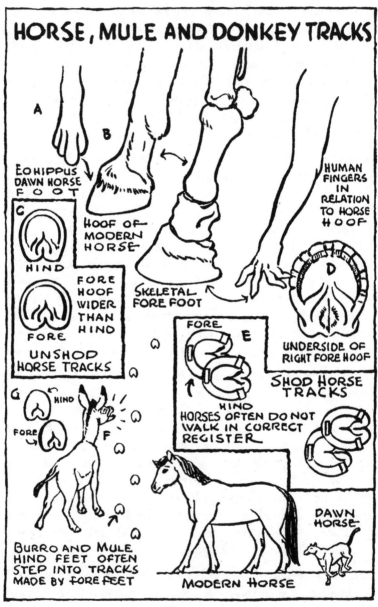

HORSE, MULE AND DONKEY TRACKS

A

B

Eohippus Dawn Horse Foot

Hoof of Modern Horse

C

Hind

Fore

Fore Hoof Wider Than Hind

Unshod Horse Tracks

Skeletal Fore Foot

Human Fingers in Relation to Horse Hoof

D

Underside of Right Fore Hoof

Fore

E

Shod Horse Tracks

Hind Horses Often Do Not Walk in Correct Register

G

Hind

Fore

F

Burro and Mule Hind Feet Often Step into Tracks Made by Fore Feet

Dawn Horse

Modern Horse

Plate 23

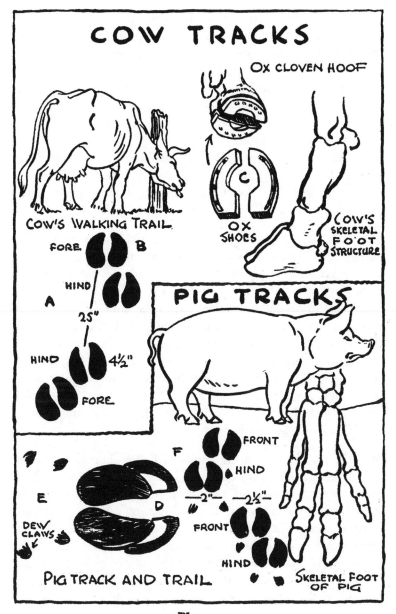

COW TRACKS

OX CLOVEN HOOF

COW'S WALKING TRAIL

FORE B

HIND

A

25"

HIND 4½"

FORE

OX SHOES

COW'S SKELETAL FOOT STRUCTURE

PIG TRACKS

FRONT

F

HIND

E

—2"— —2½"—

D

DEW CLAWS

FRONT

HIND

PIG TRACK AND TRAIL

SKELETAL FOOT OF PIG

Plate 24

two toes commonly register when she walks. Like most animals her front hoofs are wider than the hind. Note this characteristic in the drawing (B). The hind feet may be placed ahead, beside or behind the tracks made by the forefeet but they rarely register directly upon the tracks of the forefeet. See drawing (A) Plate 24. Another common sign of cattle are the large flat cakes of dung. Shrubs, too, are often trimmed into rounded shapes by cattle feeding in pasturage.

In the old days when oxen were commonly used, their cloven hoof tracks were frequently found on backwoods roads. Often oxen were shod like horses but their shoes were made in two pieces instead of one (C) to fit their cloven hoofs.

Pig. The pig, like the cow, has been a resident of men's barnyards for thousands of years. Like the cow, the pig, too, is a "toenail walker" and has cloven hoofs (D) Plate 24. Since this track closely resembles the deer's in size, the bluntness of the hoofs commonly distinguishes it from that of the antlered animal. The clouts or dew claws of the pig usually show in the track unless the ground is hard (E). The hoofs are commonly spread since the animal is heavy in comparison to the size of its feet. The pig is not a "quiet walker" and so its hind feet rarely register in the tracks made by its forefeet (F). "Quiet walkers" place their hind feet exactly in the tracks made by the forefeet, thus making less disturbance as they walk.

Sheep. Sheep belong to the family of hollow horned ruminants known as *Bovidae*. They go so far back into men's lives, little is known regarding their origins. Sheep were domesticated by man in Europe and Asia in the dawn of history, but were unknown in America until the coming of the Spanish Conquistadores. Like many other animals, sheep make scent trails. Between the cloven hoofs in most species is a gland which secretes an unctuous and odorous substance that adheres to the vegetation as the sheep wander about. They are very sociable animals and usually congregate in flocks or family groups. The old males, however, generally keep apart from the rest.

The tracks of the sheep show that they are "toenail walkers" with cloven hoofs. Although sometimes mistaken for deer tracks the sheep's hoofs are more blunt and do not have the shapely grace of the deer (A) Plate 25.

Goats. Goats are ruminants, members of the genus *Capra* and are closely allied to sheep. Domesticated goats are thought to have descended from the pasang (*Capra aegagrus*) and the East is probably their original home.

Unlike sheep, goats do not have the interdigital gland between the hoofs. They have two well developed hoofs like the sheep, however, and two secondary hoofs or dew claws on each foot (B) Plate 25. The goats at home among the rocks and crags are very surefooted animals.

The milch goat not only gives very rich and delicious milk but its winter undercoat furnishes the delicate wool which is used in the weaving of famous cashmere shawls. Angora goats have long silky fleece which is made into fabrics.

Chicken. The domestic chickens, though they perch and roost, are really ground birds. This is indicated by their tracks (C) Plate 25. They have three front toes armed with peculiar toenails well adapted to scratching and raking. The rear toe (sometimes two or more) scarcely touches the ground and is useful in perching (D). Chickens belong to the pheasant family but are the only members of that family which have fleshy combs. For this reason the genus is called *Gallus* meaning "comb." The chicken probably originated from the red jungle fowl of India and southern Asia (E) Plate 25, but domestication and breeding have produced numerous strange varieties.

Pigeon. All domestic varieties of pigeons have been developed from the rock pigeon, a wild species common in Europe and Asia. This pigeon and the doves are the only birds which can drink

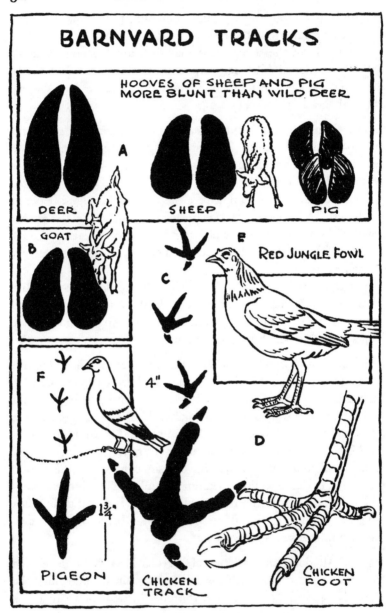

Plate 25

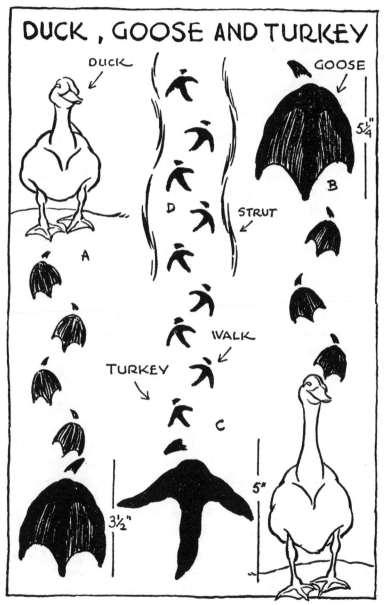

DUCK, GOOSE AND TURKEY

DUCK

GOOSE

5¼"

B

D

STRUT

A

WALK

TURKEY

C

3½"

5"

Plate 26

like a horse with their heads down in the water. The feeding of the young, too, is most peculiar. Secreted in the crops of both parents is a cheesy substance called "pigeon milk." The parent seizes the beak of the squab and pumps this food into the young. The action of the pigeon's head seems to be closely related to its gait, for its head moves back and forth as it walks. The drawing (F) Plate 25 shows the footprints of the dove and pigeon. Note in this track the hind toe points straight back.

Duck. The wild mallard duck is perhaps the ancestor of all domestic ducks with the exception of the muscovy duck. When selecting the kind of feet to carry them through life, both the ducks and the geese were evidently like-minded, for the only difference in their feet is in size. The rear toe of the diving duck's foot is larger but, taken as a whole, these two aquatic tribes have feet much alike. Their webbed feet are well adapted to swimming. Because the legs of the ducks are shorter and set farther back on the body than those of the geese, the ducks are not as good travelers upon land. The drawing of the duck's tracks (A) Plate 26 shows that it toes-in as it walks, the webs between the toes plainly registering.

Goose. The common domestic goose is thought to have descended from the wild goose of the British Isles known as "grey lag." The white varieties were evidently developed by domestication and selection. The ancient Britons were thought to have kept geese and other fowl for amusement rather than for food. The legs of the goose are much longer than those of the duck and are not set as far back on the body. Because of this the goose is a much better runner. The track of the goose is triangular with two scallops made by the webs between the three front toes (B), Plate 26. The hind toe is placed higher up on the leg.

Turkey. The turkey today has become a symbol of holiday time. Little did the early Pilgrims realize when they served the "gobbler" at their first Thanksgiving celebration that they were establishing a feast day tradition. To those pioneers, the trail of the turkey was of more interest than it is today. It was the trail that showed them where important food could be procured.

The size of the turkey track is distinctive for the turkey is our largest game bird. Note how it toes-in as it walks. The middle toe is slightly curved inward, adding to the toeing-in effect (C) Plate 26. When strutting, the stiff wing feathers often leave their mark on either side of the trail (D).

The turkey is distinctly American and its family contains only two species, the Yucatan turkey and our native species, from which have been bred the several varieties common to our barn-yards.

ANIMAL TRACKS OF
FIELD AND FOREST

7

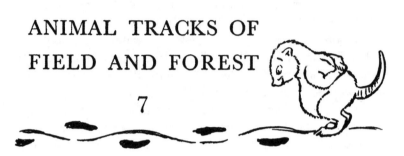

The North American continent offers, perhaps, the finest collection of animal tracks of all places on earth. While there are some, especially birds, that have become extinct since the coming of the white man, most of the tracks of our wild creatures that first thrilled the early explorers can still be seen. It is true that the tracks of one of our great game animals, the buffalo, which nearly disappeared forever, can now be viewed only in a few national parks and game preserves. Most of our smaller animals' and birds' footprints, however, are still common in field and farm wood lot. The larger game animals, in most cases, have retreated to the remaining wild places, although our whitetail deer seem to be fairly common throughout our rural areas. Beaver too are coming back to their old haunts and it is not unusual to find beaver tracks in the mud of some alder shaded creeks of our countryside.

The animals of our fields and forests are covered by the three divisions as set forth in "The Anatomy of Animal Tracks" in Chapter 4, namely the flat footed group, the toe walkers and the toenail walkers. Predaceous animals, who stalk their prey, and the "quiet walkers" usually set the hind foot in the same track made by the front foot of that side. This correct register enables these animals to move quietly. Tree climbers, when traveling on the ground, bound and pair their front feet in a line across their body.

Ground animals trot. If they bound they set their front feet in a line along their body.

CARNIVORA

The tracks of the cat family can be found all over this continent. The smallest and most familiar to us are those made by our own domestic cat. This animal, of course, is not native to the New World, but was originally brought from Europe by the early colonists. However, there is little difference in the track of our house cat and that of its wild American relatives except in size. The cat is a perfect tracker, placing its hind feet in the tracks made by its forefeet. Since all the American cats have retractile claws, they do not register in the footprint. Only four toes are imprinted in both the fore and hind foot tracks in each case. Cats are also "toe walkers."

Wildcat or Bay Lynx (*Lynx ruffus*). The smallest of our North American cats is the wildcat, bobcat or bay lynx. Larger than our domestic cat and smaller than the Canada lynx, its tracks are found in almost all wooded sections of the United States. The tracks are much like those of the domestic cat's though larger. On close scrutiny, its track reveals a more complicated palm and heel pad outline than do those of other cats (A) Plate 27. Unlike the Canada lynx, the bobcat does not grow heavy fur moccasins in winter. It, however, follows most of the predaceous animals in being correct in its fore and hind foot register. Like the Canada lynx it has a short, stubby tail, wears sideburns and has slightly tufted ears.

Canada Lynx (*Lynx canadensis*). The Canada lynx is larger than the bobcat and has a range from Alaska to northern United States. It has larger tufts upon its ears but wears sideburns and has a stubby tail like the bobcat. As in all of the cat family only four toes register in the tracks of both fore and hind feet. Like the domestic cat its feet make a perfect register. The tracks look

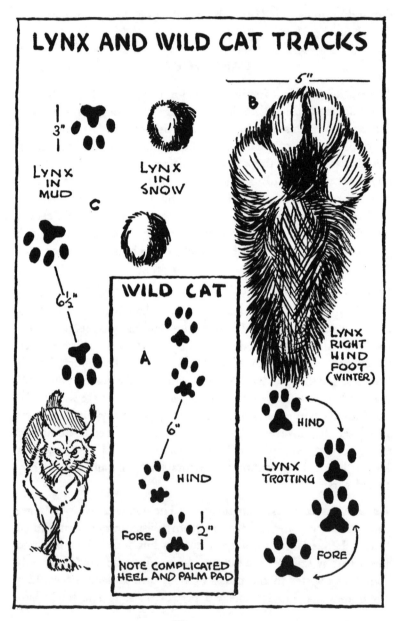

LYNX AND WILD CAT TRACKS

5"

B

LYNX
IN
MUD

3"

LYNX
IN
SNOW

C

6½"

LYNX
RIGHT
HIND
FOOT
(WINTER)

WILD CAT

A

6"

HIND

FORE

2"

NOTE COMPLICATED
HEEL AND PALM PAD

HIND

LYNX
TROTTING

FORE

Plate 27

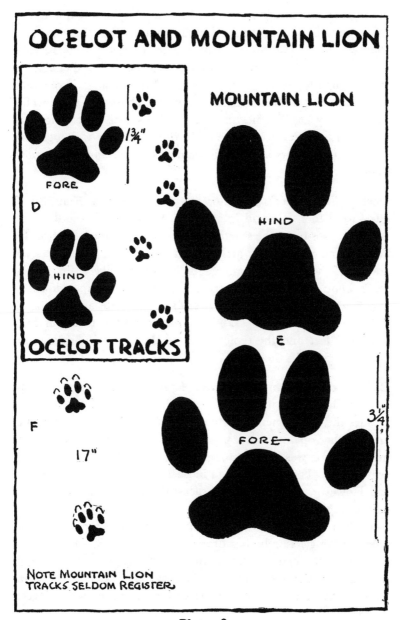

Plate 28

enormous in contrast to the size of the animal, largely due to the thick growth of hair on its feet in winter. The drawing (B) Plate 27 shows how covered with fur are its feet during the cold months. The stiff hair growth acts as "snowshoes" and enables it to walk lightly upon the deep drifts. This of course is of great advantage to it in hunting. It has a strange characteristic of walking on every log it comes to. Another is its trick of leaping suddenly ten to fifteen feet in the midst of its ordinary walking. The drawing (C) shows its tracks in mud in summer and in the snow in winter.

Ocelot (*Felis pardalis*). The ocelot, one of the most beautiful of our furred folk, is found in southern Texas, Mexico and South America. It is twice the size of our domestic cat, about that of the bobcat, and is generally at home on the ground or in trees. It knows all the tricks of trailing, for it can run like a fox, backtrack, blind hop and double cross its trail. It is an expert in making its way through the thorny scrub of mesquite and cactus of its range. The drawing (D) Plate 28 shows the tracks of fore and hind feet and the typical trail of the ocelot indicating the perfect register in the tracks.

Cougar or Mountain Lion (*Felis couguar*). The cougar or mountain lion has had a number of names in the course of its history. Besides the above mentioned names, a few of the most common are panther, painter and puma. One hundred years ago the mountain lion was found throughout the United States and southern Canada. The tracks, except in size, are like those of any other cat. However, unlike most cat tracks, those of the mountain lion seldom register. It often oversteps the tracks made by its forefeet when in haste, or does not quite cover the forefoot tracks when walking leisurely. See drawing (E) Plate 28, which shows the size of the cougar's track, the out-of-register trail (F) and trails made when sneaking up on its prey (G) Plate 29 and when trotting (H) Plate 29. The tracks of the male are usually larger

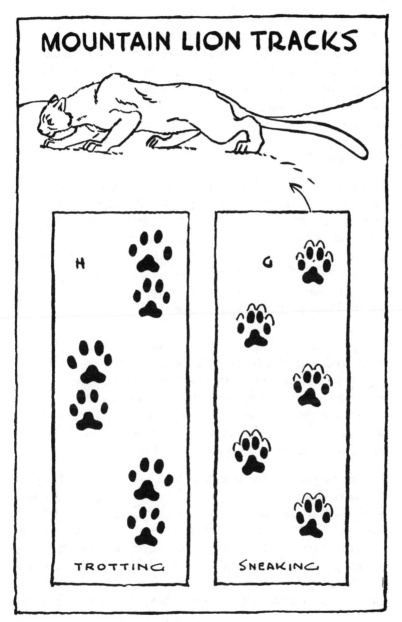

MOUNTAIN LION TRACKS

H

G

TROTTING

SNEAKING

Plate 29

than those of the female although the female may be the larger animal. When pursued, the mountain lion may leap 30 feet in a bound. On level ground a single leap of 20 feet is not uncommon. You will note in the drawing of the tracks (E) Plate 28, that the forefoot print is wider than that of the hind foot, a common characteristic in most animal tracks. The mountain lion is an expert tree climber and has keen vision, a thing to remember when hunting it. To mark its cache, the mountain lion covers its kill with brush.

Jaguar (*Felis onca*). The name "jaguar" is the native American name for this largest of American cats. It ranges from Texas, Arizona and Mexico through South America. Since it weighs from 160 to 300 pounds, its tracks may register deeply in soft ground. The characteristic four toes of the cat family without claw marks is also typical of the jaguar track. The footprint of this cat is more stubby than that of the mountain lion. The drawing (I) Plate 30 shows the track of a small jaguar.

Unlike the tracks of the cat family, those of the dog, both domestic and wild, clearly show claw marks. In the case of the dog family, the claws are non-retractile. The dog family have five toes on the forefoot. However, the innermost or fifth toe is located so far up on the leg it does not register in the track. All members of the dog family are "toe walkers." As in other animals the forefeet of the dogs are wider than the hind feet.

Grey or Timber Wolf (*Canis Mexicanus*). If you find a footprint of a large dog in the mud, you will have a very good idea of a wolf's track. In fact there is not one reliable feature that will distinguish a wolf's track from that of certain dogs. A wolf may often be a better walker than the dog. Its tracks sometimes register, but not at all times and in some individual wolves rarely. Woodsmen and naturalists agree, it is next to impossible to tell definitely the tracks of a wolf from those of a dog. In most in-

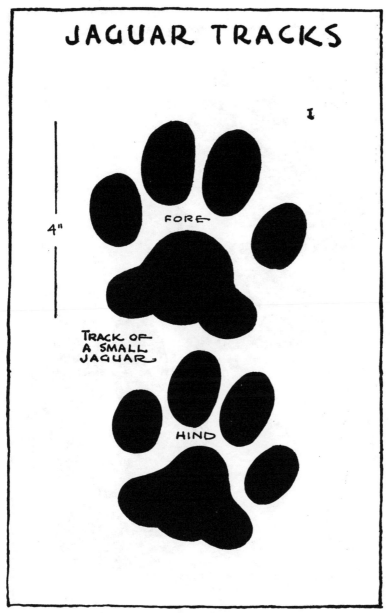

JAGUAR TRACKS

I

4"

FORE

TRACK OF
A SMALL
JAGUAR

HIND

Plate 30

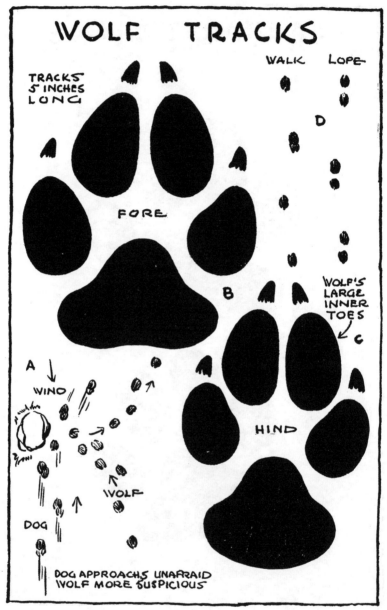

Plate 31

stances, it is true, dogs do not have the shy and suspicious characteristics of their wild relatives, and approach objects that interest them openly, while wolves and other wild dogs will make use of every bit of cover. The drawing (A) Plate 31 shows this difference of approach. The drawing (B) shows the fore and hind wolf track.

An interesting feature in the wolf and coyote track is the fact that the inner toes of the hind foot of the wolf make a larger track than do the outer toes, while the outer toes of the coyote make the larger impressions. This variation is sometimes noted in dogs as well. The collie, for instance, has relatively small outer toes like those of the wolf (C) Plate 31.

The summer range of a wolf may be fifteen to twenty miles while the winter range is double that because of the scarcity of food. The range of predatory animals is usually much greater than that of other animals. The drawings (D) Plate 31 show the walking and the loping trail of the wolf.

Coyote (*Canis latrans*). The coyote, being a "toe walker," is literally "on his toes" at all times, for though every man's hand seems to be raised against him, he still holds his own. The coyote track is like that of a smaller dog and similar to that of the wolf's except in size. It is the "in between" track of our native canines, not as large as the wolf's yet not as small and delicate as the fox's. See the drawing (E) Plate 32 showing comparative size of the wolf, coyote and fox tracks. Being a wild dog, its claws are always in evidence. As mentioned in the section on the wolf, the track of the outer toes of the hind foot is larger than that of the inner toes. The drawing (F) shows the walking and running track of the coyote.

Red Fox (*Vulpes fulva*). As is the case with most of the wood folk, the signs and tracks of the red fox are more often seen than the animal itself. Being a member of the dog tribe, the claws are prominent, but the track itself is more delicate than those of other

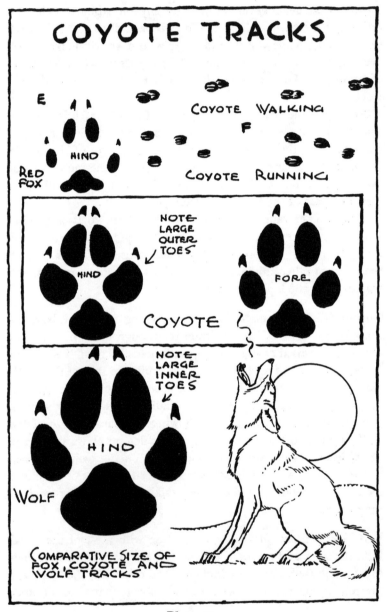

Plate 32

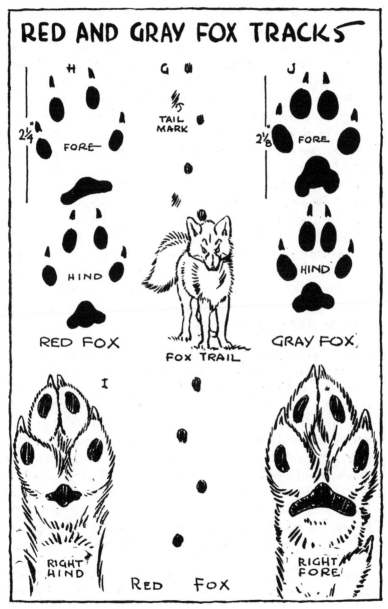

RED AND GRAY FOX TRACKS

RED FOX

FOX TRAIL

GRAY FOX

RED FOX

Plate 33

members of the canine group. The small pad impressions, widely spaced, are very characteristic. The fox trail is an excellent example of perfect register in tracks, for being a "good stalker it is a perfect walker" and its hind feet actually step into the tracks made by its forefeet. Its trail is almost a straight line (G) Plate 33.

When walking in the snow the fox leaves little evidence of dragging its feet, for the snow is seldom ruffled. Occasionally the tail or brush of the fox touches the ground. See (H) Plate 33 in the drawing which also shows the tracks made by the fore and hind foot.

Color variations of the red fox are the black, silver and cross foxes. Occasionally a freak phase of this family known as a "scorched fox" is also found. This freak fox has no long fur, nothing but wool. Though the colors be different from the red variety all the phases make the same type of track. The drawing (I) Plate 33 shows the under side of the right fore and hind foot. The fox's diggings are also a sign of its presence. These resemble somewhat the work of the skunk but are narrower and deeper than the holes dug by the skunk.

Gray Fox (*Urocyon cinereoargenteus*). The gray fox resembles somewhat the red fox but it has a grizzly gray coat and cap and a more or less black tail with a black tip. It does not have the rank odor of its red relative. It is also less swift than the red fox and may often climb sloping trees. Like the red fox, it is an expert at trick trailing. Although its track is somewhat smaller than its red relative's, the toes make a larger print. The heel and palm prints also differ. The gray fox track resembles that of a small dog more than it does the red fox's. See drawing (J) Plate 33. Being perfect trackers, the trails of all the foxes are similar to that of the red fox, stretching along in nearly a straight line, and differing only in the size of the individual track.

Desert Fox (*Vulpes macrotis*). Should you be so fortunate as to catch a glimpse of the desert fox in flight, it will seem not to be of flesh and blood but of thistledown, so lightly does it float as it runs. The desert fox is a resident of the Southwest and Lower California. Like many animals of the desert, this fox has large ears, much larger than those of the kit fox, whose habits are very similar. Although about the same weight, the desert fox is more stream-lined than the kit fox. It is also paler in color. Its track is shown in drawing (K) Plate 34.

Kit Fox (*Vulpes velox*). No larger than a house cat, the kit fox is found only on the prairies. Its general coloration is pale buffy yellow becoming deeper yellowish brown on the back of the ears, across the lower neck, on the outside of the forelegs and on the back of the hind legs. The underside is pearly white. Its back is covered with a beautiful silver gray mantle with gray-brown under fur. The tail is a yellowish gray above, strong yellow below with a black tip. The ears are small in contrast to the big ears of the desert fox.

The kit fox track (L) Plate 34 resembles a domestic cat's in size and shape, except that the claws register and the trail is almost straight like that of all other foxes.

Arctic Fox (*Alopex lagopus*). The circumpolar range of the Arctic fox extends from the timber line northward as far as land reaches. Like some of the northern dwellers, it has two suits, a sooty gray for summer and beautiful white fleecy flannels for winter. Occasionally some members of its family wear a smoky blue-gray winter coat instead of white. This blue phase is merely a color freak since both white and blue may occur in the same litter.

The drawing (M) Plate 34 shows the feet of the Arctic fox in summer, when the pads are exposed, and in winter, when it has woolly moccasins covering the whole foot. Its tracks are smaller than those of the red fox and in winter look like little oval pads. See drawing (N) Plate 34. The trail itself is like those of other foxes, differing chiefly in the size of the footprints.

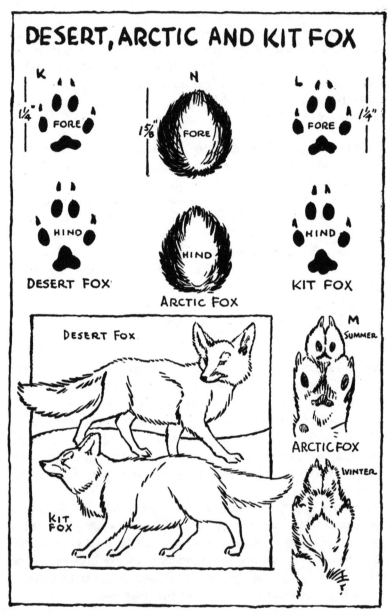

DESERT, ARCTIC AND KIT FOX

K

1/4"

FORE

HIND

DESERT FOX

N

1⅝"

FORE

HIND

ARCTIC FOX

L

FORE

1/4"

HIND

KIT FOX

DESERT FOX

KIT FOX

M

SUMMER

ARCTIC FOX

WINTER

Plate 34

The bears belong to the flatfoot fraternity for they walk upon the flat of their feet. All bears have well developed claws, the grizzlies having the largest of all. While the young bears are excellent tree climbers, only the black bear carries this activity into adulthood. The grizzly's claws are too long for climbing, their chief use being digging.

Bears are great trail makers. They carefully select the best and shortest route to an objective and then follow the same trail for generations until it becomes deeply rutted. The bear trail sometimes looks like a very narrow double rutted cart track. See drawing (A) Plate 35. In thickly forested country, the underbrush is worn away on the trail only to the height of the bear walking on all fours, and so travel is difficult along these trails as far as a man is concerned.

Bears, being omnivorous, eat a great variety of vegetables and living creatures. Evidences of their eating habits often tell of their presence when their tracks are not visible. Their characteristic dung, ripped open rotten logs (B) Plate 35, areas dug up for edible tubers, all announce the presence of bears in the neighborhood. Often the claw marks can be seen on the bark of the trees they have climbed. This is especially so of aspen trees, which show the injury made by the claws upon their bark for years (C).

Along bear trails, the well known bear tree is often found. This is a sort of bulletin board or signpost used perhaps to communicate with all the bears who pass along the trail. At least all bears seem to register there when passing. The bear tree trunk is usually scraped free of bark in large areas and the wood is gouged and splintered. Deep grooves, the marks of their teeth, can be seen in the green bark and wood.

Coming to a bear tree, bruin will examine the signpost for several minutes, sometimes looking around and testing the air with his nose. After an interval it will rise on its hind legs and scratch and tear the bark and wood with its claws and teeth, even gnawing and ripping out slabs of living wood. Sometimes

BLACK BEAR SIGNS

E

6"

D

5"

BLACK
BEAR
TRACKS

11"

A
DOUBLE RUTTED
BEAR TRAIL

CLAW
MARKS

C
OLD
CLAW
MARKS
ON
ASPEN

B BEAR SIGN - RIPPED OPEN ROTTEN LOGS

Plate 35

the bear tree is also plastered with mud and hair. See (I) Plate 12.

Black Bear (*Ursus americanus*). The black bear, the clown of the wilderness, is found from the wooded sections of the Arctic down into Mexico. In the West the black bear often has a blonde in its family, for a cinnamon cub may often be born to a black bear mother. However, this strange phenomenon occurs only in the West.

The black bear's track greatly resembles the grizzly's and the giant brown bear's except for size and claw marks. The black bear's hind foot often registers with the front when walking (D) Plate 35. Since the claws of the black bear are not as large as the grizzly's they are not prominent, often not registering at all. The fifth toe of this bear, although well developed on both the front and hind foot, at times leaves little sign of its presence, sometimes none at all. The tracks of the hind foot measure about 6 inches (E). Normally the black bear hibernates all winter and so his tracks are seldom seen in the snow. However, on occasion, bears in bad physical condition may not hibernate.

Grizzly Bear (*Ursus horribilis*). The trail of the grizzly bear will be found only in the West, for it is a giant of the Western mountains. A strong characteristic in its tracks are the marks of its extraordinary long claws. The claws are a great help in digging for tubers, ground squirrels and other burrowing animals. The length of the claws on its right or left forepaws often reveals if it be right or left handed. The paw it uses most will have the shortest claws. In spite of its huge claws, it does not climb trees when full grown. Unlike the black bear, all five toes usually register in its trail. The track of its hind foot is double the length of the black bear's and will often measure 12 inches. See drawing (F) Plate 36. Drawing (G) shows the relative size of the grizzly, black bear and brown bear claws. The grizzly often covers its kill with fresh earth, thus marking its cache. Like the black bear, the

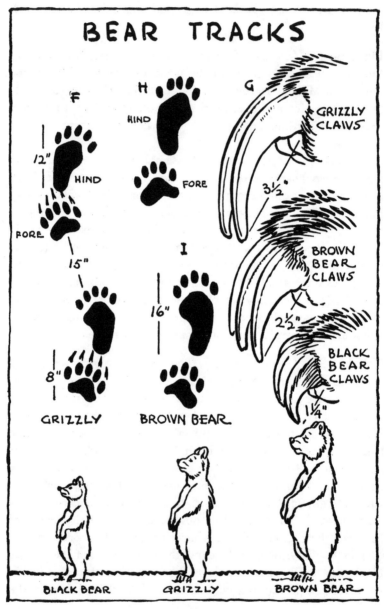

Plate 36

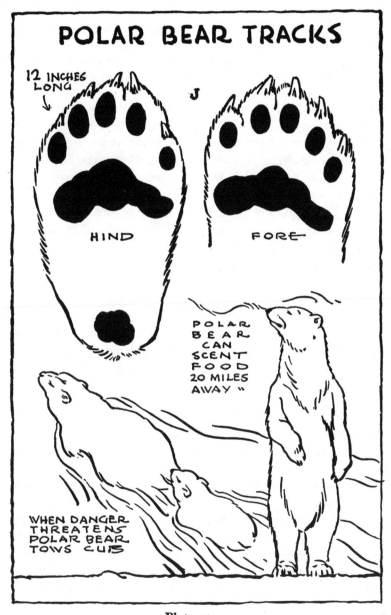

Plate 37

grizzly makes use of bear trees for communication with others of its kind. It also makes use of ancestral trails, carefully stepping into the same footprints year after year until they are deeply indented into the earth. However, like many animal trailmakers it never clears away obstructions but walks around them.

Giant Brown Bear (*Ursus gyas*). This brown bear giant is the largest meat eater alive in the world today and it weighs from 1200 to 1400 pounds. Its trails and tracks are found on the Pacific coast from Alaska to British Columbia. Here may be seen its many definite trails deeply worn by generations of these giants. The trails which the bears constantly use show a continuous series of alternate footprints worn quite deeply in the soil, for each bear steps into the same tracks. Thus these trails often resemble very narrow double rutted cart tracks. The brown bear's hind foot often registers with the front foot (H) Plate 36. Claw marks are not generally found. As with the black bear, the fifth toe in both the front and hind feet is well developed, yet it leaves little evidence of its presence in the track, at times none at all. This giant flat-foot reveals its size by its immense hind track measuring 14 to 16 inches long (I). Like other bears, it posts its preserve by rubbing its body against rocks or clawing and chewing convenient trees.

Polar Bear (*Thalarctos maritimus*). There is little chance that the average person will see the tracks of the polar bear except in the zoo, for its range is in the cold regions of the northern hemisphere.

If you traveled to the polar bear's Arctic home in winter, the chances are you would see more male tracks than female, for the mother bear usually goes into winter hibernation every other year in expectation of young. The fur of the polar bear is white or yellowish white and is dense and oily, almost wholly covering the soles of the feet. The cubs, when first out of their hibernation nursery, leave tracks no larger than the size of a silver dollar. The mother's track may measure 15 inches long and 9 inches broad. The drawing (J) Plate 37 shows the fore and hind foot track of the polar bear.

The raccoon family, the *Procyonidae*, are middle-sized animals related to the bears, having naked feet with five toes on each foot, rounded noses and tails bushy and usually ringed. The raccoon name evidently comes from the Virginia Indian name "Arocoun." Seton calls them the "woodland barber poles" because of their characteristic striped tails.

Raccoon (*Procyon lotor*). Most of us recognize the raccoon by its mask and ring tail, yet few of us know its track. Long ago the coon wore out its shoes and socks and decided to go barefoot. So today when you see its track, you will always find its bare toes and soles plainly imprinted. The coon has five well developed toes with claws on each foot and like many animals its hind feet are longer than its forefeet. Being a tree climber it places its front feet together when running (A) Plate 38. At times a small coon track may be mistaken for that of a muskrat, for like the rodent, it steps upon the track of the palm of its forefoot with its hind foot as it walks (B). The forefoot tracks of a full grown coon usually measure 3¼ inches in length and the hind feet about 4¼ inches (C). Raccoons patrol the banks of streams night after night so that they sometimes make well trodden trails. The raccoon den is usually in a hollow tree. Often coon hairs caught in the rough wood and bark identify the homestead.

Coati-mundi (*Nasua narica*). The coati of the genus Nasua are raccoons which differ from the true raccoon in their long snout, long tapering black and gray ringed tail and coarse fur. In color they are warm brown with dull white under parts. Because of the snout they are sometimes called "the hog nosed coons." Like the raccoon they have a mask of pale brown. There are seven known races. From South America this animal's range reaches as far

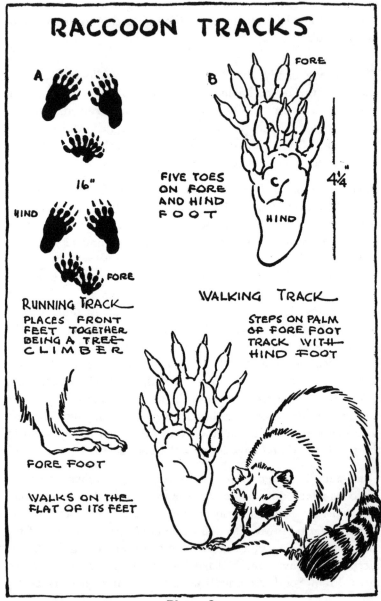

RACCOON TRACKS

A

B

FORE

FIVE TOES
ON FORE
AND HIND
FOOT

16"

HIND

C

HIND

4¼"

FORE

RUNNING TRACK

PLACES FRONT
FEET TOGETHER
BEING A TREE
CLIMBER

WALKING TRACK

STEPS ON PALM
OF FORE FOOT
TRACK WITH
HIND FOOT

FORE FOOT

WALKS ON THE
FLAT OF ITS FEET

Plate 38

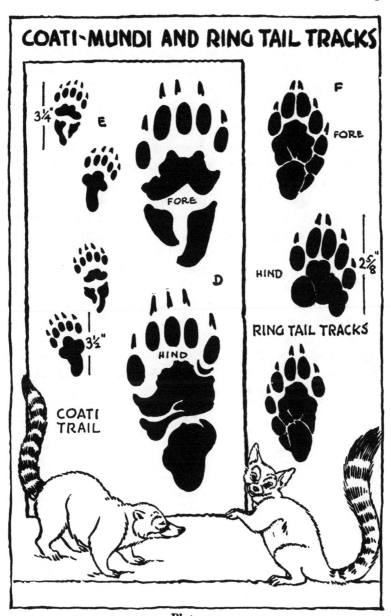

COATI-MUNDI AND RING TAIL TRACKS

E

3¼"

FORE

F

FORE

D

HIND

2⅝"

RING TAIL TRACKS

3½"

HIND

COATI
TRAIL

Plate 39

north as Texas, New Mexico and Arizona. It is a tree climber and usually comes down head first. When walking on the ground the ring tail is carried straight up, bent a little near the top.

The front and hind foot tracks are very much alike, the forefoot having a fold in the shape of a crude letter "T." Both tracks are shown in (D) Plate 39. The trail of the coati is shown in (E).

Ringtail (*Bassariscus astutus*). The ringtail belongs to the *Procyonidae* or raccoon family and resembles the raccoon but differs in being smaller and more slender with a longer and bushier tail. In color it is pale yellow-gray. A darker shade extends over the back and head. Under parts are yellowish white. The mask of this raccoon is only a blackish patch around the front half of the eye. The black rings extend only half way around the tail.

It is found in the mesquite and chaparral of Texas, New Mexico and Arizona, extending down into Mexico.

The ringtail is a toe walker. Unlike the flat footed tracks of the coon, the ringtail's are more like the cat's except that there are five instead of four toes on each foot. The hind and fore tracks are shown in drawing (F) Plate 39. The ringtail likes a high place for its home. If in a hollow tree, the wood and bark are gnawed off around the hole. It keeps this opening freshly gnawed. If it is not, the animal has deserted its den.

ANIMAL TRACKS OF
FIELD AND FOREST
8

The members of the weasel family have at least one thing in common and that is a powerful nauseating scent. All the weasel family have these poison gas scent glands. This identifying odor, especially among skunks, usually makes their presence known long before you see their tracks. While some members are bloodthirsty, others like the skunk and otter make affectionate pets. The skunk members of this family are especially valuable in insect control. A single skunk is known to devour as many insects as two acres of land will produce.

Common Skunk (*Mephitis mephitis*). Dead skunks are more often seen along our highways than any other animal, for the automobile has become a major enemy of our skunk population. The black skunk, with its white "V" for Victory on its back, is at home from Hudson Bay in Canada south to Guatemala. It is definitely a "flatfoot" and has five toes on each foot. Since it often digs for its dinner, the claws of its forefeet are well developed and are an important part of the forefoot track. No claws usually show in the track of the hind foot. See drawing (A) Plate 40. The diagonal character of its tracks when galloping, is its most characteristic trail (B). The diagonal formation also

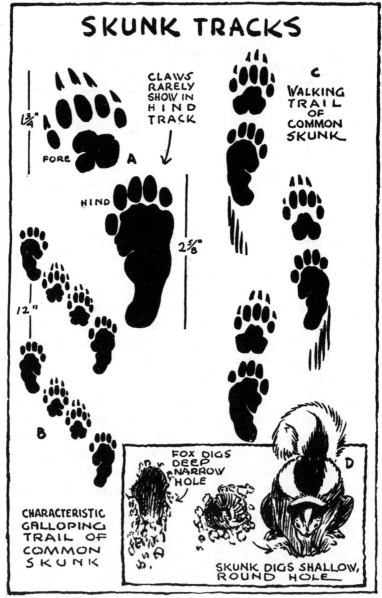

SKUNK TRACKS

CLAWS RARELY SHOW IN HIND TRACK

WALKING TRAIL OF COMMON SKUNK

FORE A

HIND

CHARACTERISTIC GALLOPING TRAIL OF COMMON SKUNK

FOX DIGS DEEP NARROW HOLE

SKUNK DIGS SHALLOW, ROUND HOLE

Plate 40

indicates that it is a ground dweller. In walking it toes in a bit and places the fore and hind foot of the same side close together, the forefoot slightly ahead of the hind track. Its tracks look somewhat like those of a very small bear's (C). Another sign of the skunk's presence are shallow, round, funnellike holes, which it digs when hunting for insect grubs (D). The fox also digs but its excavations are deeper and narrower than the skunk's.

Little Spotted Skunk (*Spilogale putorius*). The little spotted skunk is the smaller member of the skunk group. It ranges in size from a very large chipmunk to that of a fox squirrel. Its track, too, somewhat resembles a squirrel's since the forefeet tracks are paired behind the tracks of the hind feet. This track formation is especially interesting for it reveals the climbing ability of the little spotted skunk. See drawing (E) Plate 41. On close examination of the individual track, however, the skunk characteristics are clearly seen. First, the tracks are more stubby-toed than the squirrel's. Second, the spotted skunk forefoot track registers all five toes plainly while the squirrel shows only four toes (F) Plate 41.

The spotted skunk's track differs from the common skunk's for the latter's footprints when galloping are diagonal. Like the common skunk, the spotted skunk's claws of the hind feet are not always visible in the track. The spotted skunk too is a "flatfoot," for it walks upon the soles of its feet.

This skunk is known as "civet cat" in the fur trade and lives in scattered areas of Southern, Central and Western United States.

Common Weasel (*Mustela cicognanii*). The weasel is one of the bloodthirsty members of his family. In winter the northern weasels change their coats from brown to white. Only the black tips of their tails remain the same. However, where there is no snow this change does not occur.

The drawing (G) Plate 41 shows the tracks of the fore and

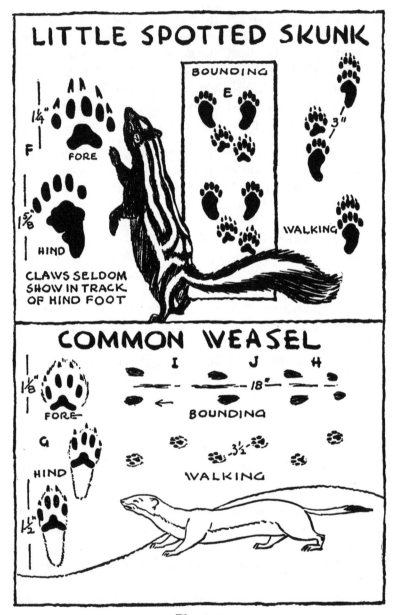

LITTLE SPOTTED SKUNK

BOUNDING

E

1¼"

F

FORE

1⅝"

HIND

CLAWS SELDOM
SHOW IN TRACK
OF HIND FOOT

3"

WALKING

COMMON WEASEL

1⅛"

FORE

I   J   H

18"

BOUNDING

G

HIND

3½"

WALKING

1½"

Plate 41

hind foot. Although the weasel has five toes on both the fore and hind foot, only four show in the track. When running, a weasel may take 18 inch bounds, the tracks of the hind feet being placed ahead of the forefeet. The change in the length of spacing between the fore and hind feet is often characteristic of the weasel's track (H). Being a "bounder" the lengths of jumps will of necessity vary in distance and so leave a wide range of spaces between his tracks. When in a hurry it may leap six feet. The tail mark may or may not be present (I). At times the weasel trail resembles a very small mink's. Some woodsmen say the weasel when running often leaves but two footprints at each bound instead of the usual four. In this instance the hind feet land exactly in the tracks made by the forefeet (J). A few weasels in an area make an astonishing number of trails twisting and interlaced and decorated here and there with the red stains of their woodland murders.

Least Weasel (*Mustela rixosa*). These are the dwarfs of the weasel family, varying from a half to less than a fourth the size of the larger members. The most northern species, *Mustela rixosa*, often called the "mouse weasel," is at home in Alaska and northern Canada and is the smallest of the family. The tail of this member is very short and is never tipped with black. Like the larger species they change their summer brown to winter white. Unlike other weasels these tiny fellows spend their lives destroying field mice, although they are smaller than a good sized meadow mouse. The least weasel tracks are similar to those of the rest of his family except of course in size (K) Plate 42.

Mink (*Mustela vison*). The mink is a "betwixt and between" member of the weasel family. That is, it usually hunts on the margins between land and water. Its relative the otter likes the water, while the weasel likes the land for a hunting ground. Although the mink uses both elements when hunting, it can equal neither the weasel on land nor the otter in the water. And so its

LEAST WEASEL TRACKS

TAIL WITHOUT BLACK TIP

FORE

HIND

K

$\frac{12}{16}"$

BOUNDING TRAIL

MINK TRACKS

$1\frac{3}{8}"$

FORE

L

HIND

N

ANOTHER MINK TRAIL

M

TAIL

← 12" →

TYPICAL MINK TRAIL

Plate 42

tracks and signs are usually found along the muddy shores or upon flat stones and projecting logs.

Although the mink has five toes on each foot only four register. A typical mink track is that illustrated in drawing (L) Plate 42. Sometimes the tail leaves its impression between the tracks of the paws. When bounding, from 12 to 24 inches may be cleared at each leap. The hind feet are placed ahead of the tracks of the front ones, when running. The drawing (M) shows a typical mink trail including the mark of the tail. (N) is another variation of this animal's trail.

Marten or Sable (*Martes americana*). One of the most beautiful and graceful of our forest animals, it is perhaps one of the shyest and few men can say they have seen it alive in its native home. Its rich brown coat is highly prized in the fur market. It lives in the wildest forest areas from the northern limit of trees to southern United States. A great tree climber, it is equally at home on the ground.

Although the track resembles a weasel's, the marten's track is much larger, this animal being 3 feet in length. The drawing (O) Plate 43 shows the footprints and a typical marten trail.

Fisher or Pekan (*Martes pennanti*). The fisher, like the marten, is a forest weasel and is even more at home in the trees than the marten. Its home range is in Canada and the United States. This is perhaps the only animal that can kill a porcupine without getting full of quills. It very dexterously places its paw underneath the unprotected belly of the porcupine and flips him over.

Both fore and hind feet tracks of the fisher look somewhat like those of the mink except that a fifth toe seems to have been added as an afterthought. See drawing (P) Plate 43. When bounding it makes a typical weasel trail except for the large size of the tracks (Q).

Otter (*Lutra canadensis*). In the New World otters are found from the northern timberline to southern South America. There

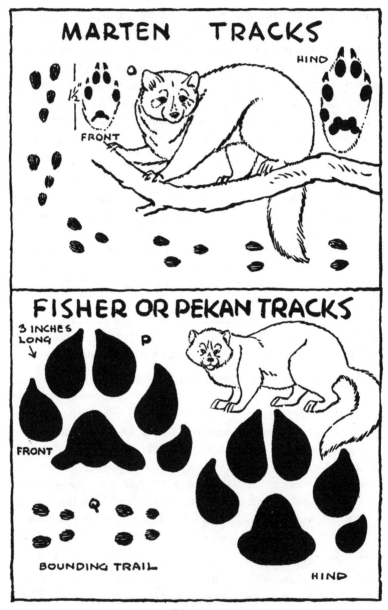

Plate 43

are a number of species and geographic races but the Canadian otter is common throughout Canada and the United States. It is a graceful, dusky brown animal about 4 or 5 feet long frequenting streams and other waterways where fish are to be had. Like the weasels the otter is short legged, poorly adapted to land traveling. However, in the water it is most graceful and agile, easily overtaking fish. In winter it travels great distances over land, searching for open water. It is then that you can see its characteristic trail. It travels in a series of bounds, each leaving a well defined, full length impression in the snow.

It looks like a continuous furrow in the snow with the otter's padded footprints often imprinted (R) Plate 44. The porcupine and beaver leave a similar trail but their footprints identify their trails.

The otter slide, too, is a very characteristic sign. Otters are most playful and spend hours sliding down slippery mud banks made smooth and slick by their wet bodies.

Both the fore and hind feet have five toes but, like the fisher, the fifth toe seems to be an afterthought. The toes are all curved like the fisher's too. Both feet make a rounded track but the hind foot is a little longer (S) Plate 44. Its relationship to the ground is indicated in its running trail for the hind feet are placed ahead of the forefeet tracks in a diagonal pattern (T). When jumping, the hind feet cover the forefoot tracks so that only the hind feet seem to be used. In this instance the tracks are paired but the heavy tail of the otter leaves a very characteristic diagonal mark (U) Plate 44.

Sea Otter (*Euhydra lutris*). This otter is the seagoing member of the weasel family for it is more at home in the Pacific Ocean than upon land. However, like all sailors it does come ashore and occasionally leaves its tracks in the sand and mud. Almost exterminated by fur hunters, mammalogists today are encouraged by the comeback of this animal in recent years. The sea otter adults are 5 feet in length, the young about 15 inches.

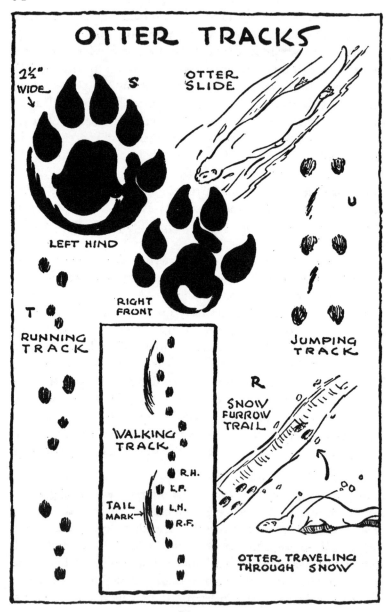

Plate 44

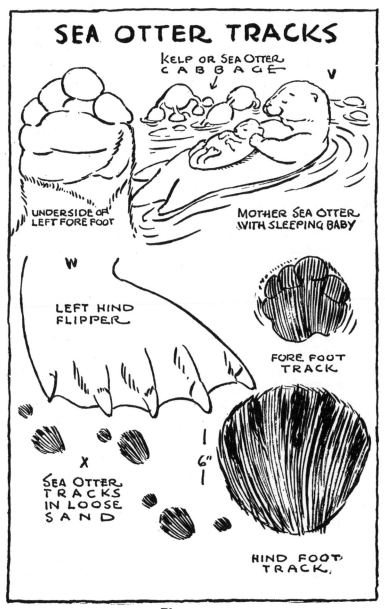

SEA OTTER TRACKS

KELP OR SEA OTTER CABBAGE

V

UNDERSIDE OF LEFT FORE FOOT

MOTHER SEA OTTER WITH SLEEPING BABY

W

LEFT HIND FLIPPER

FORE FOOT TRACK

X

SEA OTTER TRACKS IN LOOSE SAND

6"

HIND FOOT TRACK

Plate 45

The mother sea otter may sometimes be seen floating on her back amid the kelp or sea otter cabbage, her baby asleep on her breast. See drawing (V) Plate 45. When resting the animals are most sociable and gather in herds. They separate, however, when foraging. Only one baby at a time seems to be the rule.

The forefoot is very stubby, the four toes seemingly squeezed together. The hind foot has developed into a webbed flipperlike paw with five toes present, each equipped with claws. The hind flipper is furred on both sides. See drawing (W) Plate 45. On land the sea otter's tracks, when walking, show the imprint of the broad hind flipper just back of the round depression of the forepaw. See drawing (X) Plate 45.

Badger (*Taxidea taxus*). The badger is at home in the West and Middle West from Canada to Mexico and wherever it may be, there too are its diggings, for it spends the night digging out small rodents, its chief food. The trail of the badger in a single night is often marked by numerous holes, each with its fresh mound of earth upon which its tracks are imprinted. The marks of the huge digging claws of its forefeet are most characteristic in its tracks. Its hind claws do not seem to register. Like the skunk it has five toes imprinted in each track and its hind feet, too, somewhat resemble the skunk's. See drawing (Y) Plate 46.

Its trail when walking is composed of a double row of footprints close together, indicating it to be a heavy, clumsy animal. Its hind footprints are toed-in somewhat and touch the tracks made by the forefeet (Z) Plate 46. When running it makes a peculiar diagonal track with both hind and forefeet, placing the tracks of its hind feet ahead of its front tracks (XX) Plate 46.

The badger looks like a low slung bear cub, silver-gray and marked with black and white on the head.

Wolverine (*Gulo luscus*). The northern part of this continent is the home of this animal, which is so hated by trappers, both red and white alike. No cache seems to be safe from its depredations.

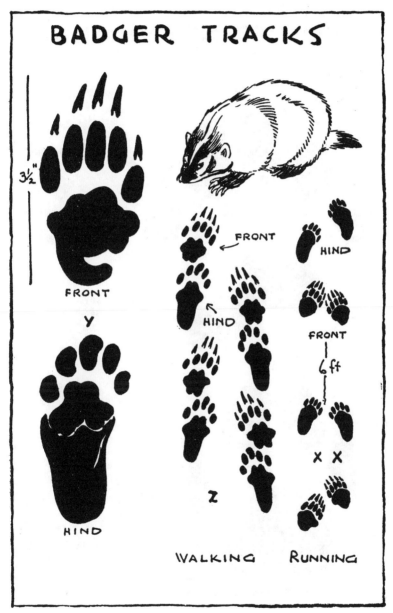

Plate 46

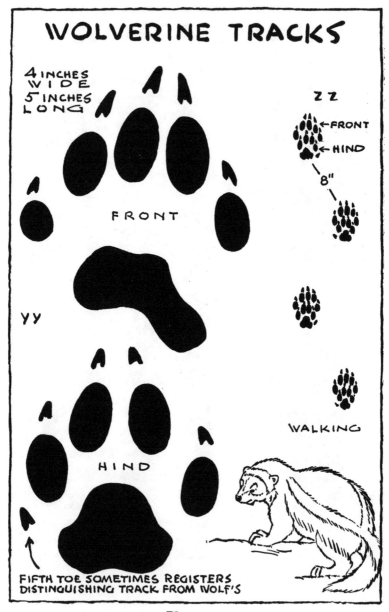

WOLVERINE TRACKS

4 INCHES WIDE
5 INCHES LONG

FRONT

YY

HIND

FIFTH TOE SOMETIMES REGISTERS
DISTINGUISHING TRACK FROM WOLF'S

ZZ

←FRONT
←HIND

8"

WALKING

Plate 47

Once it has befouled the cache with its scent, no animal or human will want to touch it again. The wolverine has scent glands like other weasels and they give off a heavy yellow-brown colored secretion with a most evil odor. This is its mark.

Its tracks at first glance resemble the wolf's. However, in deep snow, the furrow it ploughs tells of the heavy squat animal that made it. It has five toes on each foot but the fifth toe shows up only slightly even under perfect tracking conditions (YY) Plate 47. The forefoot track is larger and wider than the hind and measures about 5 inches long. When walking, the wolverine's tracks are slightly out of register. See drawing (ZZ) showing its walking trail. Like the wolf the wolverine is a toe walker. Its relative the skunk, however, is a flatfoot.

HOOFED ANIMALS (UNGULATA)

The hoofed animals long ago got rid of their surplus toes, one, three or four, according to their choice of domain and have walked upon their toenails ever since. All living native ungulates have two well developed toes ending in hardened hoofs or toe-nails. We call these cloven hoofed. They make a two-petallike track, large or small according to the animal. Some also have two additional toes, which are known as dewclaws or clouts, all except the antelope, who lost its dewclaws in distant ages. The peccary has two dewclaws on the forefeet but only one on the hind.

The dewclaws are important to the hoofed animals, when walking in snow or upon soft ground, for they help to spread the weight of the animal over a greater area (A) Plate 48. In many instances the dewclaws do not register unless the animal walks upon soft ground or lands more heavily upon the earth, as in running.

In dry weather or sometimes in winter, as with caribou, the inner part of each hoof often dries up, leaving only the crescent shaped outer shell. See drawing (B) Plate 48 of the caribou foot.

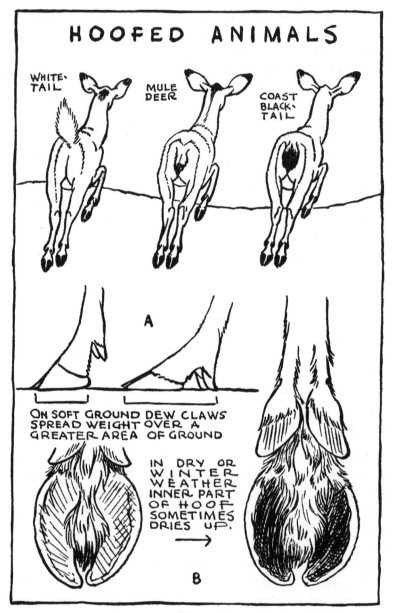

Plate 48

This often aids the animal in getting a better grip on slippery surfaces of rock or ice.

Whitetail or Virginia Deer (*Odocoileus virginianus*). The whitetail or Virginia deer is the common deer of the East. To most of us it is the symbol of the wild, yet strange to say it thrives in the farming areas of civilization. Here most of its enemies have been exterminated by man, and farm crops, such as young lettuce, cabbage, etc., are greatly relished.

Thus the whitetail's tracks are often found in the woodlands and fields close to long established communities. Regardless of this habit, however, its tracks will always be reminiscent of the wildwood, of buckskin shirt and flintlock rifle. When we find its beautiful petallike tracks in the nearby woodlot, we still get a thrill that only wild Nature can grant.

The tracks of domestic sheep, goats and even the unromantic pig are often mistaken for deer, but a close examination of the footprint of the deer reveals its aristocracy. Though the domestic animals have cloven hoofs, often the same size as the deer's, they lack the shapely grace of this wild creature's.

Since the deer is a "quiet walker" it often steps with its hind feet exactly into the tracks made by its forefeet. This, however, is not always true since the deer tracks often show the forefoot track projecting from under the track of the hind foot (C) Plate 49. When bounding the deer shows its kinship with ground dwellers by the diagonal arrangement of its tracks (D).

The tracks of the doe are smaller and slimmer and point straight forward or inward, while the buck points his toes outward (E) Plate 49. As in most instances in the deer family, the buck spreads his feet more widely than does the doe. Especially during the rutting season the buck drags his feet like a lazy schoolboy (F). Pawed-up ground, and trees or bushes scraped by antlers are other buck signs. The fawn's track is a miniature replica of its parents' (G) Plate 49.

When a deer speeds in an all-out effort, it strings out its tracks

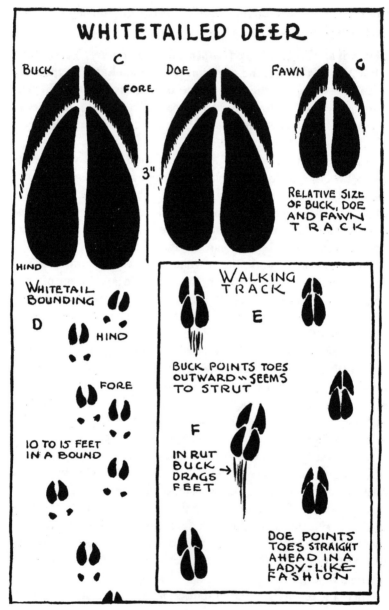

Plate 49

in almost a straight line with a space of 16 to 24 feet between bounds. A deer at full speed also spreads its hoofs more widely than when walking and the dewclaws also register (H) Plate 50. A deer with a broken foreleg drags the injured member and makes a trail as shown in drawing (I). Some woodsmen say a young buck places his hind feet ahead of his front feet in the walking track, while an old buck's hind feet lag behind the fore-foot print (J) Plate 50. A full-grown buck's track measures about 3 inches, a doe's about 2½ inches and a fawn's ¾ of an inch in length.

The matted circular beds on grassy hillsides are other signs of the whitetail's presence in the neighborhood (K) Plate 50. In winter the whitetail often "yard" (L) Plate 50, that is, they frequent areas where the food is best and here their numerous trails cross and crisscross in a maze of trails kept open by daily use. Outside this yard the drifts grow deep, often keeping the deer imprisoned until spring.

Mule Deer (*Odocoileus hemionus*). The mule deer's large butterfly ears (A) Plate 51, its black tassellike tail and the large scent gland slits on the lower part of its hind legs easily identify this western deer. Since the mule deer places its feet firmly upon the ground when walking, its tracks are somewhat rounder in appearance than the whitetail's. The walking and trotting trails are similar to the whitetail's, but when speeding it has its own peculiar method of bounding as if it were on springs. There is seemingly little leg movement, sailing lightly into the air from all four feet and landing again on all four. This characteristic gait produces curious, closely grouped tracks of all four feet, very unlike the bounding tracks of the whitetail (B) Plate 51. The mule deer's track measures about 3¼ inches long and is shown in drawing (C).

Like the whitetail deer, it makes rounded nests on grassy hillsides about 4 feet across. During the rutting season the bucks also paw "scrapes," small wallows about a yard square, in moist

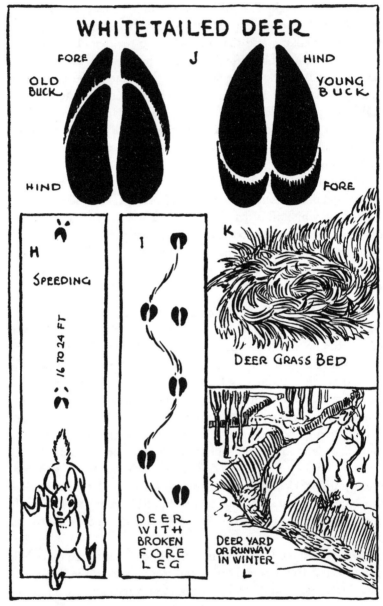

WHITETAILED DEER

FORE   J   HIND

OLD BUCK   YOUNG BUCK

HIND   FORE

H SPEEDING   16 TO 24 FT

I

K

DEER GRASS BED

DEER WITH BROKEN FORE LEG

DEER YARD OR RUNWAY IN WINTER

L

Plate 50

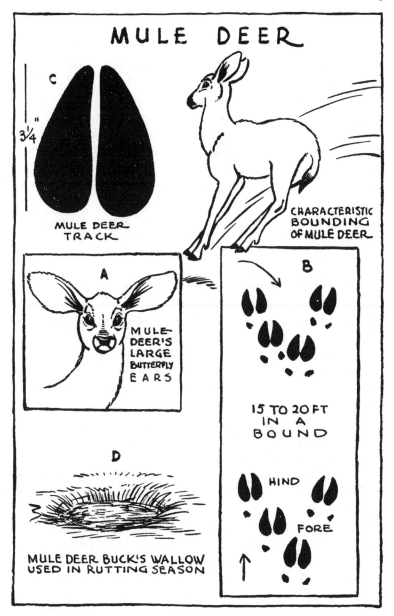

MULE DEER

C

3¼"

MULE DEER
TRACK

CHARACTERISTIC
BOUNDING
OF MULE DEER

A

MULE-
DEER'S
LARGE
BUTTERFLY
EARS

B

15 TO 20 FT
IN A
BOUND

HIND

FORE

D

MULE DEER BUCK'S WALLOW
USED IN RUTTING SEASON

Plate 51

ground (D) Plate 51. The buck also drags his feet at this time.

Coast Blacktail Deer (*Odocoileus columbianus*). The Columbia blacktail is the deer of the Pacific coast, ranging from Alaska to California. Except in California where it can be found as far east as the Sierras, its range is only 150 miles wide in the wet forest belt of the coast. One of its distinguishing marks is the black tail faced with white underneath. The antlers of the blacktail buck resemble those of the mule deer. It weighs less than the mule deer, seldom more than 150 pounds, while the mule deer may reach 200 pounds.

The tracks of the blacktail resemble those of the mule deer especially when bounding, an action characteristic of the species (A) Plate 52. Its walking track is like that of any other deer (B).

Elk or Wapiti (*Cervus canadensis*). Although elk are found only in the West today, they were distributed much more widely in the past. The elk is one of the larger members of the deer family and its tracks, when full grown, often measure 4½ inches in length and 3 to 3½ inches in width. A strange characteristic of the bull and cow elk is the difference in the spread of the hoofs. The bull's hoofs are very close together (A) Plate 53, while the cow's are spread more widely apart (B). Due to the habit of pawing the ground, the bull's hoofs are more blunted. The dewclaws too are thicker and blunter in the bull's. However, the dewclaws only register in mud or snow.

Like the buck deer, the bull elk points his toes outward, while the cow points hers straight ahead. The bull's feet too are spread farther from the center line of the trail than are the cow's (C) Plate 53. The larger the bull the wider the space between the right and left footprints. The young bull oversteps his forefoot track with his hind. However, if the larger track (the forefoot) be in front, it is that of an old bull. When trotting, the elk trail stretches out in a straight line (D) Plate 53. In galloping

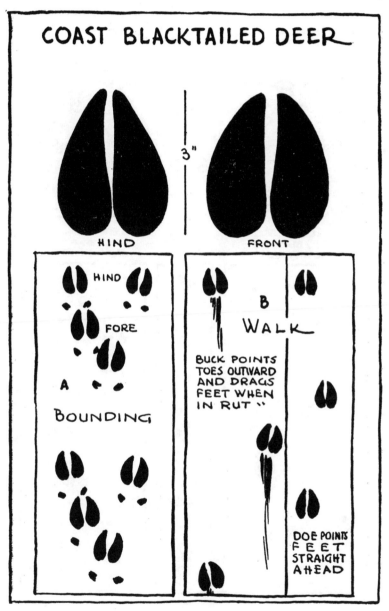

COAST BLACKTAILED DEER

3"

HIND

FRONT

HIND

FORE

A

BOUNDING

B

WALK

BUCK POINTS
TOES OUTWARD
AND DRAGS
FEET WHEN
IN RUT

DOE POINTS
FEET
STRAIGHT
AHEAD

Plate 52

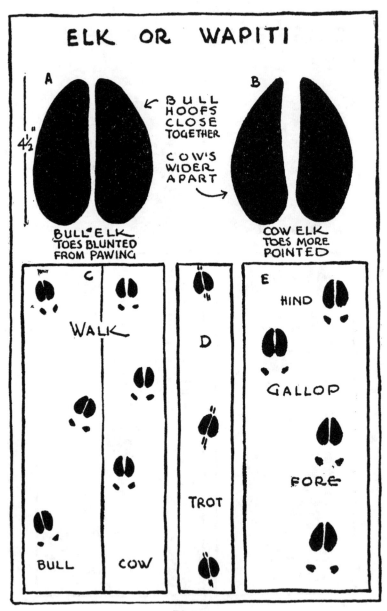

ELK OR WAPITI

A — BULL HOOFS CLOSE TOGETHER — COW'S WIDER APART — B

4½"

BULL ELK TOES BLUNTED FROM PAWING

COW ELK TOES MORE POINTED

C — WALK — BULL — COW

D — TROT

E — HIND — GALLOP — FORE

Plate 53

the hind feet are placed diagonally ahead of the fore footprints (E).

Moose (*Alces americanus*). Moose are northern residents and are found in Canada and some parts of northern United States. In summer, to escape insect pests and to feed upon their favorite water plants, they frequent lakes and streams. Uprooted aquatic vegetation usually indicates moose have been recently feeding. Since moose use their hoofs as weapons, they are long and pointed and perhaps the largest of our native ungulates. The average moose track is about 7 inches long. The great size, pointed shape and long stride easily distinguish it from that of a domestic cow's.

The bull's track is usually rounder and blunter than that of the cow moose (A) Plate 54. There is also a greater distance between the dewclaws and the hoofs of the bull. The bull points his toes outward, the cow straight ahead. As in other antlered relatives, the bull tracks are farther from the center line than are the cow's (B). He also takes strides of 3 to 5 feet while the cow's are considerably less. The drawing (C) shows tracks of a moose trotting and at a gallop. Note the diagonal character of both front and hind tracks indicating a ground dweller.

Other signs of a bull's proximity are twigs and branches broken by his antlers, pawed ground and his strong smelling wallows. These are shallow depressions which he paws into the mud about 3 or 4 feet wide and irrigates with his urine (D) Plate 54. In this mess he wallows and although he is perhaps the most outstanding example of "B.O." after this mud pack, he seems to be very popular with the lady moose.

Caribou (*Rangifer caribou*). The caribou, the American reindeer, are the only members of the deer family where the female normally has antlers. The name "caribou" is that given to this animal by the New England Indians. The dewclaws or accessory hoofs of the caribou are so long, they commonly reach the ground like the heels of high-heel slippers (A) Plate 55. Most

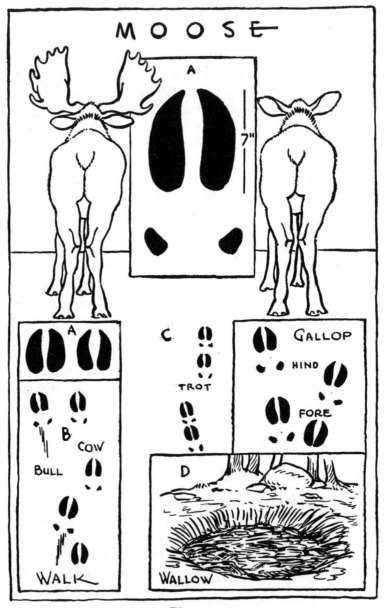

Plate 54

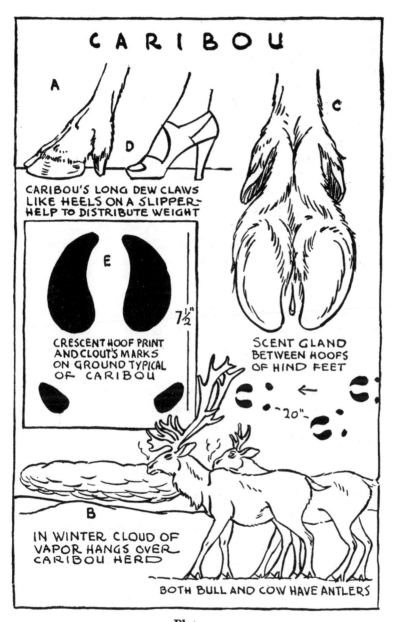

CARIBOU

A

D

CARIBOU'S LONG DEW CLAWS
LIKE HEELS ON A SLIPPER-
HELP TO DISTRIBUTE WEIGHT

C

E

7½"

CRESCENT HOOF PRINT
AND CLOUT'S MARKS
ON GROUND TYPICAL
OF CARIBOU

SCENT GLAND
BETWEEN HOOFS
OF HIND FEET

~20"~

B

IN WINTER CLOUD OF
VAPOR HANGS OVER
CARIBOU HERD

BOTH BULL AND COW HAVE ANTLERS

Plate 55

animals have a comparatively small home range. In the case of the caribou, however, it travels the whole year round and often migrates long distances to escape the deadly cold or the equally deadly insect hordes.

In winter, caribou herds may be spotted from a distance by the cloud of vapor that often hangs over the animals caused by the body warmth of the closely packed herd and by the collective vapor from their breathing (B) Plate 55.

The scent glands of the caribou are located between the hoofs of the hind feet and give off an unctuous secretion (C) Plate 55. Like the mule deer, the inner part of the caribou's hoofs is absorbed or dries up and the outer edges develop into sharp thin ridges. This enables the caribou to walk securely upon ice and snow and will be described fully in Chapter X on "Woodland Snowshoe Tracks." The large crescent-shaped hoofprints are easily identified. Since it travels much on snow and in swamps it has wide spreading hoofs and the elongated dewclaws act as additional supporting stilts (D) Plate 55. Thus the caribou has a square inch for every two pounds of its weight, while the moose has eight pounds to the square inch. The drawing (E) shows characteristic caribou tracks.

Antelope (*Antilocapra americana*). The antelope is a unique creature for it combines the peculiar features of the giraffe, the deer and the goat. It has only two hoofs, the dewclaws being entirely absent. It has hollow horns like the goat family but these are branched and are shed every year like antlers.

The antelope, according to Hornaday, seems to have at least three gaits. When in danger it runs with its head low like a sheep. Sometimes it gallops with its head high. Again it may take stiff-legged leaps like the mule deer. These perhaps are for the purpose of getting a better view of the countryside.

The antelope's tracks are narrow and more tapering than those of the deer (A) Plate 56. They resemble somewhat the tracks of the mountain sheep in length and those of the domestic sheep

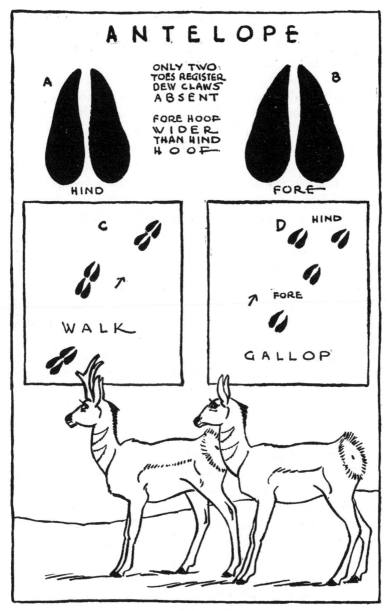

Plate 56

in the back portion of the hoof. The front hoofs are wider than the hind (B). The tracks, too, are larger than those of domestic sheep. The drawing (C) and (D) Plate 56 shows the walking trail and that of a galloping animal.

Rocky Mountain Goat (*Oreamnos montanus*). This big white goat of the mountains is found from Alaska to Montana and Washington. It is a true mountaineer and challenges the fierce winter gales on the high peaks. Just behind each sharp black horn is a black mass, its scent glands. As it wanders about, it often blazes a scent trail by rubbing its head and horns against the scrubby brush. It has four hoofs on each foot but only two register in the tracks. The goat's track reveals its relationship to the sheep and antelope. However, it wears "rubber heels," that is, the heel pads are so large and rubberlike, the track is rarely as sharp as other hoofed animals. The rubbery cushions act somewhat like suction cups when the goat climbs slippery rocks. The drawing (A) Plate 57 shows a track with its characteristic widely spread hoof tips. The ordinary walking track and that of a bounding animal are shown in (B) and (C).

Mountain goats are very fond of various minerals and salts found in the mountains and these characteristic "licks" are often seen (D) Plate 57. At times, too, dusty hollows are scraped out by the goats in which they roll and sprawl. They also make snow beds, probably to ease the irritation of insect bites.

Big Horn Mountain Sheep (*Ovis canadensis*). These mountain dwellers range from British Columbia possibly to northern New Mexico. In fact many ancient rock petroglyphs in New Mexico show that horned sheep were familiar to the prehistoric Indians there. Although it enjoys the higher mountain elevations in summer, winter storms drive it down to the foothills.

Its breath-taking leaps from crag to crag indicate its mountaineering ability. Its hoofs seem to be especially made for this work. The hoof spreads easily but the toes are not as widely

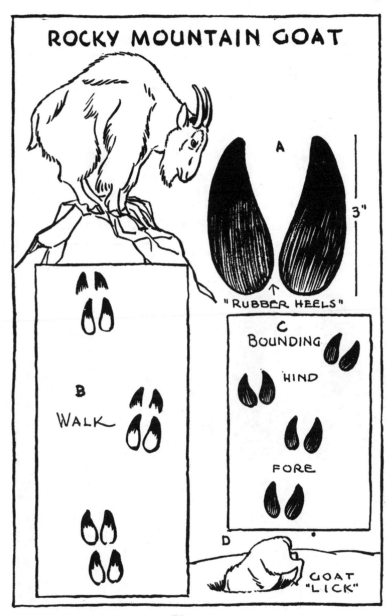

ROCKY MOUNTAIN GOAT

A

3"

↑
"RUBBER HEELS"

B
WALK

C
BOUNDING
HIND

FORE

D

GOAT
"LICK"

Plate 57

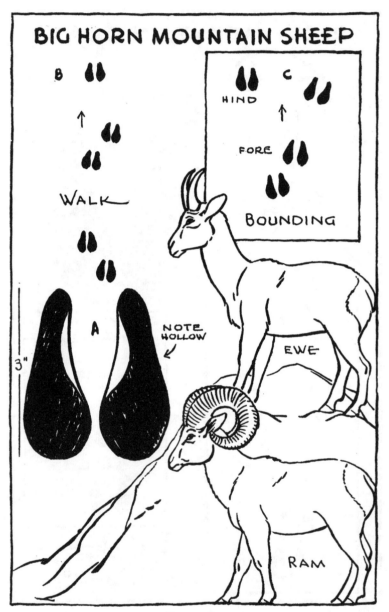

Plate 58

spread as the mountain goat's. The toes are more blunted than the deer's and the hollow on the outer edge of the hoof is very characteristic (A) Plate 58. The dewclaws, while present, rarely register in the track. At times the mountain sheep is a "perfect tracker," that is, it steps with its hind foot exactly into the track made by its forefoot. A characteristic walking trail and that of a bounding sheep are shown in (B) and (C) Plate 58.

Muskox (*Ovibos moschatus*). The muskox is an unusual animal found on the polar plains of Canada anatomically somewhat resembling the American bison. Its horns, however, are different from those of any other American mammal, being more like those of the African buffalo. It has rather an ancient lineage, for its fossil remains can be traced back to the Pleistocene.

The musk, from which it gets its name, is perhaps secreted by small skin glands and may serve as a protection against the insect hordes so common in its Northland home.

The muskox has four well developed hoofs on each foot (A) Plate 59, but only the forward two seem to register. The drawing (B) shows the tracks of the fore and hind foot and (C) illustrates the walking trail. Like other cloven hoofed beasts, the age of the animal is perhaps indicated by the position of the hind foot track in relation to that of the forefoot, the younger animals usually placing their hind foot track ahead of the forefoot, the older behind the forefoot track. See (C) Plate 59 the drawing of the walking trail.

The American Bison or Buffalo (*Bison bison*). The American bison, having a wide range in its habitat, produced a number of different races. In the north was found the large wood buffalo, in the Rockies the small dark mountain bison, in the plains a medium-sized lighter colored plains animal, and in the forests of some of our Eastern States the black Pennsylvanian variety.

Although it is estimated that the prehistoric numbers of buffalo must have been around 60 to 75 millions, today there are com-

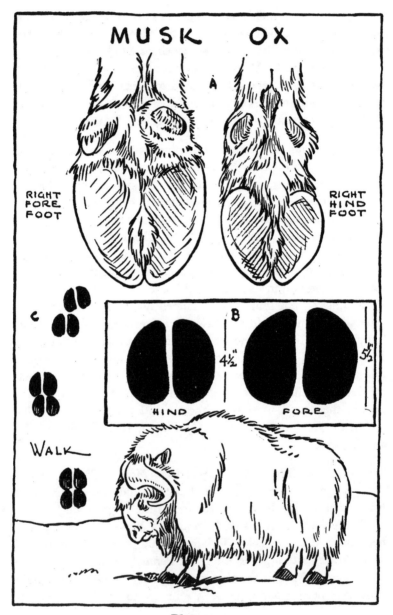

Plate 59

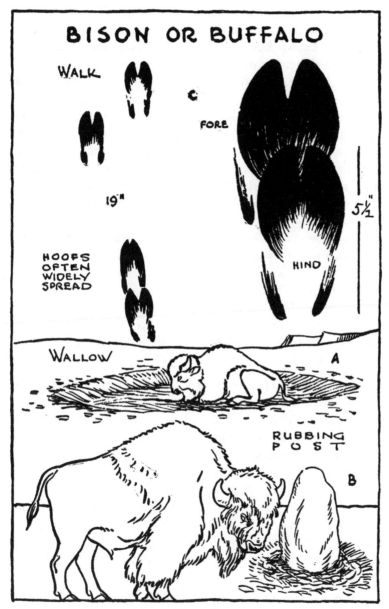

BISON OR BUFFALO

WALK

C

FORE

19"

5½"

HOOFS
OFTEN
WIDELY
SPREAD

HIND

WALLOW

A

RUBBING
POST

B

Plate 60

paratively few in small scattered herds in the United States and Canada. The most outstanding physical characteristic of the bison is its well known hump on the shoulders produced by a well developed elongation of the vertebral spines in that region.

One of the signs of the buffalo's presence in an area was the muddy wallow used as a mud bath against insects (A) Plate 60. Another buffalo sign was the rubbing post, convenient tree trunks and large boulders often worn smooth by countless generations of bison (B). The dung or "buffalo chips," as they were called, were flat cakes of dung often used for fuel on the plains. The sun-dried chips burned with a hot clear almost smokeless flame.

In the early days the buffalo trails were the most convenient paths for men and many of our roadways today were the buffalo trails of yesterday. While the tracks of the buffalo were common 200 years ago, they can only be found today in a few national parks and ranches. Like many of the cloven hoof family the buffalo has four hoofs on each foot, the rear two, the dewclaws, higher and smaller than the front two. The drawing (C) Plate 60 shows the tracks of a buffalo with the accessory hoofs registering. Since the bison is a heavy animal, the hoofs are often widely spread.

Peccary (*Pecari angulatus*). Today these strange little piglike animals are round from the southern parts of our Southwest south to Patagonia. They are equally at home in the dense growth along river bottoms or in the chaparral on the plains.

The peccary likes the company of its fellows and bands of 20 or 30 may be found led by an old grandparent. Unlike most hoofed animals it sleeps in some sort of a den, in a hollow log or hole. The peccary is omnivorous, that is, it eats almost anything, vegetable or animal. One of the signs of its presence is its characteristic rooting up of the ground (much like that of our domestic pig) in its search for edible roots, bulbs and grubs.

While it makes a piglike track, its hind feet are unusual, having

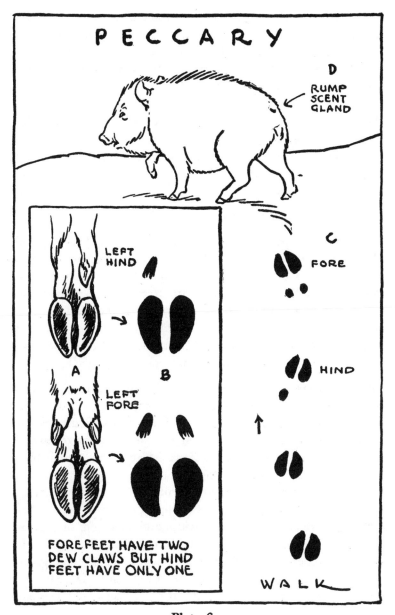

PECCARY

D
RUMP
SCENT
GLAND

LEFT
HIND

FORE C

LEFT
FORE

A

B

HIND

LEFT
FORE

FORE FEET HAVE TWO
DEW CLAWS BUT HIND
FEET HAVE ONLY ONE

WALK

Plate 61

only three toes. The forefeet are like those of most of the hoofed animals, having four toes (two front hoofs and two dewclaws). The drawing (A) Plate 61 shows the front and rear feet. The fore and hind foot tracks are pictured in (B) and a trail made by a peccary when walking in (C).

This animal also makes scent trails, having a scent or musk gland located on the back about 8 inches from the tail (D), Plate 61. The peccary will often rub its back against low shrubbery, probably marking its territory. When danger threatens it also emits musk to warn its relatives.

RODENTS (RODENTIA)

The rodents are perhaps the most numerous in the animal world. Most of this family are small, the largest in North America being the beaver, and all are distinguished by.the two gnawing teeth in each jaw. Some of this family are tree climbers. Others are ground dwellers. Many are bounders, that is, their hind legs are longer than their front ones. Some walk on the flat of their feet, like the beaver and porcupine. Many members of this order have only four toes on the front feet, while others have five toes.

Meadow Mouse (*Microtus pennsylvanicus*). The meadow mouse is found over a wide area of this continent, from the frozen tundras of the North to the arid desert lands of the Southwest. Its shredded nests of grass may often be found and were used as tinder in fire making by the Indians. Meadow mice often blaze trees and shrubs by gnawing the bark.

The meadow mouse is a great trailmaker, covering its range with a network of tiny runways leading in all directions. These little trails are about an inch in width and lead from the burrow to various feeding areas. The little runways are kept spick and span, with all obstructions carefully removed so that nothing shall impede its getaway when hard pressed by enemies (D), Plate 62. The meadow mouse is a ground dweller and, like all of this group, its places its forefeet diagonally behind its hind feet when it runs (E), Plate 62. Since its tail is very short it never registers in the tracks. The walking track of the meadow mouse is like that of the bear, the fore and hind foot registering together (F) Plate 62. The front feet have only four toes, the hind feet five.

Deer Mouse (*Peromyscus leucopus*). In contrast to the meadow mouse, the deer mouse, or white-footed mouse, has a much longer tail and its mark is always present in snow or dust. The deer mouse is the most attractive of the mouse family, having large ears and eyes and is colored a soft tan or gray above and pure white below. This mouse is a tree climber (A), Plate 62 and its nests are often found in old deserted bird nests (B) roofed over, in hollow trees and other elevated shelters. Its tree climbing ability is indicated in its tracks, for like the squirrel it pairs its forefeet behind its hind feet when running (C). The delicate tracery of its tracks is often seen on new fallen snow in the woods. Like many rodents, it has four toes on the front feet and five on the hind. The deer mouse has cheek pouches in which it carries supplies to its storehouses. Like the red squirrel and rabbit it often signals by drumming. It does this by rapidly beating any near object with its paw.

Grasshopper Mouse (*Onychomys leucogaster*). Another ground dweller of the mouse family is the grasshopper mouse, whose fairy rabbitlike tracks reveal the ability of keeping its feet on the ground (A), Plate 63. It places its forefeet diagonally behind its hind feet as it runs. The hind feet of the grasshopper mouse have only four well developed toes. The fifth is so stubby it is barely noticeable (B). In this it differs from the meadow and deer mouse, who have five toes on the hind feet. The tail seldom or never shows in the trail. The grasshopper mouse lives in burrows on the treeless areas of the West. Its liking for grasshoppers has given it its name, but its appetite for flesh is so strong it often kills other small animals.

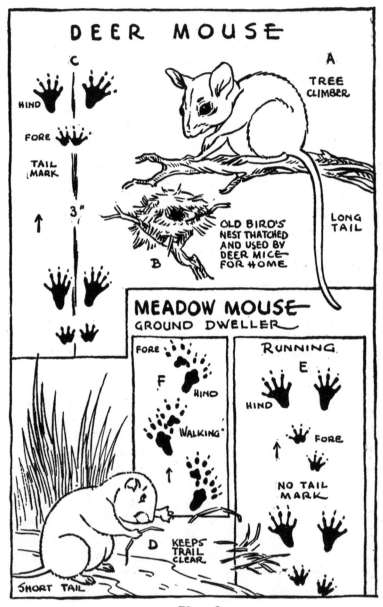

Plate 62

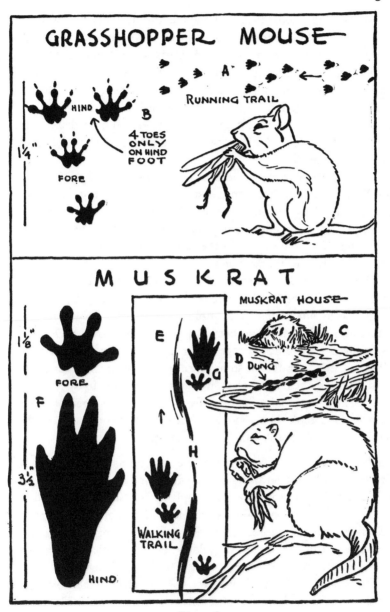

GRASSHOPPER MOUSE

A RUNNING TRAIL

HIND

B

4 TOES ONLY ON HIND FOOT

1¼"

FORE

MUSKRAT

MUSKRAT HOUSE

1⅛"

FORE

E

G

C

D DUNG

F

3½"

H

WALKING TRAIL

HIND

Plate 63

Muskrat (*Fiber zibethicus*). Although the muskrat is a stay-at-home and seldom wanders far from its home marshland unless forced to, it is one of the most widely distributed animals on this continent. Its rounded lodges of cattails and marsh grass are perhaps the outstanding advertisement of its presence in the neighborhood (C), Plate 63. The muskrat itself is about three or four times the size of the common house rat with brown dense fur. It has partly webbed hind feet and a nearly naked scaly tail flattened vertically.

A pile of empty clam shells on the bank is another sign the muskrat is around. Sometimes it sticks the clams into a blistering hot sand bank to save itself the job of opening the shells. Another muskrat sign is its musky dung placed upon logs projecting into the water (D), Plate 63. Like the beaver it sometimes digs canals and these also are muskrat signs.

The tracks of the muskrat (F), Plate 63, show that it has only four toes on its forefeet but five on its hind. Its trail (E) weaves from side to side as if it had imbibed too much "firewater." Its tracks also look as if it had been stepping upon its own heels with its forefeet (G). This strange effect is created by the fact that although it is a flatfoot it steps more heavily upon the toes of its hind feet and thus does not obliterate the track made by its forefeet when it walks upon it. It really steps upon the forefoot track with its hind foot. The wavy line between its footprints is made by the sharp edge of its tail (H), Plate 63.

Pack or Trade Rat (*Neotoma cinerea*). The name of this rat is descriptive of its characteristic activity, that of carrying off an object and leaving something in its place. It is in this way that it establishes its museum mounds, visible evidence of the pack rat's presence. The mound is a large ever-growing pile of sticks, leaves, cactus and rubbish and trash galore that the rat has picked up from time to time and brought to its nest (A), Plate 64.

The tracks of the pack rat resemble somewhat the common rat's, but being a climber it often pairs its forefeet (B). The fore-

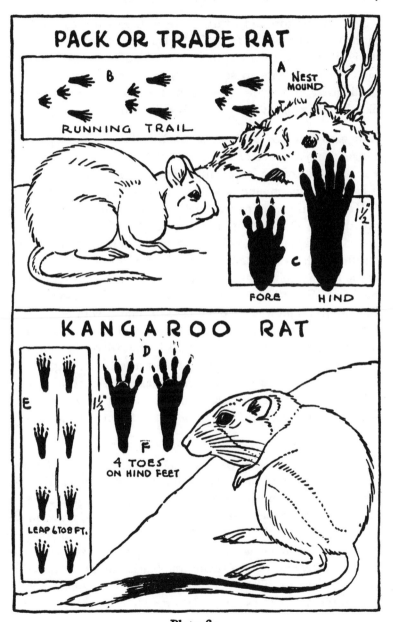

PACK OR TRADE RAT

B

NEST MOUND

A

RUNNING TRAIL

FORE   HIND

C

1½"

KANGAROO RAT

D

E

1½"

F

4 TOES ON HIND FEET

LEAP 6 TO 8 FT.

Plate 64

foot shows four toes and a very stubby fifth. Five toes clearly show in the track of the hind foot (C). When the animal is in a hurry, the heel print sometimes is absent in the hind footprints. The pack rat evidently resorts to scent trails for it has a strong musky smell, given off perhaps by glands on the belly of the animal. Unlike the common rat the pack rat's tail is hairy.

Kangaroo Rat (*Dipodomys spectabilis*). For the most part the kangaroo rat's choice of home are dry areas from Manitoba to Panama. One of the most conspicuous signs of this rat's presence is its large home mound of sand with its numerous entrances.

However, the little paired tracks of this beautiful desert sprite are the best evidence of its nearness (D), Plate 64. Since it bounds like a kangaroo, only its two hind feet register in the track together with its long tail (E). Its forefeet are small in contrast to the long jumping hind legs and there are only four toes on the hind foot (F). When in danger it can leap 6 to 8 feet in a bound. Its powerful hind legs are often used in combat with others of its kind. Since it is nocturnal, only the tracery of its tracks is usually seen and even these are soon erased by the wind. For the keen noses of its kind, the kangaroo rat has a large scent gland between the shoulders that secretes a waxy substance of strange odor. With this little scent pad it blazes its trails on the low hanging scrub for all to read. This scent pad is shown in Plate 12 (G), page 26.

Gray Squirrel (*Sciurus carolinensis*). In winter when the trees are bare, a mass of dried leaves and twigs may be seen lodged high in the top-most branches. This is the gray squirrel's temporary shelter for occasional naps (A), Plate 65. The gray squirrel is found only in the East from southern Canada to southern United States. While it is commonly a pepper and salt gray color in the United States, in Canada the black variant or melanistic phase is the rule. The black variety seems to be found only in the northern part of its range. Both the black and gray, however,

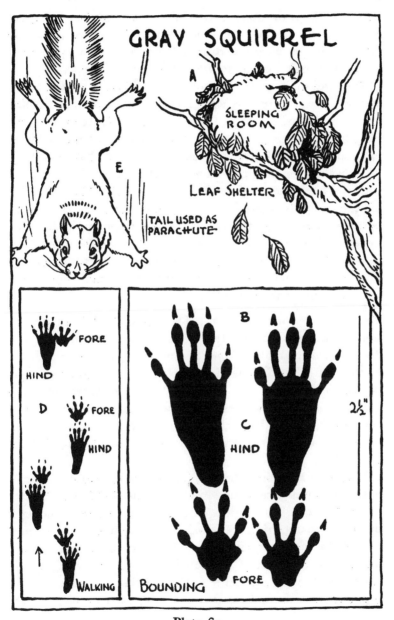

GRAY SQUIRREL

A

SLEEPING ROOM

E

LEAF SHELTER

TAIL USED AS PARACHUTE

B

FORE

HIND

D   FORE

HIND

C

HIND

2½"

FORE

HIND

↑

WALKING   BOUNDING   FORE

Plate 65

may come from the same nest. While the average home range of this squirrel is usually not more than a few acres, it and its fellows often get the wanderlust and at times make migrations of hundreds of miles, often crossing large lakes and rivers.

The gray squirrel is a flatfoot, that is, it walks on the palms and the soles of its feet. When running it reveals its tree climbing habits by the pairing of its front feet behind its hind feet (B), Plate 65. It has only four toes and a knoblike thumb on its forefoot, but there are five well developed toes on its hind foot (C). When walking on the ground, however, it makes an alternate track with the hind and forefeet close together (D), Plate 65. This indicates it is also a ground walker. In soft snow its large fluffy tail sometimes leaves its mark as it bounds. Ordinarily the gray squirrel will take a half dozen hops and then take time out for a look around. When in a hurry it can increase its leaps from 2 feet to 5 feet. In making high jumps from trees it fluffs out its tail and uses it as a parachute (E), Plate 65.

Fox Squirrel (*Sciurus niger*). The fox squirrel is larger and stockier than the gray squirrel, being almost twice the size. The eastern hardwood forests from the southern tip of the Great Lakes to southern United States form its range. It makes two types of nests in the trees. One is just a platform of sticks without a roof covering. The other nest has a well built weatherproof roof covering. This type is usually built high up in some tall tree. A more permanent den is usually made in a woodpecker hole or hollow tree.

Like the gray squirrel the fox squirrel has four toes and a stump of the fifth on its forefeet and five toes on the hind feet (A), Plate 66. Although it is more of a ground dweller, when bounding it makes the characteristic tree dweller track by pairing the forefeet behind the hind feet (B). When foraging, it pairs its forefeet ahead of its hind feet (C). The tail, however, never registers in the track. The fox squirrel has special eating perches and often a pile of nutshells and rejected nuts advertise its dining haunts.

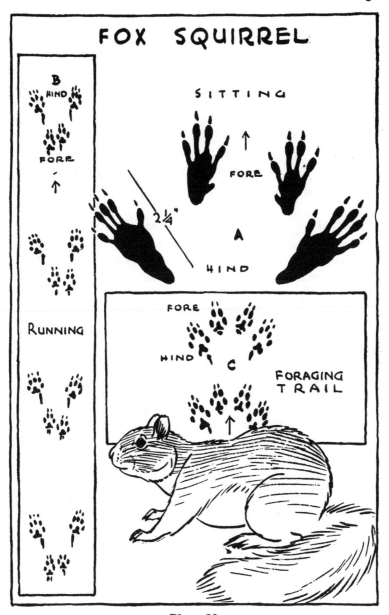

Plate 66

Red Squirrel (*Sciurus hudsonicus*). The red squirrel's red coat and white underparts are a distinctive uniform easily identified. It not only leaves its autographs all over the winter woods but makes its presence known with its rich and strong red squirrel vocabulary as well. Every red squirrel has several dining platforms, stumps or logs where it husks and shells nuts and cuts up cones. These eating spots are easily discovered for heaps of cone scales and shells are found about the spot (A), Plate 67. Another sign of the red squirrel's presence are such foods as mushrooms, fruits, etc., that are cached in the branches of trees (B), Plate 67. Like other squirrels, it often makes rounded and roofed platform nests.

The red squirrel sleeps only during the coldest and darkest days and so it's often found frolicking in the winter snow. At times it digs tunnels in the soft snow for recreation and to reach buried food. There are usually numerous entrances, which form perhaps a labyrinth of passages (C), Plate 67. Like other squirrels, the red member of the family has four toes and a knob on the forefoot and five on the hind (D), Plate 67. When making its greatest leaps, which are not more than 5 feet in length, it places its forefeet diagonally behind its hind feet as do the ground dwellers (E).

Chipmunk (*Tamias striatus*). The eastern chipmunk is the most common of the several chipmunk groups. The black and white stripes on the warm tan of its livery easily identify it. Although it can climb, it usually prefers the ground, and its round little burrow openings may often be found in dry, sunny, wooded spots.

Since it hibernates during the winter, its tracks are seldom seen in the snow. One of the strange customs of the chipmunk is its awakening song in the spring and its farewell to summer in the fall (A), Plate 68. Its tracks readily tell of its ground dwelling preference, for it places its forefeet diagonally behind its hind feet, typical of the ground dwelling animals who bound (B), Plate 68. It too, has four toes on the forefeet and five on the hind.

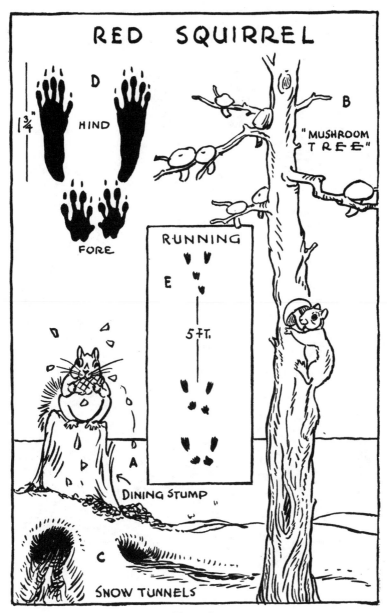

Plate 67

Plate 68

The chipmunk track is delicate and beautiful, as the drawings show (C).

Woodchuck (*Marmota monax*). The woodchuck or ground hog hole is common in all countrysides in eastern Canada and United States. The woodchuck's burrow is perhaps the best sign of its presence and is usually found in open woods and pastures. The burrow often has two or more openings, one, the original digging has an earth pile at the entrance, the other, without an earth pile, was dug from below. The woodchuck hibernates during the cold months and since it does not store food in its den, it stores it under its skin. Although it is known as one of the "seven sleepers" it often comes out of its winter den in February, especially if it is an open winter, and its tracks may then be found in the snow.

While only four toes register in the track of the forefoot, the woodchuck has also a knoblike thumb with a nail. The hind feet have five well developed toes (A), Plate 69. In walking, the "chuck" alternately places its fore and hind feet close together as do most of the ground dwellers (B). The tracks made when the animal is speeding, resemble the formation made by the chipmunk (C).

Hoary Marmot (*Marmota caligata*). Next to the beaver and porcupine, the hoary marmot is the largest rodent on this continent. It is almost twice as big as its relative, the woodchuck (D), Plate 69. This marmot is native to the Rockies from latitude 45° almost to the Arctic Circle. The French Canadians call it "Sif-fleur" (whistler), because of its shrill whistle which can be heard at a great distance. Since it lives in high places where the cold-maker comes early and leaves late, its winter sleep is often six months long. Like the woodchuck, its winter pantry is located under its skin.

The burrow is usually among heaps of tumbled rocks large enough to offer protection from even the giant grizzly. Often well

Plate 69

beaten trails diverge from the burrow in various directions. Dung is usually found in abundance near the den. Like the woodchuck, the hoary marmot has only four toes on his forefoot and five on his hind. Its tracks resemble the woodchuck's except in size (E), Plate 69, and its walking trail is similar to other ground animals, who place their front and hind feet close together alternately (F). It, too, is a flatfoot, for it walks on its palms and soles.

Beaver (*Castor canadensis*). The beaver, perhaps, was responsible for more exploration of the New World than any other factor. Since its range covered most of the northern hemisphere and its fur was much sought after, fur trappers and traders went ever deeper into the wilderness to secure its pelts. The beaver is one of the most intelligent wild creatures on this continent and its works clearly advertise its presence. It is a great water conservationist and builds dams with uncanny engineering skill. Then, too, its lumbering activities may be seen wherever it lives, for it cuts down with its chisellike gnawing teeth trees both large and small (A), Plate 70. Typical chips cut by beaver are shown in the drawing (B).

The beaver lodge, too, indicates its presence. A typical beaver house is a mound of gnawed sticks and mud often 20 feet in diameter, and 4 to 6 feet high (C), Plate 70. Among the beaver's amazing works are its canals, ditches that are dug by this animal to float its logs to the home pond. Like canals made by man, the beaver's have small dams along them, which act as locks to raise the water when the ground rises.

The dam is also a common beaver sign. This is constructed of branches and sticks cut by the beaver and cemented with mud and roots. The dam is well built and a cross section is shown in (D), Plate 70. Often the beaver has several landing places with well cleared trails leading some distance into the bush.

The beaver's mud pies (E), Plate 70, advertise its matrimonial objectives. These are mud patties carefully molded by the beaver upon which is placed a few drops of castoreum or beaver scent.

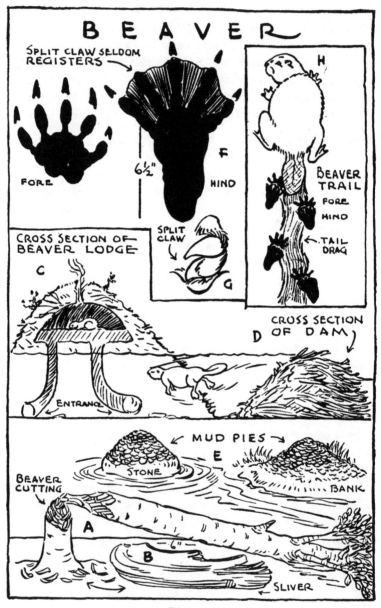

Plate 70

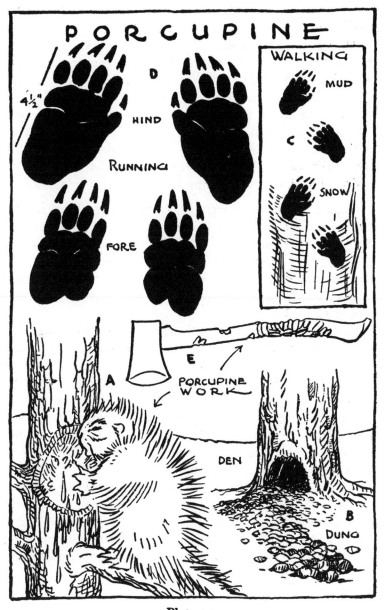

Plate 71

Beaver castoreum not only holds a fascination for the beaver but other animals are often lured with it by trappers.

These characteristics may be noted in its tracks. The beaver has five toes on both front and hind feet. The hind feet, however, are webbed (F), Plate 70, the beaver being an aquatic animal. All toes have claws, but the claw on the second toe of the hind foot is split and may be used as a comb. This split claw seldom registers (G). Its tail is broad, flat and scaly and usually drags in the trail. In walking it toes-in somewhat like a woods Indian and treads upon its front foot track with its hind foot. The tail makes a broad, flat trail weaving from side to side (H), Plate 70.

Porcupine (*Erethizon dorsatum*). Unlike its intelligent relative, the beaver, the porcupine is the "dim-wit" of the wildwood. Everyone is acquainted with this quill "pig," for it is famous for its armament of barbed quills. The porcupine is a stay-at-home and may spend days in one spruce tree. Since it prefers the bark of evergreens for food, these trees are often well gnawed and even girdled (A), Plate 71.

Its signs are easily read. The floors and woodwork of old cabins usually show the characteristic porcupine gnawing. It is also generous with its dung, and usually places frequented by porky are liberally covered with the fibrous oval pellets (B), Plate 71.

Since it does not hibernate, its tracks may often be found in the snow. At that time its trail is a deep furrow with its footprints at the bottom. Like the beaver it also toes-in, stepping upon the tracks of its forefeet with its hind feet (C), Plate 71. It has only four toes on the front foot and five on the hind. Both fore and hind feet have strong climbing claws and these are always visible in the track (D). The porcupine's characteristic gnawing marks may often be found upon ax handles (E), Plate 71, or canoe paddles, for porky is a great salt addict and salty perspiration upon these implements encourages its destructive work.

ANIMAL TRACKS OF
FIELD AND FOREST
9

HARES AND RABBITS (LAGOMORPHA)

Like the order of rodents, the rabbits are small animals that have no canine teeth but four incisors or gnawing teeth in the upper jaw and two in the lower. The tails are small and in the case of the coney or pika, the external tail is entirely absent. Most of the members of this order have long ears and long hind legs. They also have five toes on the forefeet and four toes on the hind. However, only four toes of the forefeet register in the tracks. The rabbit family are "bounders," that is, they place their hind feet ahead of the tracks made by their forefeet. Their ground dwelling habits are revealed by the diagonal position of the forefoot tracks.

Cottontail Rabbit (*Sylvilagus floridanus*). The common identification of this little rabbit is its white powder puff tail on the seat of its brown breeches. The cottontail is a small rabbit with ears not as long as the jackrabbit's and snowshoe hare's. Its home range is small, perhaps not more than an acre. It seems to be a creature of habit and follows the same path every day. The cottontail has been blamed for much of the winter damage to the bark of trees, which in most instances is the work of mice. If the trees are damaged by rabbits the marks of the teeth will be

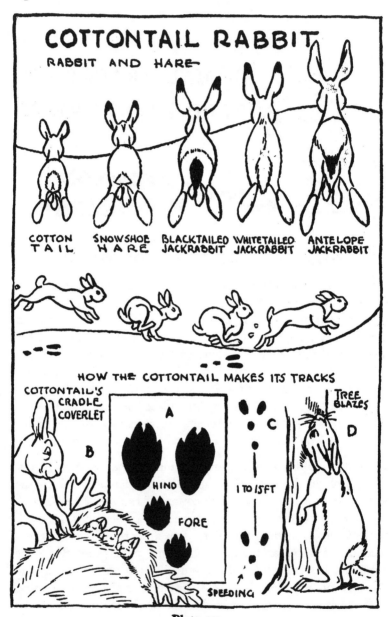

Plate 72

large and the bark next to the gnawings will hang in strips. Then, too, rabbit work will be above the snow; that of mice below. The dung pellets and the tracks will also identify the culprit.

The cottontail never trots or runs like a dog, but hops and bounds. In the cottontail track, the hind feet are paired ahead of the tracks of the front feet, which are placed diagonally (A), Plate 72. The position of the front feet is characteristic of all rabbits and hares. The mark of the tail of the cottontail is seldom if ever present in the tracks. From 10 to 15 feet in a bound can be made by this rabbit (C), but this great exertion cannot be kept up for long. The cottontail usually resorts to tricks rather than speed and may often double, backtrack and side leap to throw pursuers off the trail.

The nest of the cottontail is a shallow hole in the ground in which a bed and coverlet is made of dry grass and fur plucked from the mother's breast. The coverlet is spread over the babies when mother cottontail is away (B), Plate 72.

Like the bears, rabbits may stand on their hind legs and rub their chins on the bark of trees (D), Plate 72, as far up as they can reach. Buck rabbits especially seem to do this. These blazes may mark the boundaries of its home range or may also serve as a sort of bulletin board where scent messages are left for others to read.

Snowshoe Hare (*Lepus americanus*). The snowshoe rabbit or varying hare is a northern resident, although it may be found as far south as the mountains of New Mexico. Like many animals of the north, the snowshoe rabbit has two suits, a brown tweed in summer and white flannels in winter (A), Plate 73. Like some other dwellers in Winterland it also grows "snowshoes" upon its feet, hence the great size of its tracks, which so readily identify it(B). When not in a great hurry it makes a track like (C), pairing its hind feet ahead of the forefoot tracks, which are almost paired, too. However, when speeding it stretches both fore and hind tracks out diagonally as in (D). This track struc-

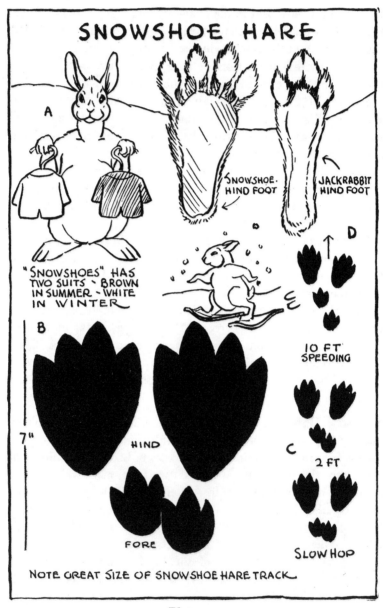

SNOWSHOE HARE

A

SNOWSHOE.
HIND FOOT

JACKRABBIT
HIND FOOT

"SNOWSHOES" HAS
TWO SUITS ~ BROWN
IN SUMMER ~ WHITE
IN WINTER

D

10 FT
SPEEDING

B

7"

HIND

C

2 FT

FORE

SLOW HOP

NOTE GREAT SIZE OF SNOWSHOE HARE TRACK

Plate 73

ture is also common to the jackrabbits. The snowshoe's tail, being small, never registers in the track except when it is in a sitting position. When speeding it takes from 8 to 10 feet in a bound.

Whitetailed Jackrabbit (*Lepus townsendii*). The jackrabbits are large hares with long legs and ears. In color the whitetail or prairie hare is silvery gray with a white tail and underparts. The white tail is its conspicuous mark, for it is held straight out or switched about like the white tail of the Virginia deer (A), Plate 74. This jackrabbit is the largest hare in temperate North America and is widely distributed throughout the Northwest. It is perhaps the fastest wild four-foot on the plains today and when hard pressed may take leaps of 20 feet.

The whitetailed Jack takes high, long bounds like a deer (B), Plate 74. The blacktail jack's bounds are lower and shorter, regularly interspersed with high observation hops (C). All jackrabbits make this bound straight in the air, but the whitetail does it least of all, since perhaps all of its bounds are high (D). At times it may double back on its track, make a long side leap and then freeze. The running tracks of the whitetail and blacktail jackrabbits are very much alike except in the distances between bounds. The whitetail's bound is greater. Both the tracks of the hind and forefeet are placed diagonally (E), Plate 74, by jackrabbits, thus indicating their terrestrial habits.

Blacktailed Jackrabbit (*Lepus californicus*). The black top of this jackrabbit's tail has given it its name. It carries this appendage in its own way, that is, hanging downward, so that it sometimes leaves its mark on the trail (A), Plate 75. The blacktail is typically of the West, its range extending from Missouri to the Pacific and from South Dakota into Mexico and Lower California.

Jackrabbits always look like gangling adolescents with their long thin necks, long ears and legs. Unlike the cottontail and like all jackrabbits, the tracks of both the hind and forefeet of this

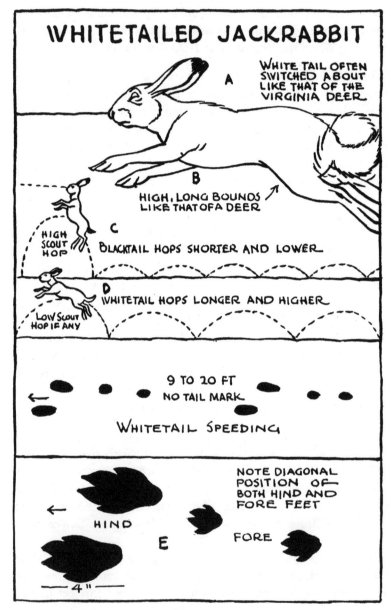

Plate 74

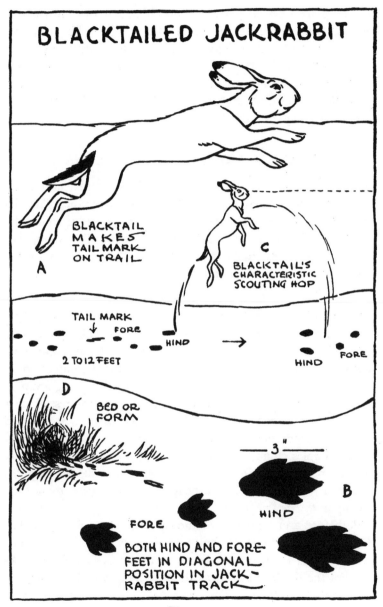

BLACKTAILED JACKRABBIT

BLACKTAIL MAKES TAIL MARK ON TRAIL

A

C

BLACKTAIL'S CHARACTERISTIC SCOUTING HOP

TAIL MARK

FORE

HIND

2 TO 12 FEET

HIND

FORE

D

BED OR FORM

3"

HIND

B

FORE

BOTH HIND AND FORE-FEET IN DIAGONAL POSITION IN JACK-RABBIT TRACK

Plate 75

hare are placed in a diagonal position (B), Plate 75. The distance between hops is not usually more than 12 feet. The blacktail bounds are shorter than the whitetail, but the observation hop is much more accentuated. This is shown in drawing (C) in Plates 74 and 75. Jackrabbits make beds or forms. These are scraped out under some scrub and are smooth hollows (D), Plate 75, without any lining material whatsoever.

POUCHED ANIMALS (MARSUPIALIA)

The marsupials or pouched animals are of a most ancient lineage, for they can trace their ancestry back to the Mesozoic. The outstanding characteristics of this order are the pouch in which the young are carried and the lack of a placenta. The young are among the smallest of all mammal babies. The opossums are the only American marsupials and they are found from Lake Ontario to Patagonia.

Opossum (*Didelphis virginiana*). The opossums are strange leftovers from an earlier day, furry creatures with naked prehensile tails and pouches in which they carry the tiny almost microscopic young. In fact, the young are so tiny at birth that eighteen could be placed in a teaspoon (A), Plate 76. Since the young are only partly developed at the time of birth, they spend the rest of their unfinished babyhood in the mother's pouch (B), each attached to a teat. Underdeveloped though they be, these strange embryonic babies climb hand over hand up the fur of the mother into her pouch the minute they are born. They develop rapidly, and after 5 or 6 weeks in the pouch the young venture out and ride upon the mother's back.

Both fore and hind feet of the opossum have five toes (C), Plate 76. The hind feet, however, have a very characteristic thumb which is the outstanding sign of the opossum's trail. All toes but the thumb have claws. Its trail looks as if it had walked along on its hands (D). The opossum is a waddler and seems to

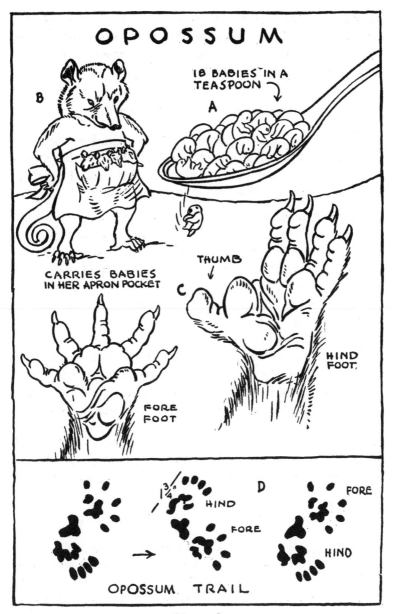

Plate 76

move the legs of one side at the same time. The tracks are usually not more than 1¾ inches in width and are often found along woodland streams. Since the opossum is nocturnal, its tracks are more often seen than the animal itself.

ARMADILLOS (EDENTATA)

While the order Edentata includes animals of varied forms, they all are alike in respect to the absence of all teeth in the front of their jaws. Since they are insect eaters, they have long sticky tongues which they shoot among insect gatherings.

Common Armadillo (*Dasypus novemcincta*). The armadillo seems to have taken a hint from modern military equipment and has become a little walking tank. Its body, head and tail are covered with a bony armor, the armor of the body being made up of nine bony plates so beautifully constructed it seems to have been hammered out by the best of the King's armourers (A), Plate 77. Since it has a stiff little trot a good descriptive name for it might be "little armored pig."

The armadillo is found from Texas to Argentina and its shells are made into baskets and sold in curio shops. It has strange lizardlike feet with four toes on the front foot and five on the hind (B), Plate 77. All toes have long, strong digging claws. Well trodden trails lead from its burrows in various directions, and its clawed toes make hooflike tracks in the dust and mud (C), Plate 77. At water holes the marks of its nose and its armorplate are printed into the mud as it roots about or takes a mud bath.

INSECT EATERS (INSECTIVORA)

These small creatures are often mistaken for mice, yet their teeth are very different from the gnawing teeth of the rodents, since theirs are sharp, pointed and set close together. Their eyes and ears are very poorly developed. In fact, their eyesight is such that

ARMADILLO

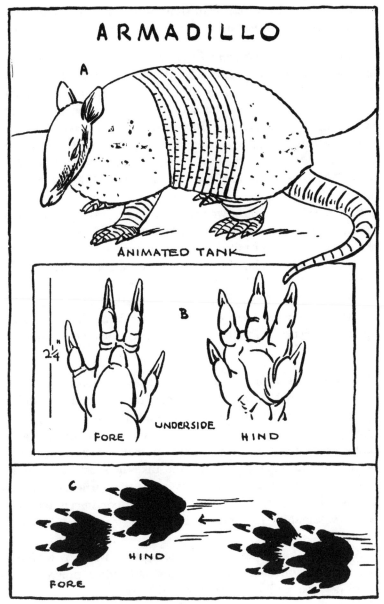

A

ANIMATED TANK

B

2¼"

FORE   UNDERSIDE   HIND

C

HIND

FORE

Plate 77

they can barely distinguish light from dark. Both the shrews and the moles belong to this order.

Short-tailed Shrew (*Blarina brevicauda*). The most numerous and common animal in eastern North America is the short-tailed shrew (A), Plate 78. This is a dark colored mouselike animal with a short tail. It occurs almost everywhere in woodlands, fields and along banks of streams. Its runways, scarcely half an inch wide, are usually partly sunken in the woods mold. They are made by pushing aside the loose earth and form an irregular network. The shrew also uses the runways of mice and even the tunnels of moles.

In winter it often burrows under the snow, leaving tiny ridges on the surface like a mole's track. When walking on the surface of the snow, the short-tailed shrew has a curious wavy trail made by its tail with tiny alternate footprints bordering each side of the tail mark (B), Plate 78. When running it makes a jumping trail, the footprints being paired with the tail mark in the center (C). In spite of their size these tiny animals are fierce killers and feed upon all varieties of insects, as well as mice much larger than the shrew.

Common Shrew (*Sorex personatus*). The common shrew is the smallest mammal in the northern part of this continent and is lighter in color than its larger short-tailed relative, being of a grayish brown in tone (D), Plate 78. This shrew uses the little pathways of mice and other small animals whenever possible, but it also makes runways of its own. Like the short-tailed shrew, it, too, raises slight, rounded ridges in the snow whenever it tunnels, and like its larger relative it also feeds upon insects and flesh when obtainable. In spite of its size it is a most ferocious hunter.

All shrews have musk glands, the odor of which is evidently obnoxious to other animals, for they are seldom preyed upon. The odor, too, perhaps serves as a trail marker.

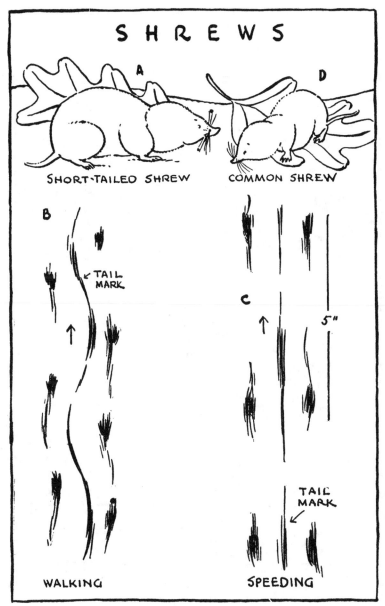

SHREWS

A

D

SHORT-TAILED SHREW

COMMON SHREW

B

← TAIL MARK

C

5"

TAIL MARK

WALKING

SPEEDING

Plate 78

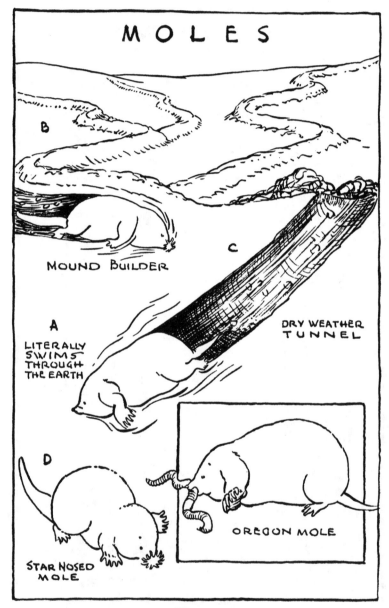

MOLES

B

MOUND BUILDER

C

A
LITERALLY
SWIMS
THROUGH
THE EARTH

DRY WEATHER
TUNNEL

D

STAR NOSED
MOLE

OREGON MOLE

Plate 79

Oregon Mole (*Scapanus townsendi*). This animal is highly specialized for its tunneling work, having a sharp nose, a short neck, a compact body with strong ribs and short digging forefeet equipped with strong claws. The mole is found in the United States and Canada except in the broad, dry belt of the interior. The Oregon mole is the largest of this group.

Where the earth is soft, it seems literally to swim through it (A), Plate 79. In moist weather it tunnels near the surface of the ground and its subways are marked by a slight ridge (B). When the weather is dry it digs more deeply and pushes the surplus soil through the tunnel and out through the opening at the surface (C), where little "dumps" are found similar to those of the pocket gopher. It and its mole neighbors have regular subway networks covering a considerable area often having many branches. The courses of the many branched tunnels are marked by a series of mounds varying up to 10 inches in height and from 5 to 20 inches wide.

Star-nosed Mole (*Condylura cristata*). The star-nosed mole is easily identified, for it wears a fleshy star at the end of its nose (D), Plate 79. It is found in eastern Canada and the United States westward to Manitoba and Minnesota. Damp, marshy ground is preferred by these animals who spend more time above ground than do other moles. Their open surface runways are found among the grass roots and matted vegetation. However, they constantly add to their surface ridges and extend their tunnels, forcing up the loose earth through the tunnel entrances and forming mounds much like those of the Oregon mole. The food of most moles is earthworms and scores of underground insects.

WOODLAND
SNOWSHOE TRACKS
10

Snowshoes in Nature. The type of country in which an animal lives, often shapes its feet and determines the type of track it makes. Snow and ice may influence the seasonal changes that occur in mammals' and birds' feet to enable them to travel more easily during the months of deep drifts and glare ice. Long before primitive man invented snowshoes, Nature fashioned such footgear for a number of animals living in the snow country.

Sometimes she merely gave them furry moccasins to protect their toes from the intense cold. The Arctic fox grows such furry footwear in winter (A), Plate 80. In fact, its toe pads are entirely covered with these woolly moccasins so that its winter track differs from his summer footprints (B).

When Linnaeus named the Arctic fox *Alopex lagopus*, he did so because of these winter moccasins, for *Alopex* means "fox" and *lagopus* means "hare footed," since this fox had hair covered soles like the hare. Although the coat of the Arctic fox may sometimes be bluish gray instead of its regulation winter white, the woolly soles of its feet are always a dull yellow-white.

Another northern woods dweller, whose winter tracks differ from those of the summer, is the lynx. The feet of this member of the cat family look enormous (C), Plate 80, so enlarged are

ARCTIC FOX WINTER MOCCASINS

TRAIL

B

A

SUMMER WINTER

LYNX SNOWSHOES

LYNX TRAIL
IN SNOW

C

D

LYNX SNOWSHOE

Plate 80

they, especially during the cold months. At that time a stiff growth of bristly hairs covers its feet, which act not only as warm socks, but as snowshoes as well. A lynx may weigh 30 or 40 pounds, yet it can walk over snowdrifts, in which even a fox will flounder (D). Its snowshoes, however, are useful only as long as it walks or trots. Should it become alarmed and try to bound, it will sink into the snow and quickly become exhausted.

Oddly enough, though the varying hare is also a member of the snowshoe fraternity, its membership does not prevent its being the principal item on the menu of the lynx. Like the lynx, the varying hare or snowshoe rabbit has large feet with wide spreading toes that are covered with stiff bristly hairs (A) Plate 81. With these it can skim over the drifts as readily as an Indian with snowshoes. Perhaps the Indian was inspired by this hare. Like many of the winter company, the snowshoe rabbit changes his brown tweeds for white flannels when the snow comes.

The arrival of winter sometimes changes the footwear of certain birds. The grouse family, especially, are charter members of the Aboriginal Snowshoe Club. The ruffed grouse have a curious fringe of strong horny points that grow around the toes (B), Plate 81. It looks like a row of flat yellow balsam or hemlock needles and forms a racquet or snowshoe on each foot, enabling the grouse to traverse the drifts of winter. Each autumn these snowshoes sprout in time for the first snow and drop off when the snow disappears in the spring.

The ptarmigan is another snow child, who likes to keep its feet warm and to skim over the drifts. Each year when the snows around its home grow deep, the ptarmigan's feet become entirely covered with a marvelous growth of feathers which serve as warm socks as well as snowshoes (A), Plate 82. Thus, unlike many birds who migrate as far as possible from the cold and snow, the ptarmigan changes itself to meet winter conditions. Like the snowshoe rabbit, this bird, too, changes its summer uniform of tweed to white.

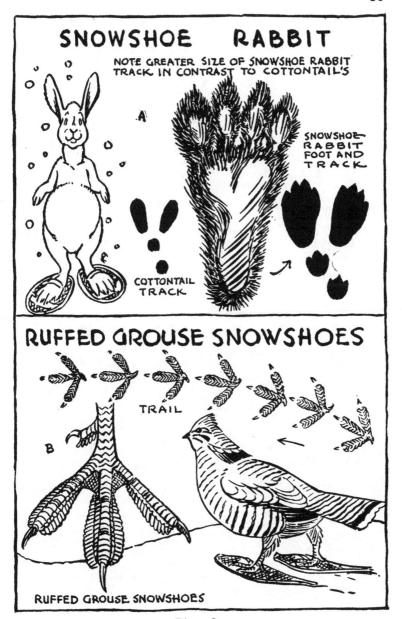

SNOWSHOE RABBIT

NOTE GREATER SIZE OF SNOWSHOE RABBIT TRACK IN CONTRAST TO COTTONTAIL'S

A

SNOWSHOE RABBIT FOOT AND TRACK

COTTONTAIL TRACK

RUFFED GROUSE SNOWSHOES

TRAIL

B

RUFFED GROUSE SNOWSHOES

Plate 81

PTARMIGAN'S SNOWSHOES

A

TRACKS
IN WINTER

ENTIRE FOOT COVERED
WITH FEATHERS

MOOSE OR DEER YARD

B

Plate 82

Members of the deer family, who do not have snowshoes to combat the drifts of winter, often resort to other measures. When snow becomes deep, moose and deer will seek out a protected spot in the woods that offers ample browse, and there will create a maze of paths which become wider and more numerous as the animals use them day after day. Such a spot is called a "yard." The yard is not deliberately cleared of snow, as some people think, with the broad antlers of the moose used as snow shovels. Nor is it a wide clearing with snow piled high all around it. The yard is merely a number of pathways interwoven as the animals move about, trampling down the snow (B), Plate 82. The yard not only makes it easier for the deer family to secure food, but gives them an opportunity to defend themselves from attack by predators without becoming snowbound.

One member of the deer family, however, does not need the security of the yard. This is the caribou. It may be difficult to imagine an animal with hard, sharp hooves, weighing about 300 pounds, crossing snowdrifts without floundering deeply. However, the caribou can cross over deep snow, into which a man or even a wolf would sink deeply. When walking on deep snow, it spreads its hoofs widely and also makes use of the well developed dewclaws or accessory hoofs, which spreads the weight of the animal over a much greater surface (A), Plate 83. By this simple trick, it converts its feet into wide snowshoes.

The caribou can also use its hoofs as at kind of skate, when crossing glare ice. In winter the inner section of each hoof is absorbed or shrunken, leaving only the outer part of the hoof. This outer shell, resembling an oyster shell in shape, grows rapidly and gives the caribou an advantage on ice that few animals have (B), Plate 83. The hollow hoof like hollow ground skates, grips and glides safely over glazed surfaces (C).

Indian Snowshoe Tracks. The formation of the tracks of a human snowshoer is much the same regardless of the type of snowshoe he may be wearing. The snowshoer who uses his snow-

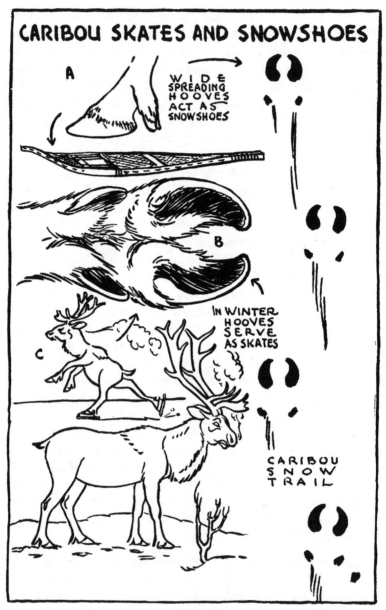

Plate 83

INDIAN SNOWSHOE TRACKS

B
TRAIL OF
CORRECT
SNOWSHOEING

A.

PROPER SNOWSHOE STRIDE

C

REAPPEARANCE OF
TRACKS COVERED IN
WINTER, WHEN SPRING
THAW COMES

Plate 84

shoes correctly will make a trail in which each snowshoe track fits perfectly with that of the opposite shoe. The drawing (A), Plate 84, shows this correct pattern and the method of walking on snowshoes.

Walking on snowshoes is very much like sliding along in an old pair of slippers. The shoe is lifted only high enough to clear the snow and the stride not too long, just enough to clear the frame of the opposite shoe. If this is done correctly the trail will resemble (B), Plate 84, in the drawing.

Reappearance of Tracks. Often the tracks made in early winter will be covered over time and again with many layers of snow, but when the spring thaws come, many of these hidden trails will reappear, making it difficult for the inexperienced tracker to distinguish the old trails from the new.

When mild weather causes the snow to melt, at first slight depressions occur scarcely larger than the original track. Later the surrounding snow may melt to the same level and the old tracks again disappear. However, when the softer snow surrounding the tracks continues to melt faster than the hard packed and often frozen tracks, the footprints may again appear, resembling a row of crude mushrooms (C), Plate 84, several inches above the surrounding snow, strange reminders of travelers who had passed months before.

Type of Country Influences Snowshoe Pattern. The type of country often influenced the shape of the Indian snowshoe. The oval pattern or "bear paw" is best suited for woodland country. The long, tapering style with the long tail is used in the open areas where snow is light and powdery. This type of snowshoe makes a well packed trail for dog teams to follow. The oval pattern or "bear paw" is perhaps the oldest type, so named because of its resemblance to the shape of a bear's track (A), Plate 85. In fact the Ojibway have an old legend that tells of a bear who once wore snowshoes.

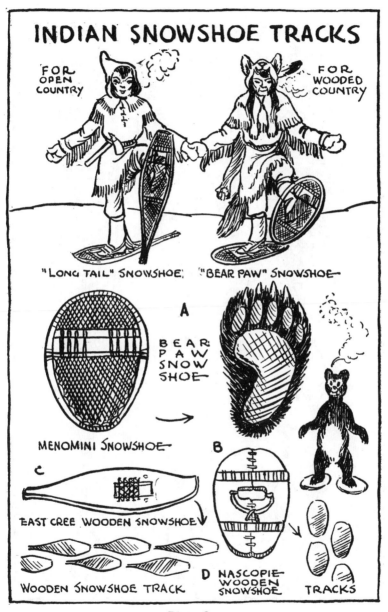

INDIAN SNOWSHOE TRACKS

FOR OPEN COUNTRY

FOR WOODED COUNTRY

"LONG TAIL" SNOWSHOE "BEAR PAW" SNOWSHOE

A

BEAR PAW SNOW SHOE

MENOMINI SNOWSHOE

B

C

EAST CREE WOODEN SNOWSHOE

WOODEN SNOWSHOE TRACK

D NASCOPIE WOODEN SNOWSHOE

TRACKS

Plate 85

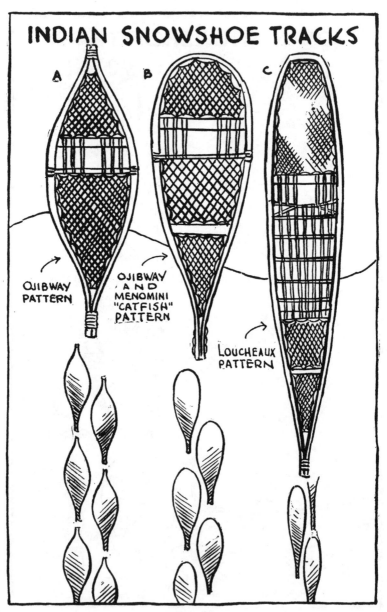

INDIAN SNOWSHOE TRACKS

A   B   C

OJIBWAY
PATTERN

OJIBWAY
AND
MENOMINI
"CATFISH"
PATTERN

LOUCHEAUX
PATTERN

Plate 86

Wooden Snowshoes. Not all snowshoes have the characteristic rawhide webbing inside the frame. In fact, some of the old time snowshoes were made of thin boards split from straight grained birch or ash. One pair, which resembled the oval bear paw pattern was made by the Nascopie Indians of eastern Canada, of two flat boards lashed together with rawhide (B), Plate 85. Another wooden snowshoe in the shape of the long narrow type was made by the Eastern Cree of Canada (C). In this instance, a small area in the center was laced with rawhide. The tracks made by the wooden snowshoes resembled the drawing (D).

Snowshoes with Rawhide Lacing. Another early type of snowshoe, made by the Ojibways, had a frame of two separate pieces, in the shape of two bent bows opposite each other and lashed together at the toe and heel and spread apart with a thin wooden crosspiece. The whole interior was laced with rawhide webbing. Its trail resembled (A), Plate 86.

Both the Ojibway and Menomini made a snowshoe pattern called "the catfish," which was rounded at the toe and elongated at the heel (B), Plate 86, resembling the blunt headed bullhead of our fresh water streams. A square-toed snowshoe was also made by the Menomini Indians (A), Plate 87. This pattern is also found in Manitoba.

A Loucheaux, South Mackensie River snowshoe, is a very much elongated shoe. It resembles one of the models adopted by the U. S. Army and is particularly well suited for snowshoe travel in the open tundras. Its track resembles (C), Plate 86.

From the Northwest Territories came a wider snowshoe somewhat similar to the square-toed Manitoba model, but of greater width and a less square toe (B), Plate 87.

The Iroquois model (C), Plate 87, is the most common pattern found in sporting goods establishments today. This is perhaps the most familiar snowshoe shape and is also found among the Menomini. In this pattern the toe of the shoe is bent up slightly, so that it can slide more easily over the snow surface (D).

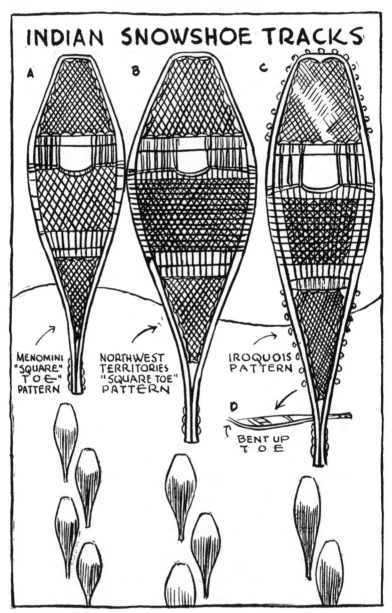

Plate 87

Plate 88

A very wide pot-bellied sort of snowshoe is made by the Nascopie of eastern Canada. This is shaped almost like the oval bear paw model except that it has a tail at the heel (A), Plate 88. A similar snowshoe is also found in Labrador.

An early bear paw snowshoe made by the Ojibway and still quickly made by them when caught in a snowstorm in the woods, is this primitive type that somewhat resembles a huge bear track (B), Plate 88. The more common oval bear paw is also made by these Indians as well as by their neighbors the Menomini (C).

Snowshoe Dance Tracks. In the early days explorers nearing an Indian village after the first fall of snow might come upon a circle around an upright pole, that had been trampled in the snow by numerous snowshoes (D), Plate 88. These tracks were left by the dancers of the Snowshoe Dance, a celebration of the coming of the first snow. The Indians knew the delights as well as the terrors of winter, and they also understood how dependent they were upon the snowshoes to aid them in winter travel and hunting. And so they danced around a pole, from which snowshoes were suspended in supplication and thanks to the good spirits, who gave them the snowshoes and for good medicine in safe and speedy travel with them.

TRACKS IN
JUNGLE
AND ZOO

11

In pioneer days a track or trail was called a "trace." In Africa a track is known as a "spoor." Few of our readers will ever follow the spoors of the great animals of the hot veldts or in the jungle fastnesses of Africa or India, yet many will see these animals in the zoo or circus and will thrill at their size and majesty. However, with air transport developing in leaps and bounds, it may soon be within the reach of almost everyone to journey to faraway places in a day or so and see the herds of zebra, hartebeest and giraffe amid their native thorn trees, or a group of lions taking their afternoon siesta in the shade of scrub.

The natives of Africa are the best trackers on the continent. They are far superior to the white man, and in East Africa, natives known as the "Wa-Ndorobo," a tribe of outcaste Masai, are perhaps the finest trackers in that whole area.

Tracking by Sound. The native trackers not only use their eyes to follow the tracks of animal footprints, but they also use their ears and noses, just as our American Indians did in tracking their game. As was stated in previous chapters, an animal's presence may be indicated by a number of things. For instance, if a tick bird is heard in the country where the rhinoceros is found, it is an excellent idea to go very carefully, for the tick birds are frequent companions of the rhino.

In elephant country, the sounds made by these great beasts are many and varied. In fact, elephants are often noisy in their everyday occupations, and various sounds tell they are near. Common sounds in an elephant herd are intestinal rumblings. The flapping of their tremendous ears against their withers and the noisy munching of vegetation are other sounds commonly heard. Often their pleasure is expressed by a rumbling purr made in the throat. Cows sometimes trumpet shrilly in anxiety or resentment, and calves often squeal or make short coughing sounds.

Tracking by Dung. One of the commonest signs of an animal's presence is its dung. Each species has a characteristic dung with which the trained tracker is familiar. It may be different in size, shape or color. Often the best way to tell the age of a spoor is by the freshness of the droppings. For instance, in following an elephant, the dung soon dries and becomes light yellow in color if dropped in the sun. However, it will still be dark and moist inside even after several hours in the sun.

Blood Spoors. The blood color varies with different types of wounds. If the animal is shot in the lung, the blood is often light in color with froth on it. From a kidney shot the blood is almost black, but body wounds emit the usual colored blood. The blood is commonly brushed off upon the vegetation as the animal passes by. Sometimes, too, when badly hit, the game will drop very soft excreta, much softer than the usual type from the animal.

Experienced African hunters have told me that the best way to track game is to go slowly. Many important details may be missed otherwise. There should be no loud conversation and as little of it as possible. Always work into the wind. The native trackers often gauge the direction of the air currents by dropping a little dust. Watch carefully for details. For instance, a few spider webs across a track will tell at a glance that the track is far from fresh. The native tracker never wastes time when the trail is lost. He quarters back and forth and often picks up the trail again in a few minutes.

The animals of jungle and zoo, like the animals of our own country, are divided into various groups such as the cat, dog, antlered and horned families, etc. The animals in this chapter are not confined to Africa alone, but those from India, Australia and other places are included. However, their native habitat is indicated in each case.

CARNIVORA

Lion (*Felis leo*). The lion once roamed over quite an area of this earth. Today, however, it is found only in Africa and occasionally in northern India. The male wears a mane, a luxuriant growth of hair covering the head and chest. In the wild the mane may be torn and ragged because of the thorn scrub. The female does not have a mane and is smaller than the male.

Lions are extremely sociable and may be found at times in groups or "prides" of four to a dozen or more. They make a lot of noise on occasion and hold their heads close to the ground, giving forth reverberating thunderous roars.

The lion has five toes on the front foot and four on the hind, but only four padded toes register in each track (A), Plate 89. The lion's track is like that of most of the cat family in that the claws are retractile and do not register in the track. It looks almost like the footprint of the ordinary house cat except, of course, it is many times larger. The lion steps with its hind feet exactly into the tracks made by its forefeet (B).

Tiger (*Felis tigris*). While the tiger in the zoo is the gaudiest of the cat family, in its native jungle of dark shadows and brilliant sunlight, its coat becomes almost invisible. Although the tiger is

Plate 89

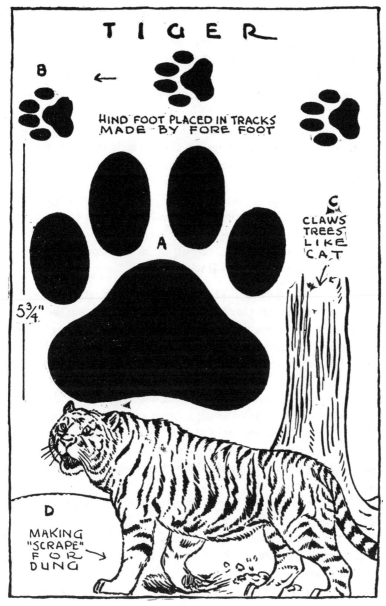

Plate 90

commonly known to be a native of India, other races are found in Siberia, China and in Sumatra.

The track of the tiger is very similar to that of the lion (A), Plate 90. Four padded toes show in the print of both the fore and hind foot. The tiger, like the lion, walks in perfect register, that is, it places its hind feet exactly into the tracks made by its forefeet (B), Plate 90.

Like the domestic cat, the tiger has clawing trees. It stands upon its hind legs and drags its claws down through the bark several times (C), Plate 90. Often along jungle roads, places are found where this big cat has taken its dust baths. It also scratches out depressions where it buries its dung like an ordinary house cat (D), Plate 90. These depressions usually measure a foot in length and are about 6 inches in width. A characteristic feeding habit of the tiger is to tear out the entrails of its kill from between the buttocks. It also covers its kill with brush.

Leopard (*Felis pardus*). The rustlings, squeals, and a thousand other noise of the jungle come to an abrupt halt when the sawing cough, like the thrust and return of a saw cutting through wood, is heard. This characteristic sawing call is that of the leopard, one of the most destructive predators, found both in Africa and India.

The leopard's colorful coat of yellow-orange and white is covered with a multitude of black spots, some markings looking for all the world as if the animal had taken its paws and placed their tracks upon the coat. Even the albinos (white) and the melanistic (black) leopards show their spots, making the coat look like watered silk.

Unlike the tiger, the leopard is a tree climber. In fact, its habit of parking its kill up in trees often tells of its presence in an area. Like the tiger, it has clawing trees (C), Plate 91, and often scratches depressions for its dung.

The track of the leopard is a typical cat track, smaller than that of the lion or tiger, and perhaps a little more elongated (A),

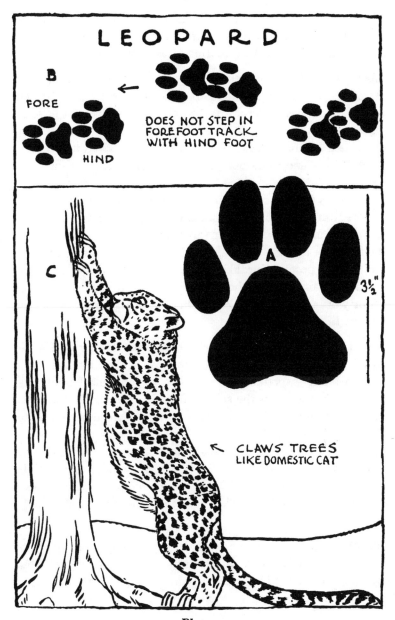

LEOPARD

B

FORE

HIND

DOES NOT STEP IN
FORE FOOT TRACK
WITH HIND FOOT

C

A

$3\frac{1}{2}"$

CLAWS TREES
LIKE DOMESTIC CAT

Plate 91

Plate 91. Its trail, however, differs from that of both the big cats, since the leopard does not place its hind feet in the tracks made by its forefeet. All footprints show clearly in the trail (B).

Cheetah (*Acinonyx jubatus*). The cheetah is a cat that greatly resembles a dog. It has long, doglike legs and carries its tail upright like the dog. Also, it is the only cat that does not have retractile claws, and the claw marks show clearly in the track. The track itself is more doglike than catlike. Four clawed toes register in both fore- and hind-foot tracks. The fore track is a bit wider than the hind (A), Plate 92.

Cheetahs stalk as close as possible to their prey and then make a swift rush (B), Plate 92, sometimes attaining a speed of sixty to seventy miles an hour over short distances. They strike down their victims and kill by strangulation. Usually hunting in pairs, they have a peculiar birdlike cry resembling the call of the small green African parrot. Cheetahs were once found in the open country of both India and Africa but are nearly extinct in a wild state in India today.

Serval (*Felis serval*). The serval is one of the smaller wildcats of Africa and has long legs and a short tail. Its coat ranges from buff to orange, spotted with dark brown and black spots and stripes. Like most cats the serval depends upon stalking its prey, sprinting only as a last resort. It is a noted high jumper, leaping 10 feet or more to pull a bird from a tree (D), Plate 93.

It has a strange, rather splay-footed cat track, with the claws well hidden as is usual with the feline family (A), Plate 93. Its trail is typical of the cats (B). When bounding, it also makes a characterstic bounding track, the hind feet placed diagonally ahead of the forefeet (C).

Jackal (*Canis aureus*). The jackal, like our coyote, seems to be able to multiply its voice, and one can usually make enough noise for an entire pack. The jackal's vocal ability is most interesting. Its common cry is a long wailing howl repeated three or four

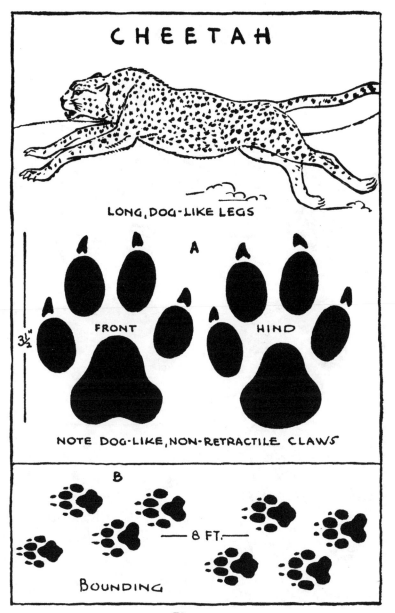

CHEETAH

LONG, DOG-LIKE LEGS

A

FRONT   HIND

3½"

NOTE DOG-LIKE, NON-RETRACTILE CLAWS

B

8 FT.

BOUNDING

Plate 92

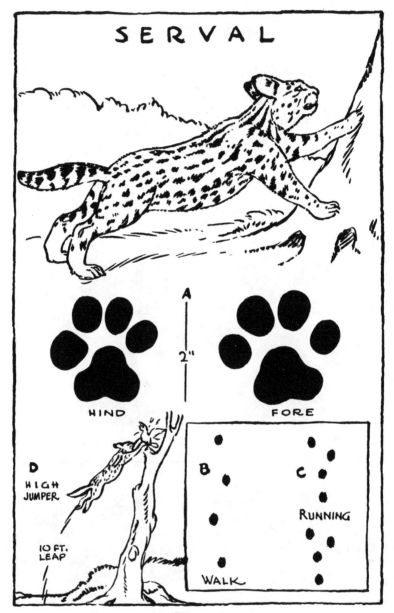

Plate 93

Plate 94

times, rising on a higher note each time and finally ending with three yelps. Just before dawn the jackals start in the east and it seems as if their cries are taken up in relays westward across the whole land.

This member of the wild dog family is commonly found in both Africa and India. It is a great scavenger, but like many of the wild dogs, it is omnivorous, eating fruits and vegetables as well as flesh.

The track of the jackal is like that of a small dog, the forefoot being wider than the hind, and four toes register in each foot, each showing a claw (A), Plate 94. The walking trail of the jackal is like that of the wolf or coyote, the hind foot registering close to the forefoot, the trail being almost a straight line (B). In running or bounding, the hind feet are placed ahead of the diagonal tracks of the forefeet (C).

Wild Dog (*Lycaeon pictus*). The wild dogs or hunting dogs of Africa run in packs of ten or more, and once on the trail of their victim, follow it to the end. They do not run at a great speed, but their tireless tenacity eventually enables them to run down their game. When in the tall grass, they often jump up on their hind legs to survey the country about them (A), Plate 95. The wild dogs have a strong odor and their coats are colored in white, black and yellow patches. Their bark is a sort of "Kak—kak—kak" and they sometimes give a long drawn "cooing" note.

The track is similar to the ordinary dog track except that it is more elongated. Only four toes register in both the fore and hind track (B), Plate 95. The walking track (C) is similar to that of other dogs—almost a straight line—with the forefeet and hind feet placed close together. When loping, it places its hind feet diagonally ahead of its forefeet (D).

Fennec (*Vulpes zerda*). The fennec is a very small foxlike animal found in Africa. In fact it is the smallest of the wild dog family, being only about 9 or 10 inches in length. What it lacks in body

WILD DOG

A
TYPICAL
LEAP
TO VIEW
COUNTRY

C

D
HIND

B

3½"

FORE

WALK

TYPICAL LONG
NARROW TRACK.

LOPE

Plate 95

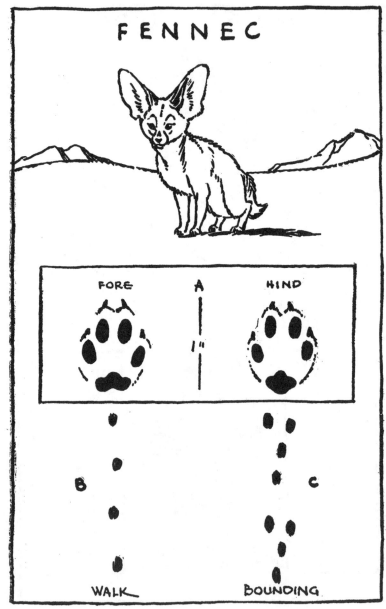

Plate 96

size, however, it makes up in ears. In fact, its ears seem as large as the whole of its body. Like most wild dogs, it is fond of a varied diet and likes fruits, insects and lizards, as well as small mammals.

The tracery of its tiny foxlike tracks is found in the dust and sands of the desert, each track showing four tiny toe pads, each with its claw mark (A), Plate 96. The walking trail is a straight line of tracks, like that of the ordinary fox (B). Like the common fox, too, it is a perfect tracker, that is, with its hind foot it steps exactly into the track made by its forefoot. When running or bounding it places both its hind and forefeet diagonally, the hind feet ahead of the forefeet (C).

Dingo (*Canis dingo*). The dingo is the only wild mammal of Australia that is not a marsupial (pouched animal) or a monotreme, and is thought to have been introduced there by the natives. At present it is more numerous in the hilly, scrubby country.

Like most dogs, the dingo has five toes on its forefeet and four on its hind, each crowned with a typical blunt doglike claw. Its track resembles the ordinary dog's, showing only four toes in both fore and hind tracks (A), Plate 97. The forefoot is wider across than the hind foot. Its walking track also resembles the common dog's, with forefeet and hind feet placed together in a somewhat straight-line trail (B). The loping trail, too, is similar to that of other dogs in that it shows the hind feet placed diagonally ahead of the forefeet (C).

Hyena (*Hyaena striata*). Although the hyena resembles the dog somewhat, it is actually more nearly related to the civets. It is a most cowardly animal, feeding by night, mostly upon carrion or the remnants of a lion's or tiger's feast. It has powerful teeth and jaws and can crack large bones with ease. It has a marvelous digestive system.

The horrible crazy laugh, the most commonly known of its voice accomplishments, is made by the spotted hyena only. The

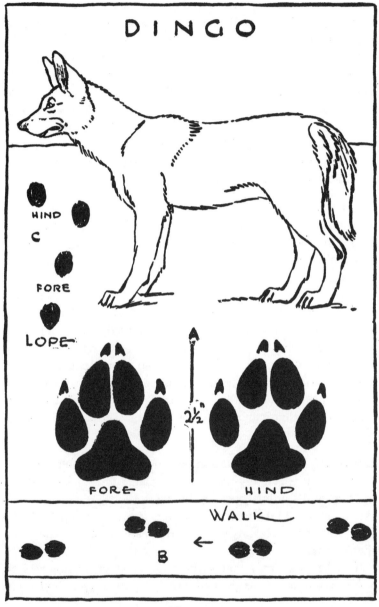

Plate 97

HYENA

B

C

A

4¾"

↑

↑

NON-RETRACTILE
CLAWS REGISTER
IN HYENA TRACKS

WALK

LOPE

Plate 98

Plate 99

front legs are longer than the hind, giving it an awkward appearance.

It is dangerous to sleep in the open where hyenas are found, for they often sneak up to a sleeping person and bite out large parts from the face and body. The striped hyena is found both in Africa and India.

The hyena has four toes on each foot, and all four register in the track. The track resembles the dog's in that it shows the claws, otherwise it might look like a large cat's track (A), Plate 98. The walking track is similar to the dog's (B), and the loping track also resembles the common canine trail (C).

Giant Panda (*Ailuropoda melanoleuca*). In the dense bamboo jungles of Szechuan, West China, the strange bearlike giant panda is found. It is a large black-and-white animal which looks like a bear, but it has no close, living relatives. It first became generally known to the outside world in 1869. Since the panda seems to feed upon bamboo shoots, its droppings contain slightly digested bamboo leaves and shoots. It sleeps in hollow trees, or beds down among the bamboo by turning around and around until the stalks are twisted into a sort of nest.

Like a bear, it rubs, claws or scores certain trees. Its tracks, too, somewhat resemble bear tracks, the fore- and hind-foot tracks being placed together as it walks (A), Plate 99. The claws register plainly in the tracks.

PRIMATES

Gorilla (*Gorilla gorilla*). The gorilla, found only in Africa, is the largest and most awe-inspiring of the primates, with powerful arms and a great barrel of a chest. The arms are especially long, reaching to the middle of the legs. The hands are elongated, with a short thumb (A), Plate 100. The toes are short and thick, and the large toe also moves like a thumb. See drawing of upright animal, Plate 100.

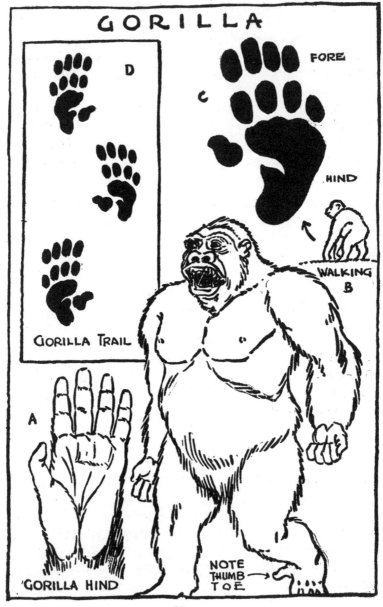

Plate 100

Plate 101

On the ground the gorilla ordinarily walks on all fours with the fingers of its hands doubled under. Resting its fists upon the ground, it takes curious half jumps forward (B), Plate 100. Only the four fingers of the hand register ahead of the track of the foot. The thumb print is absent. However, all the toes of the feet, including the thumblike large toe, are found in the track of the hind foot (C). Having a heel, it can stand upright better than other great apes, and often attacks in this position. The alternate walking trail of the gorilla is shown in (D).

Proboscis Monkey (*Nasalis larvatis*). The proboscis monkey, so called because of its comic nose development, is found only on the island of Borneo. It lives in trees in small groups. The large nose reaches its greatest development in the male. Besides its long nose, this monkey also has a long tail.

The tracks of both the fore and hind feet register four toes and thumb. The forefoot of this monkey is more like a hand, having a well developed thumb. The hind foot, too, has a thumb-like big toe. Evidently, in walking, the fingers of the forefoot are doubled under. The palm also registers (A), Plate 101. The track of the hind foot is almost like that of a human foot except for the thumblike big toe (B). The alternate track, with the fore and hind foot placed close together, is typical of this monkey (C).

HOOFED ANIMALS (UNGULATA)

Elephant (*Elephas africanus or indicus*). The African elephant differs from the Indian species, being greater in size, with larger ears. The forehead of the African is convex, while the Indian's head is concave. The number of toenails also differs in the two species, the African elephant having four nails on the front foot and three on the hind, while the Indian elephant has five on the front and four on the hind (A) and (B), Plate 102.

Elephants are social creatures and roam in herds of a half dozen to hundreds. They have definite trails which they follow

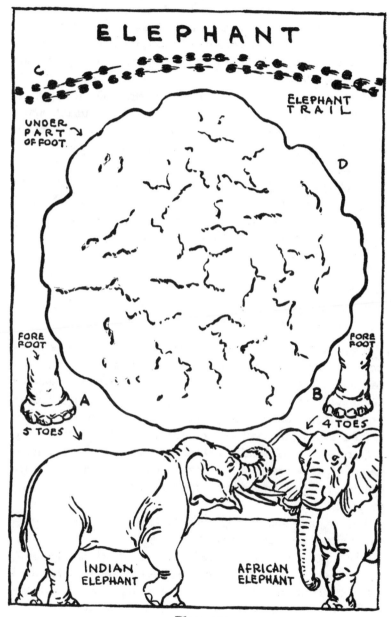

ELEPHANT

C

ELEPHANT
TRAIL

UNDER
PART
OF FOOT

D

FORE
FOOT

A

5 TOES

B

4 TOES

FORE
FOOT

INDIAN
ELEPHANT

AFRICAN
ELEPHANT

Plate 102

for generations, wearing them flat and smooth. These paths are wider than native trails and are usually straight, since the elephant can break down most obstructions. In fact, these trails are so well chosen for grade and directness, they are excellent trails for humans to follow.

Elephants have soft, spongy, cushioned feet, which makes them remarkably silent walkers. When the streams dry, elephants sometimes punch holes with their feet in the sandy bottoms to reach water. Sometimes they rub themselves against trees, which also tells a keen observer of their presence.

In wet spots elephants make deep tracks sometimes 3 feet deep or more. Often their trails are blazed with broken branches and leaves. The elephant trail of footprints is usually a double row of alternate tracks that look like telephone post holes if the ground is wet (C), Plate 102.

The elephant track is round, showing numerous cracks on the underside of the foot (D), Plate 102. These cracks differ with each elephant, and so individuals may sometimes be tracked by their characteristic "palm prints."

Hippopotamus (*Hippopotamus amphibius*). The hippopotamus frequents lakes and streams of Africa, mostly in the south central part today. They spend much of the day in the water or sunning themselves on the banks, but at night may forage long distances from the water, often raiding native fields and gardens. They live in families or herds, sometimes numbering twenty or thirty.

Since the hippo is quite a corpulent creature, its fat is much sought after by natives and white hunters alike, because the fat can be rendered by boiling into snow-white lard for cooking purposes.

The grunting and roaring of the bulls often tells of their presence quite some distance from their pools.

The hippo has four toes, and the round track clearly shows the imprints of the four stubby toes (A), Plate 103. The trail shows a double row of alternate footprints, sometimes deeply sunken if the ground is soft, for a hippo may weigh 3 or 4 tons (B).

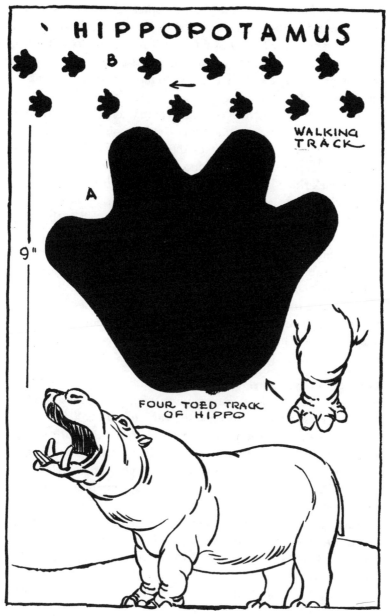

Plate 103

Rhinoceros (*Rhinoceros bicornis*). Another leftover from a pre-historic world is the rhinoceros. There are two African species, the black and the white, and another is found in Asia. Because of their bad sight and hearing, they are rather fussy and nervous. Seldom are there more than three found together and this is usually a family group.

The tick birds are their constant companions, ever searching for vermin found on the thick hides. These birds give warning to the rhino at the approach of danger, and in this way, also announce the presence of the rhino to the traveler.

The black rhino is smaller than its white relative. It has smaller horns and a prehensile lip instead of the square lip of the white species. In spite of the description "black or white," both are of the same gray color.

The rhino likes to wallow in mud and often uses trees and rocks for rubbing posts. When depositing its dung, it comes back to the same spot, raking it over with its horns and feet.

The round track of the rhino has three hooflike toes, broad and squat (A), Plate 104. When walking it makes a double trail with alternate footprints (B). In running both fore and hind feet are placed diagonally (C).

Giraffe (*Giraffa camelopardalis*). The giraffe, a native of Africa, is a most unusual animal, having an extremely long neck and long legs. It seems to walk as if on stilts with an extra stilt for a neck. In spite of the fact the neck is so elongated, the giraffe has the same number of vertebrae as the ordinary mammal, the neck bones, in its case, being unusually long. The average height of a giraffe is 10 to 20 feet, and it makes a very imposing sight in its native veldt. The giraffe is voiceless.

Each foot has two long hoofs. There are no secondary hoofs. As the animal steps upon the foot, the hoofs spread widely. When the weight is taken off the foot, the hoofs come together with a distinct clicking sound.

The track of the giraffe shows the two hoofs plainly, looking

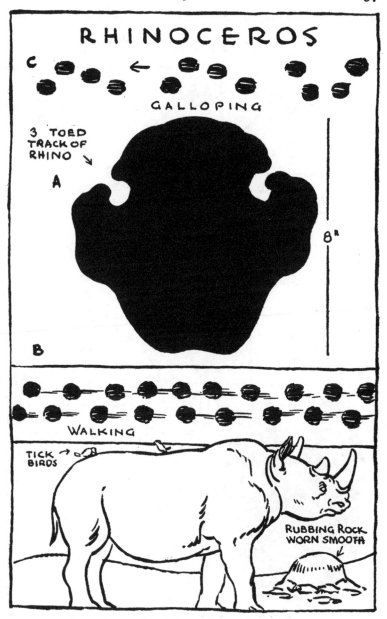

RHINOCEROS

C

GALLOPING

3 TOED
TRACK OF
RHINO

A

8"

B

WALKING

TICK
BIRDS

RUBBING ROCK
WORN SMOOTH

Plate 104

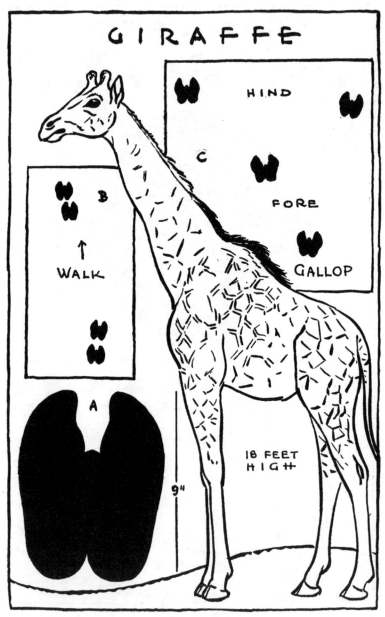

Plate 105

somewhat like two slippered feet placed close together (A), Plate 105. In walking, the legs on the same side of the giraffe seem to be lifted almost at the same time, making a track similar to (B). The long hind legs are wide spread when galloping and are placed ahead of the forefeet in a sort of straddling gallop (C).

Camel (*Camelus dromedarius and bactrianus*). There are two species of camel living today, the Arabian or one-humped camel, (B), Plate 106, and the Bactrian or two-humped camel of central Asia (A). Although ruminants, camels do not have horns, and have only three instead of four compartments in their stomachs. In the wall of the paunch of the camel stomach are a number of cells in which a quantity of water may be stored.

The hump, which is also characteristic of these animals, is composed of huge masses of fat, used as a reserve when food is scarce.

The foot of the camel has only two toes, and these are of equal size and covered with a cushionlike pad of hardened skin, which spreads under the weight of the animal. This foot is particularly well suited for traveling on desert sands. The toes have broad nails (C), Plate 106.

The camel, too, has a peculiar gait. According to E. Muybridge in his "Animals in Motion," the camel has three distinct gaits, the walk, the rack and the gallop. In the rack, he states, the legs are used in lateral pairs instead of diagonal. That is, the legs on the same side of the animal's body are lifted almost simultaneously.

The track of the camel clearly shows the imprint of two toes (D), Plate 106. The walking track is shown in drawing (E) and the running track in (F).

African Buffalo (*Syncerus caffer*). The African buffalo is, perhaps, among the three most dangerous animals in Africa. The bull sometimes has a horn spread of some 56 inches and is a most powerful animal. It is gray-black in color and is among those animals with the keenest sense of smell. It also has good hearing

Plate 106

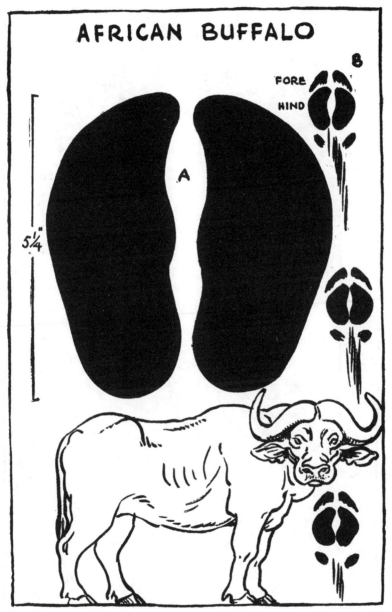

AFRICAN BUFFALO

FORE

HIND

B

A

5¼"

Plate 107

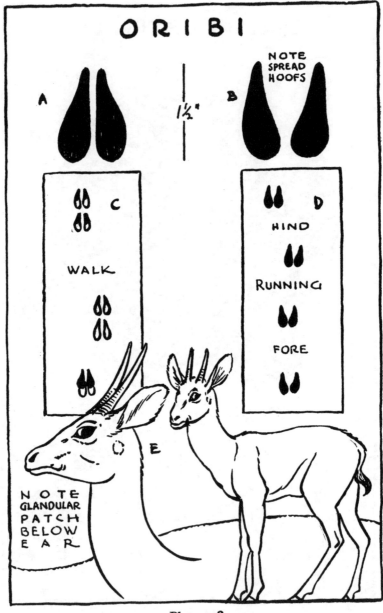

Plate 108

and eyesight. Usually found in isolated herds, it prefers a combination bush and open country.

In spite of its heavy, thick-set appearance, it is quite fast and can make its way over soft ground and through dense thorn cover with remarkable speed.

The track is usually clearly imprinted in the earth, since the buffalo is a heavy animal. It shows the two large cloven hoofs, larger than our domestic cattle's (A), Plate 107. In the trail, the prints of the forefoot hoofs project just ahead of those of the hind feet (B).

Oribi (*Ourebia ourebi*). The oribi is one of the most graceful of the smaller African antelopes, and is found in twos or threes in open country where there is grass and water.

This antelope has a small, round, bare gland patch about the size of a penny just below the ear (E), Plate 108. The females do not have horns.

The track of the cloven hoofs is like two dainty flower petals laid side by side, the points being deeply imprinted (A), Plate 108. When running (B), the hoofs are spread widely. The walking track shows the fore and hind feet close together alternately, almost in a straight line (C), Plate 108. In the running track the hind feet are placed diagonally ahead of the forefeet (D).

Impala (*Aepyceros melampus*). The impala, found in southern and eastern Africa, is larger than the oribi. It is more social than the oribi, being sometimes found in herds of a hundred or more. Only the males have horns, which are gracefully curved.

They seldom wander far from water in wooded areas. Approaching or leaving the water, they bunch together and leave a distinct narrow trail in the sand or mud. When frightened, they easily bound over bushes or other obstacles.

The track of the impala shows narrow, tapering hoofs. The forefoot is wider than the hind (A) and (B), Plate 109.

In bounding, the hind feet are placed diagonally ahead of the

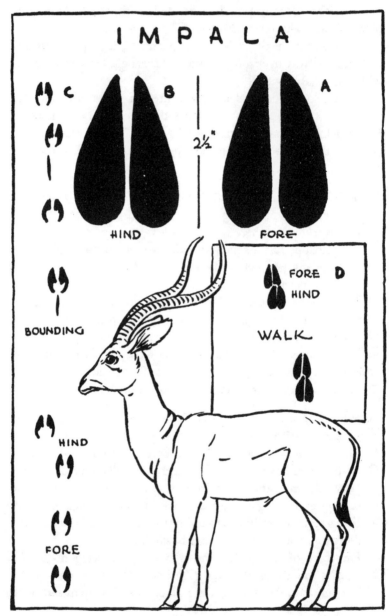

Plate 109

forefeet (C), Plate 109. The fore and hind tracks are close together in the walking trail, the tracks of the left and right alternating (D).

Dik-dik (*Madoqua saltiana*). The dik-dik is a very small animal, only about 14 inches high at the shoulders. It has a strange nose formation, somewhat trunklike in form. It likes densely forested country of Africa along rivers, where it ranges in family groups of two or three.

Like our western jack rabbit, it often takes observation hops high above the grass or scrub (A), Plate 110.

It almost obliterates the track of its forefoot with its hind foot as is shown in the alternate walking tracks (B), Plate 110. The sharp little points of the hoofs are deeply impressed. The running track, like that of many other ground animals, shows the hind feet arranged diagonally ahead of the diagonal tracks of the forefeet (C).

Eland (*Taurotragus oryx*). This is the largest of the African antelopes. Both the bulls and cows have twisted, spiral horns, the cow's sometimes being of a greater length. Both sexes have a characteristic dewlap (A), Plate 111. The usual herd consists of a dozen or so, but they may gather in great numbers at times. They usually rest in the shade during the day and leave a sweet aromatic odor behind, which tells of their presence in the area.

The greater size of the forefoot track in contrast to that of the hind is very marked in this animal. Being a heavy creature, it leaves large spoors. The points of the hoofs register more clearly in the tracks than the rear portion of the hoof. The drawing (B), Plate 111, shows a large hoof track. The walking track (C) clearly shows the greater width of the forefoot track.

Greater Kudu (*Strepsiceros strepsiceros*). The greater kudu is a magnificent antelope of Africa, large in size, and grayish blue in color with a varied number of white stripes. It has beautiful spiral horns which only the bulls usually carry. The bulls, too,

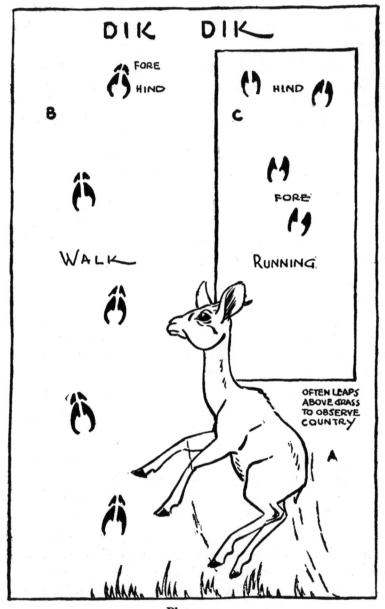

Plate 110

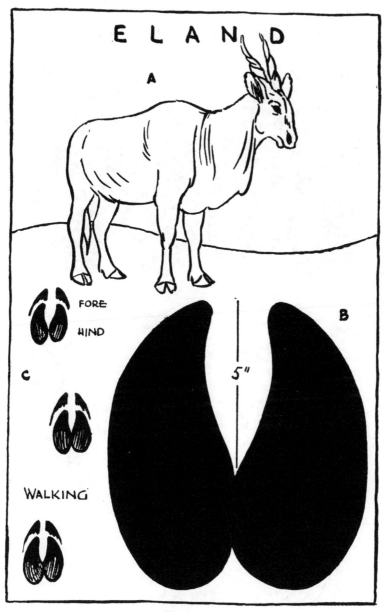

Plate III

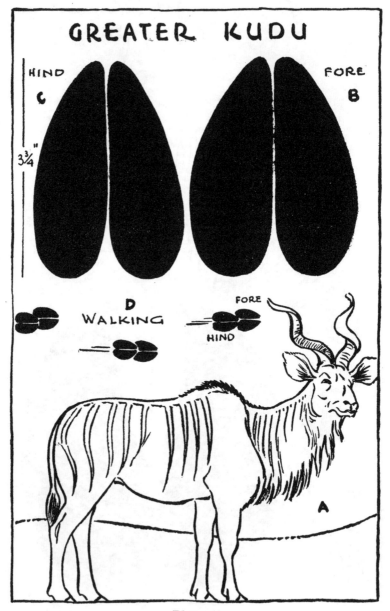

GREATER KUDU

HIND

C

FORE

B

$3\frac{3}{4}''$

D

WALKING

FORE

HIND

A

Plate 112

have a thick growth of hair on the throat (A), Plate 112. The greater kudu frequents partially wooded, hilly country, usually in small herds. The cow kudu is much smaller than the bull.

The hoofs track very close together, and for its weight this animal makes the lightest footprint of all the antelopes. The forefoot is wider than the hind, as shown in (B) and (C), Plate 112. When walking, it steps with its hind foot upon the heel of the track of its forefoot (D).

Brindled Gnu (*Connochaetes taurinus*). The brindled gnu is a strange composite animal, having the head of a buffalo, the tail of a horse, and legs and hoofs of the antelope. Both sexes have horns. The Dutch settlers of Africa dubbed them "wildebeest" or "wild cattle." Herds of gnus are often found peacefully grazing with zebra and other antelopes, and their tracks are intermingled with those of the other animals.

The hoofs of the gnu are blunt and rounded at the tips and seem to be joined together at the heel. At least the track has that appearance (A), Plate 113. The walking track (B), like those of other antelope, shows the alternately placed foretrack almost obliterated by that of the hind foot.

Warthog (*Phacochaerus aethiopicus*). When African natives wish to call each other the most insulting name they can think of, they shout "Njiri," meaning "Warthog." This animal is indeed a personification of ugliness, having a large wart-covered face with large tusks curving upward.

Warthogs run in pairs or families. They live in burrows probably excavated by ant bears, and when pursued by an enemy, try to take cover by backing into some near-by burrow. Like pigs, they enjoy mudholes in which they wallow for hours.

Their tracks, (A) and (B), Plate 114, show the cloven hoofs, blunt and round at the tips like the hoofs of swine. The walking trail shows the alternate footprints of the fore and hind feet. In

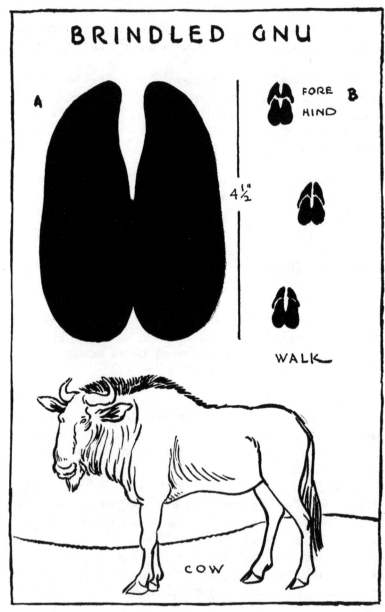

BRINDLED GNU

A

FORE B
HIND

$4\frac{1}{2}''$

WALK

COW

Plate 113

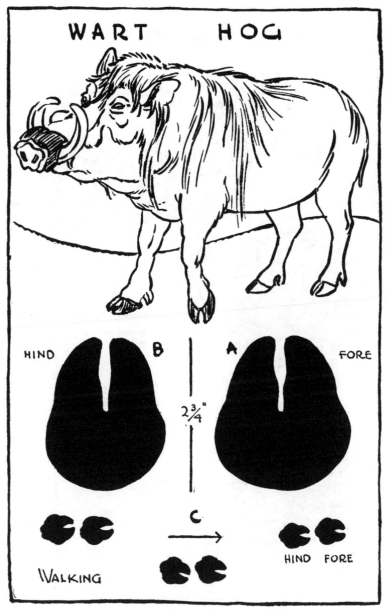

Plate 114

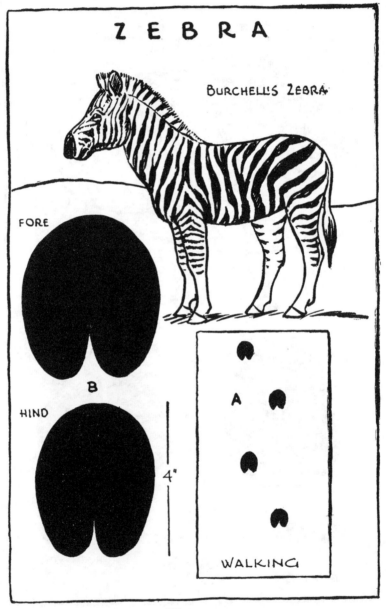

ZEBRA

BURCHELL'S ZEBRA

FORE

B

HIND

4"

A

WALKING

Plate 115

this instance, both the fore and hind tracks are separately imprinted (C).

Zebra (*Equus burchelli*). There are several species of zebra in Africa, Burchell's, Grevy's, and the mountain zebra. However, Burchell's is most numerous and ranges over a large part of Africa. Although they may sometimes gather in numbers, the ordinary group may contain only ten or twenty.

When feeding, they always wander into the wind. In this way they are kept informed of any danger ahead, since they have keen noses. They prefer open parklike areas and never live in the dense jungle.

The hoofs of Burchell's and Grevy's zebras are narrower than those of the horse, yet wider and more rounded than the donkey's. They seem to have been especially made for traveling on rocky ground, since they are deeply hollowed and very hard in texture.

Being sure-footed animals, they make a walking track similar to the donkey's, the hind foot stepping exactly into the track of the forefoot (A), Plate 115. Another characteristic, common to most mammals' feet, is the greater width of the zebra's forefoot in comparison to that of the hind (B).

ENDENTATA

Aardvark (*Orycteropus afer*). The Boers of Africa gave the name "aardvark," earth pig, to this strange creature. Being nocturnal, it is seldom seen, spending most of the day deep in its burrow. Since it feeds principally upon ants and termites, it is usually found in areas where the nest-building ants erect their huge hillocks. Here it breaks into the nests and licks up quantities of ants with its long sticky tongue. Even its teeth are specialized for insect eating, since it has only twenty crushing teeth, which have no roots and grow continually. The animal has no front or cutting teeth.

With its powerful claws it can bury itself in a few minutes,

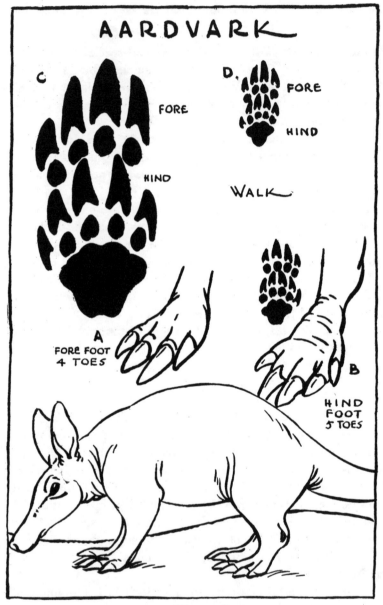

Plate 116

even in hard ground, excavating large lumps of soil as it sinks into the earth. There are four claws and toes on the forefoot and five on the hind (A) and (B), Plate 116, the claws being prominently displayed in the tracks of both fore and hind feet. In walking, the track of the forefoot is often nearly obliterated by the hind foot (C). The walking trail (D) shows the fore- and hind-foot tracks close together, the right and left feet alternately.

POUCHED ANIMALS (MARSUPIALIA)

Kangaroo (*Macropus giganteus*). The kangaroo is one of the strange, large marsupials peculiar to Australia. Like all marsupials, the young are born in a very underdeveloped embryo state and are raised in the pouch.

The great gray kangaroo and the red kangaroo are perhaps the largest of some twenty-four known species, a full grown male weighing 200 pounds. The kangaroo often makes trails through the scrub and thick undergrowth, following the easiest grades. It also makes shallow depressions in the sand and earth and uses them as dusting places.

Distinguishing characteristics of this animal are the large, strong hind feet and tail. The central toe of the hind foot is long and large (A), Plate 117. The forefoot track clearly shows the five toes and the palm pad.

When traveling slowly, it swings its hind legs forward while it rests upon the forefeet and tail (B), Plate 117. In this way it covers about 3 feet in a stride. When leaping, however, the tail and forelegs do not touch the ground, and it hops entirely upon the powerful hind legs (C), Plate 117. A slow pace will cover 4 to 6 feet, but when speeding it can make 26 feet in a single hop.

CASUARIIFORMES

Emu (*Dromaeus novae-hollandiae*). Sharing honors with the kangaroo upon the coat of arms of Australia is the emu, the sole

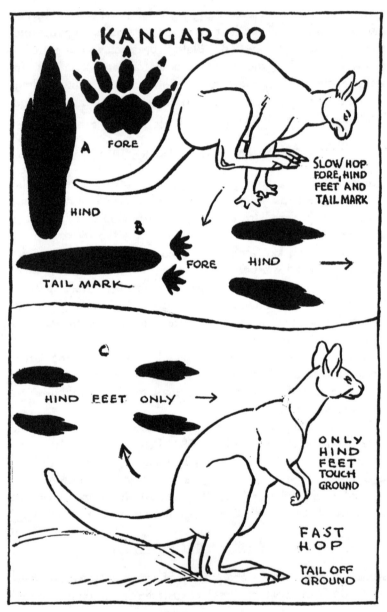

Plate 117

EMU

EMU TRACK

A

B

C

EMU FOOT

D

TRAIL

Plate 118

living species of flightless birds of the *Dromaiidae* family. This bird is unable to fly, but its long, strong legs are used most effectively, and it has been clocked at speeds of 30 to 35 miles an hour.

The feathers of this bird are most unusual, two feathers appearing to spring from a common shaft. This is due to the unusual growth of the aftershaft, which is merely a minute branch in the feathers of most birds. In the emu, however, this aftershaft is as large as the main shaft.

The large, three-toed track (A), Plate 118, is often found on the Australian plains with others of its family, for it seems to be most sociable, liking the company of its fellows. It makes the typical walking and running track of a ground bird, placing its feet one ahead of the other in almost a straight line (B). The large strong feet are shown in (C), while a drawing of the emu itself is shown in (D).

BIRD TRACKS
12

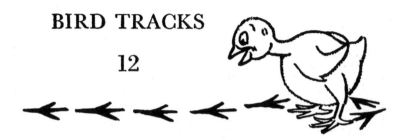

A Few Bird Signs. Many newcomers to the field of bird study often neglect important clues in establishing the presence of various birds, because they depend almost wholly upon seeing or hearing the birds. There are, of course, other ways of determining who our feathered neighbors are.

For instance, owls and sometimes crows and hawks, may re-gurgitate pellets, the undigested parts of their victims. The owl pellets vary in size according to the type of bird from which they came, and look like matted felt with shining bits of white bone scattered through it. These are usually found at the base of their roosting places (A), Plate 119.

The crow pellets, like the owl's, are composed of indigestibles, and are an inch or so in length. Unlike the owl, the crow shows its varied diet, and its pellets may contain the hard parts of insects and snails, cocoons, berries, seeds, nuts and remnants of a hundred other foods (B), Plate 119.

A shrike tells of its presence, at times, by its habit of impaling its victims upon thorns. Often, a mummified frog will be found thrust upon a thorn, forgotten by some shrike months before (C), Plate 119. It is because of this habit that this bird is often called the "butcher bird."

The whereabouts of woodcock is many times indicated by its "borings" (D), Plate 119. Woodcocks probe into the soft earth

Plate 119

for worms, and these probings are called "borings." They are certain evidence of woodcock in the neighborhood. The bill of the woodcock is most sensitive, and by thrusting it deeply into the soft earth, the bird seems to determine the nearness of a worm. The tip of the woodcock's upper mandible can be moved independently of the lower one and is used like a finger to draw the quarry up through the boring.

Birds' nests, like old-time tavern signs, advertise their owners. The mud-and-straw pot nest of the robin is easily identified (A), Plate 120. The Christmas stocking of the oriole is hung out in all oriole neighborhoods (B). The bakery oven of the ovenbird (C) is a sure sign of his presence, and the minute hummingbird's nest of lichens (D) tells that this mite is about. The cliff swallow's mud pellet retort (E) and the chimney swift's glued pocket of sticks (F) inform us of their having moved into the neighborhood.

The woodpeckers apparently admit to the saying that, "By their works ye shall know them," for the knowing observer can readily identify his woodpecker neighbors by the type of tree trunk excavation. Equipped with combination hammer-and-chisel bills, these birds dig out their food as well as their homes. Every park, orchard or grove usually has several memorials hammered into the trees by these birds, and each will identify the maker.

The downy and redheaded woodpecker and the flicker, like the three bears, in their afore-mentioned order, make a small size round hole, a middle size and a larger one (A), (B) and (C), Plate 121. The hairy woodpecker must have heard about that much-discussed square peg in a round hole, for its excavating obviously tries to reconcile the two (D). The pileated woodpecker goes in for tree excavation on a wholesale scale. Its work shows great gougings into the tree trunks (E).

The arctic three-toed woodpecker has a most distinctive technique. It flakes off the top surface of the outer bark on large areas of tree trunks, leaving the residue at the base of the tree (F), Plate 121.

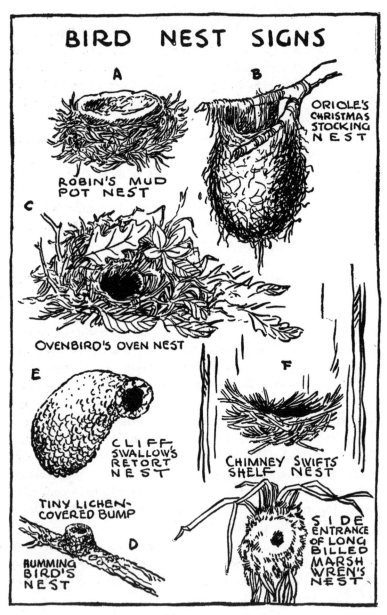

Plate 120

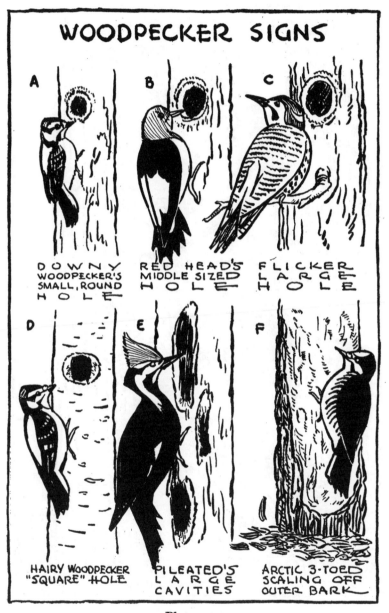

WOODPECKER SIGNS

A · B · C

DOWNY WOODPECKER'S SMALL, ROUND HOLE

RED HEAD'S MIDDLE SIZED HOLE

FLICKER LARGE HOLE

D · E · F

HAIRY WOODPECKER "SQUARE" HOLE

PILEATED'S LARGE CAVITIES

ARCTIC 3-TOED SCALING OFF OUTER BARK

Plate 121

WOODPECKER SIGNS

H

I

G

RED BREASTED
WOODPECKER
WORK

WILLIAMSON'S
WOODPECKER

YELLOW
BREASTED
SAPSUCKER

L

OTHER WOODPECKER'S
UNDULATING FLIGHT

K

LEWIS WOODPECKER'S
STRAIGHT FLIGHT

J

GILA
WOODPECKER
N

CALIFORNIA WOODPECKER
INLAYS ACORNS

Plate 122

The yellow-bellied sapsucker likely has a great thirst, for it loves to tap trees for their sap wherever it goes. It seems to have a measuring rule in attendance, since its borings are carefully and evenly spaced (G), Plate 122.

The northern red-breasted sapsucker of southern Alaska and south to Oregon, and its close relative, the southern red-breasted of California, are most handsome birds and, like the yellow-bellied sapsucker, make carefully measured borings around the trees (H). Another who leaves his blazes in a similar manner is the Williamson's sapsucker of the western mountains of southern British Columbia south to New Mexico and Arizona (I).

The tree blazes of the California woodpecker are easily identified. Nature, no doubt, inculcated a spirit of thrift in this bird, for its digging is done with an eye to a rainy day. It has a liking for fat acorns, and when the acorn crop is ripe it hammers great numbers of these nuts into little holes it has chipped into tree trunks and branches. Thus, you may come upon numerous acorn-studded tree trunks in the Southwest, which indicate the presence of the California woodpecker (J), Plate 122.

Lewis's woodpecker, another western bird, does not dig into trees for its food, but often catches its food upon the bark or on the ground. Its sky trail differs from that of many woodpeckers, for it flies in a straight line (K), Plate 122, while that of others is undulating (L), Plate 122. On the ground it makes the typical |< >| track common to most of the family (M).

The gila woodpecker of the Southwest digs its home in the giant cacti, making round openings high up, which plainly tell of its presence as do a woodman's blazes upon a tree (N), Plate 122.

Bird Tracks. Few ornithologists have given as much attention to the study of birds tracks as this subject deserves. Of course, many bird authorities have made careful observations concerning the feet of birds and their adaptations but the actual foot of a bird and the track it makes may at times have little resemblance to

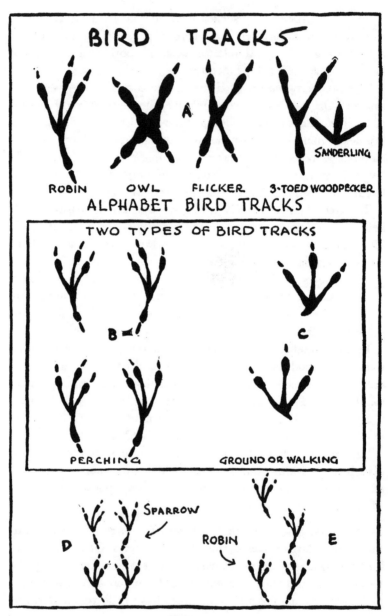

Plate 123

each other. The weight of the bird, its method of walking, the type of ground it walks upon, all have to do with the kind of track that results. Then, too, the individual bird may have some peculiarity or deformity which may or may not register.

The feet of birds differ both as to the formation of the toes and the number. A bird's foot commonly has three toes in the front and one behind. However, owls and road runners have two toes in front and two behind, forming an X-like track. The toe formation of the flicker and some of the woodpeckers is somewhat like the owl but forms a K-like track. The three-toed woodpeckers have two toes in front and one at the back, making a Y track. The sanderling makes a W-shaped track. Thus birds, like our federal agencies, seem to go in for the alphabet at times (A), Plate 123.

Roughly, there are two types of bird tracks, those made by perching birds and those made by ground or walking birds. Perching birds, like tree climbing mammals, pair their feet and hop (B), Plate 123. Ground dwelling or walking birds either place their feet one directly ahead of the other or place them diagonally, like the ground dwelling mammals (C). Each group can easily be recognized.

Some Common Bird Tracks. Some birds, such as the robin, have a combination of perching and ground dwelling characteristics, for these birds both hop and walk when on the ground. The robin track (E), Plate 123, clearly shows both its hopping and walking ability, the hopping indicated by the pairing of the feet, the walking or running by the single file tracks. If you observe a robin upon the ground, you will often see it take a number of hops and then run like any ground bird.

The English sparrow, another common bird of our back yards, belongs exclusively to the perching group, for its tracks are always paired when on the ground (D), Plate 123. The middle and inner toes are usually close together, in fact, they seem to be fast together. The hind toe is rather larger.

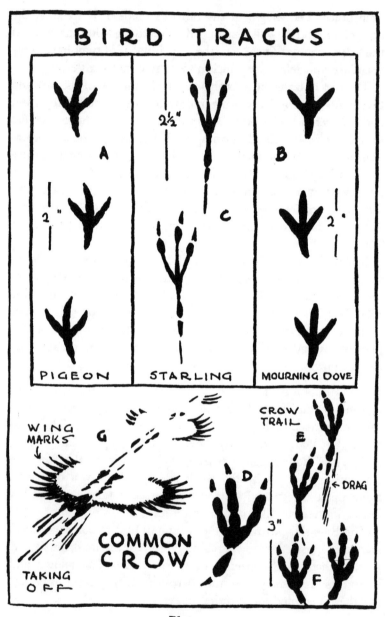

Plate 124

Another familiar bird track that we often see in the city is the common domestic pigeon (A), Plate 124. The adjective "pigeon-toed," possibly originated from this bird's habit of toeing-in slightly, although a number of other birds toe-in even more than the pigeon does. In the case of the pigeon, the middle toe seems to do most of the toeing-in.

The track of the mourning dove resembles that of the pigeon, except that the middle front toe does not seem to be bent inward so much (B), Plate 124. Both birds' tracks are about the same size.

The starling, an unwelcome immigrant, is fast becoming a national nuisance, and its tracks are found both in urban and rural areas. Its toes are rather long in proportion to the size of its track, and it walks like a ground bird (C), Plate 124.

One of the most intelligent birds that we see both in the city and country is the crow. Its "gouty-toed" tracks (D), Plate 124, are often found in sand, mud and snow. The inner and middle toes are close together, and it has a lazy habit of dragging its feet. It rarely hops, preferring to walk like a ground bird (E). When alighting upon the ground, it pairs its feet and then walks away. When both feet first touch the ground, the hind toes may not register (F), Plate 124. When springing up from the earth in preparation for flight, both feet are again paired, sometimes sinking deeply if the ground is soft. The imprints of the wing tips are often plainly marked. The drawing (G) shows the tracks of a crow taking off from a snow-covered field.

DIVING BIRDS (PYGOPODES)

Common Loon (*Gavia immer*). The tracks of the loon (a large black-and-white bird with brilliant red eyes) are seldom seen upon the land, except at nesting time. The legs of the loon are placed so far back upon the body that locomotion (A), Plate 125, upon dry land is difficult. The large feet are webbed, and traces

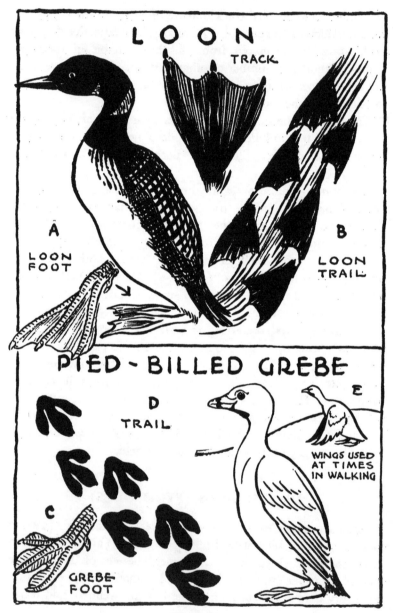

LOON

TRACK

A
LOON
FOOT

B
LOON
TRAIL

PIED - BILLED GREBE

E

D
TRAIL

WINGS USED
AT TIMES
IN WALKING

C

GREBE
FOOT

Plate 125

of its tottering, halting steps are sometimes seen in the mud or sand of lake shores (B). In the water, however, it is an expert diver and underwater swimmer.

After the young are hatched, they may be seen dressed in their nursery suits of brown down, riding upon their parents' backs. The laughter and the melancholy yodeling of the loon are its well known cries that may announce its presence, sometimes miles away.

Pied-Billed Grebe (*Podilymbus podiceps podiceps*). This is a common grebe of the eastern streams, ponds and marshes. It is an excellent swimmer and diver, but, like the loon, is clumsy in land travel. The toes of the grebe are lobed (C), Plate 125, and not webbed like the loon's. It makes a rather halting sort of track (D). The short wings at times are used as forefeet to aid its awkward progress (E).

Grebe nests are made of rushes and other aquatic vegetation in the form of rafts or islands. One of the strange baby diets of the grebe is its habit of feather eating. Several hundreds of feathers have been found in the stomach of a baby grebe only a few days old.

LONG-WINGED SWIMMERS (LONGIPENNES)

Herring Gull (*Larus argentatus*). This is an abundant member of the gull family found along the coast and on inland lakes and rivers. It nests in colonies, usually on islands, and its webbed track may often be seen in the mud. Only three foretoes register clearly, the fourth or hind toe showing only as a slight imprint in the track, being somewhat above the "heel of the foot" (A), Plate 126.

This gull has been known to take a fresh water mussel in its bill and fly to a height and drop the mollusc upon the rocks below in order to open the shell (B), Plate 126. It is also a great scavenger, aiding in the clearing up of harbors and rivers.

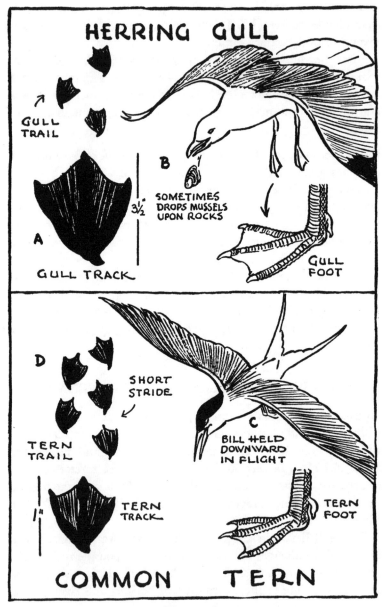

HERRING GULL

GULL
TRAIL

B

SOMETIMES
DROPS MUSSELS
UPON ROCKS

A

3½"

GULL TRACK

GULL
FOOT

D

SHORT
STRIDE

C

BILL HELD
DOWNWARD
IN FLIGHT

TERN
TRAIL

TERN
TRACK

1"

TERN
FOOT

COMMON   TERN

Plate 126

Common Tern (*Sterna hirundo hirundo*). In flying, the tern usually has its bill pointed downward, distinguishing it from the gull which carries its bill more in line with its body (C), Plate 126. Like the gull, it nests in colonies on islands, and its three-toed webbed track may frequently be found, a shallow imprint in soft mud or wet sand. The track of the tern is less than a third the size of that of the gull, being only about an inch in length. It has a short stride (D).

TOTIPALMATE SWIMMERS (STEGANOPODES)

White Pelican (*Pelecanus erythrorhynchos*). In the summer months, the white pelican frequents only fresh water, but salt water seems to be its choice when winter comes. This is one of our largest birds, having a wing spread of 8 and 9 feet.

Brown Pelican (*Pelecanus occidentalis carolinensis*). The brown pelican, on the other hand, lives around salt water at all seasons of the year. This bird secures its food by diving (A), Plate 127, while the white member of this family catches its food while swimming (B).

The four toes of the feet of both these birds are connected with webs which makes for a most unique track. The drawing shows a typical pelican track (C), Plate 127, and trail (D). The characteristic pelican sky trail is also shown in (E), Plate 127, a diagonal single file. They travel by alternately flapping and sailing, all in unison.

LAMELLIROSTRAL SWIMMERS (ANSERES)

Mallard Duck (*Anas platyrhynchos platyrhynchos*). The mallard is one of our common river ducks, and an examination of its feet shows that, like others of this group, the hind toes seem smaller than the hind toes of the sea and bay ducks. This is due to the fact that the river and pond ducks do not have a lobe upon the hind toe as do the sea and bay ducks (A), Plate 128. However,

Plate 127

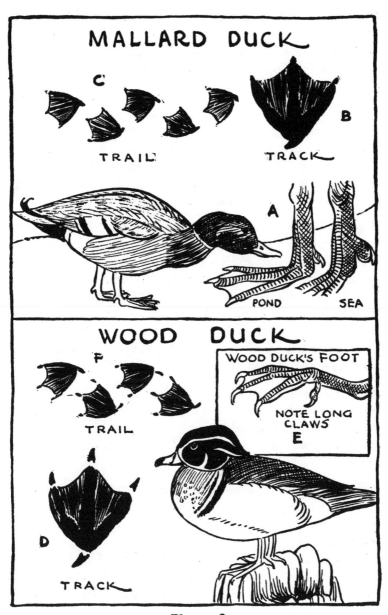

MALLARD DUCK

C

TRAIL

B

TRACK

A

POND   SEA

WOOD DUCK

F

TRAIL

WOOD DUCK'S FOOT

NOTE LONG
CLAWS
E

D

TRACK

Plate 128

regardless of this difference, the hind toes rarely register in the track, only the three front toes with their connecting web making the typical duck track shown in (B). Duck tracks are much alike, varying only slightly in size. The trail is shown in (C).

Wood Duck (*Aix sponsa*). This duck's track is shown in (D), Plate 128. The claws of this tree duck are noticeably long (E), probably so developed to aid it in its perching on trees. This is our most beautiful duck and it nests in hollow trees or stumps. It sometimes swims ahead of your canoe and on rounding a bend in the stream it will go ashore and walk rapidly away into the woods. The trail is shown in (F), Plate 128.

Canada Goose (*Branta canadensis canadensis*). The track of the goose is similar to that of ducks, except that it is larger in size. Being a heavier bird, the hind toe also registers together with the webbed three foretoes (A), Plate 129. When walking, the goose toes-in quite decidedly (B). The legs of the goose are placed nearer the middle of the body than is the case with ducks, and consequently, it can walk upon land with greater ease. The characteristic sky trail of the Canada goose is the V-shaped flight, making it easy to identify at long distances (C).

Snow Goose (*Chen hyperborea*). On the other hand the flight of this goose is also typical, and because of its characteristic flight this goose could be called "wavey" (D), Plate 129. However, the name "wavey" is a corruption of the Indian name "wa-wa" (goose).

Whistling Swan (*Cygnus columbianus*). Large numbers of these swans are often seen above the cataract at Niagara Falls during their springtime migrations, and at times many are killed going over the Falls.

The track of the swan is very similar to that of the goose except in size. In this case, the track may be a half inch to an inch longer. As in the track of the goose, the hind toe of the swan also

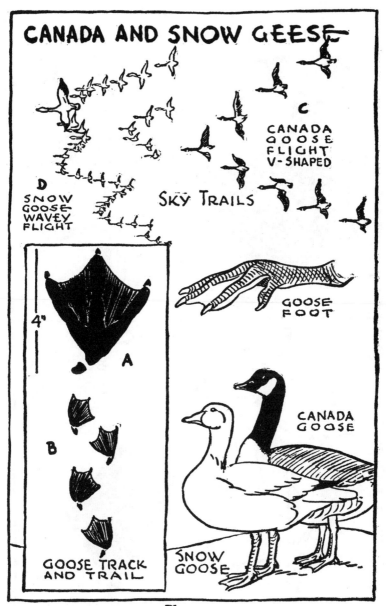

CANADA AND SNOW GEESE

C CANADA GOOSE FLIGHT V-SHAPED

D SNOW GOOSE WAVEY FLIGHT

SKY TRAILS

GOOSE FOOT

4"

A

B

CANADA GOOSE

GOOSE TRACK AND TRAIL

SNOW GOOSE

Plate 129

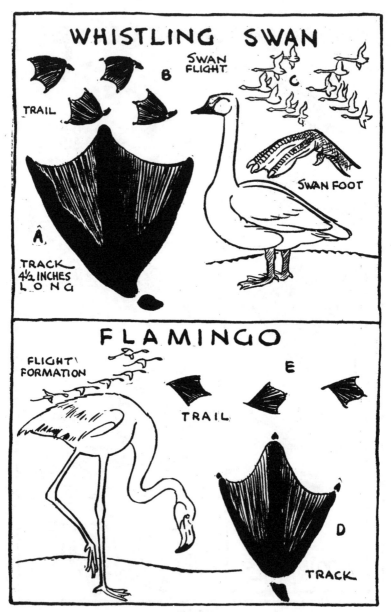

Plate 130

registers, as well as its three webbed foretoes (A), Plate 130. In walking, the swan takes short strides, toeing-in somewhat (B). In migration, they fly in V-shaped flocks, creating definite sky patterns (C), Plate 130.

LAMELLIROSTRAL GRALLATORES (ODONTOGLOSSAE)

Flamingo (*Phoenicopterus ruber*). The flamingo was formerly a common visitor to the extreme shoals of Florida, but it is now rarely seen. It is a beautiful rose-pink wader with a strange, bent bill.

The track of the flamingo shows its four toes, three webbed foretoes, and one smaller hind toe which registers as in the tracks of the swans and geese. It is a wading bird with long legs and its tracks are found on the vast mud flats. The middle toe seems to be somewhat longer than that of the geese or swans. The track and trail are shown in (D) and (E), Plate 130.

HERONS (HERODIONES)

American Bittern (*Botaurus lentiginosus*). Bitterns, unlike some herons, do not roost in flocks, but are found alone or in pairs. They usually frequent marshes and their tracks are often difficult to find, for they keep within the sedge and cattails.

However, their tracks are similar to that of a blue heron, except in size and depth of imprint. Being a smaller bird, this variation is quite in order. All four toes are slender and register distinctly in the track (A), Plate 131. The bittern has elongated wading legs and consequently takes longer strides than do ducks or geese. As it walks, it toes-in slightly, making a trail similar to the great blue heron (C), Plate 131, in the blue heron illustration, the distance between prints being shorter, however.

Great Blue Heron (*Ardea herodias*). The blue heron, frequently misnamed "crane," likes company, and although it may hunt by

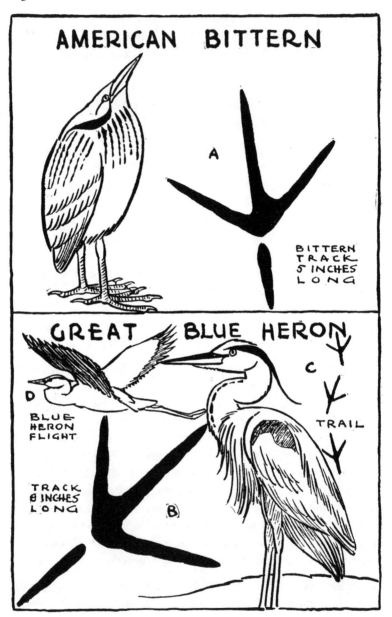

Plate 131

BLACK-CROWNED NIGHT HERON

A

TRACK
4 INCHES
LONG.

LITTLE GREEN HERON

C
TRAIL

B

TRACK
3 INCHES
LONG

Plate 132

itself during the day, it returns to join its fellows at a rookery at night.

Its track, very similar to that of the bittern, is about 3 inches longer. All four toes are visible in the track and are slightly webbed (B), Plate 131. The blue heron has long wading legs, and its strides are much greater than the bittern's. It also toes-in somewhat, making a trail as in (C). When flying, its folded neck is drawn back between its shoulders, a characteristic that readily distinguishes the heron from the crane (D), Plate 131. The crane stretches its neck out straight.

Black-Crowned Night Heron (*Nycticorax nycticorax hoactli*). These birds live in large colonies, and as their name indicates, are fond of night life, beginning their hunting after sundown. Their tracks are like those of the great blue heron but are smaller in size (A), Plate 132. The foretoes are perhaps a bit more spread, and the stride, of course, is shorter.

Little Green Heron (*Butorides virescens virescens*). Wooded streams and ponds are the favorite hunting grounds of this little heron. Unlike the night heron, it is a solitary bird and usually nests alone. It is usually active at nightfall or in the early morning, resting in some hideout during the day. The track is a miniature of the blue heron, being only a third of the size (B), Plate 132. However, it resembles the other heron tracks and trails (C).

CRANES, RAILS, GALLINULES, AND COOTS
(PALUDICOLAE)

Sandhill Crane (*Grus canadensis*). Although few in number, the sandhill crane is the more common member of this family and is found in south-central Florida. Like the herons, it has a long neck and legs, and frequents the borders of wet spots in the open places and among the pines.

In flight, it extends both its neck and feet, which distinguishes

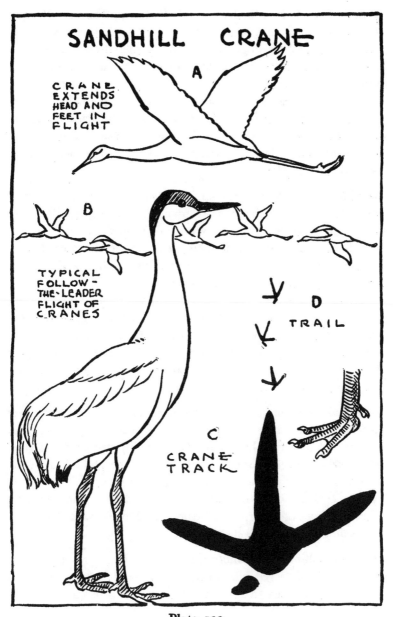

SANDHILL CRANE

A

CRANE EXTENDS HEAD AND FEET IN FLIGHT

B

TYPICAL FOLLOW-THE-LEADER FLIGHT OF CRANES

D TRAIL

C CRANE TRACK

Plate 133

its flight from that of the heron (A), Plate 133. Herons fold back their necks, forming a sort of letter "S." The flight formation of cranes commonly is single file, following their leader in a wavy line (B), although they have been reported flying in a triangular grouping.

The feet of cranes have four toes, the hind toe being smaller and higher above ground than the foretoes. The track shows the toes widely spread, with just an indication of the hind toe a little to one side (C), Plate 133. Its trail is like that of all long-legged ground walkers (D).

Virginia Rail (*Rallus limicola limicola*). The rails are swamp-loving birds, who depend more upon their legs for safety than their wings. Consequently, they have developed large strong legs and feet at the expense of their weak, rounded wings. In extremity, they take to their wings. Their flight is short and labored, with their legs dangling (A), Plate 134.

Their track is somewhat similar to that of the cranes, except, of course, only about half the size. All four toes register, but the front toes are not spread so widely as are the crane's (B), Plate 134. The walking trail is shown in (C). A piglike grunting often tells of their presence in the near-by swamp, but it requires patience and good eyes to spot them.

Sora Rail (*Porzana carolina*). The sora rail is widely spread over North America and is smaller than the Virginia rail. Its short yellow bill and gray-brown plumage readily distinguish it from the reddish Virginia rail with its long slender bill. I have not found the track of the sora rail, but according to Professor E. Laurence Palmer, in this instance, the hind toe is long, wherein it differs from the Virginia rail whose hind toe is small. The track, according to Palmer, is shown in (D), Plate 134.

Florida Gallinule (*Gallinula chloropus cachinnans*). This bluish slate bird with a red bill is commonly found in the marshes of our northern states. In appearance it seems to be a wanderer from

VIRGINIA RAIL

WALKING TRAIL

B

RAIL TRACK

SORA RAIL

LABORED FLIGHT
LEGS DANGLING
A

D
SORA
RAIL
TRACK

RAIL
FOOT

Plate 134

Plate 135

the barnyard and even its voice sometimes sounds like that of a squawking hen.

Examination of the feet of this bird shows that the hind toe is on the same level with the front ones. In this, it differs from the rails whose hind toes are raised somewhat above the foretoes. It is perhaps because of this arrangement that the hind toe is almost equal in length to the middle foretoe in the track (A), Plate 135. The toes are slender, and the trail is shown in (B).

Coot (*Fulica americana*). The coot is a slate-gray, ducklike bird with a white bill. As it swims, it moves its head back and forth like the gallinule. When taking off from the water, it runs along the surface for quite some distance, which makes a very characteristic sound and wake. The strange lobed toes of the coot produce a most unusual scalloped track (C), Plate 135. This characteristic indicates that the coot is more aquatic than the gallinule.

SHORE BIRDS (LIMICOLAE)

Wilson's Phalarope (*Steganopus tricolor*). The equal rights movement has been taken up by the lady phalarope with a vengeance. She is larger and has brighter plumage than the male. She does all the courting, and although she still lays the eggs, her husband incubates them.

The front toes of the northern and red phalarope are so lobed that the birds are almost webfooted (A), Plate 136. However, the lobes may or may not show in the track, depending upon the softness of the ground. The track of Wilson's phalarope under ideal conditions is shown in (B), Plate 136. The trail is shown in (C).

Wilson's phalarope is found in summer in prairie sloughs and ranges as far westward as California. The northern and red members are found in the northern part of the Northern Hemisphere.

WILSON'S PHALAROPE

TRAIL

B

TRACK
1⅜ INCHES
LONG

FEMALE

NORTHERN PHALAROPE

LOBED
FOOT OF
PELAGIA
SPECIES

FEMALE

TRACK
1½ INCHES
LONG

A

Plate 136

American Avocet (*Recurvirostra americana*). The avocet is another bird common in sections of the West and Middle West. It is a large shore bird with long legs and an upturned bill, which it uses somewhat like a scythe under water as it moves around. Although the avocet has four toes, the hind toe is slightly higher and does not show in the track. Only the three foretoes register, the outer toe being more widely spread. The toes are partially webbed (A), Plate 137. The avocet trail is shown in (B).

Black-Necked Stilt (*Himantopus mexicanus*). This stilt is black above and white below with very red legs. It is rightly named, for it looks as if it were walking on stilts (C), Plate 137. Today it is chiefly found in Florida and the Gulf Coast. The stilt has less webbing between its toes than the avocet, the outer toe has less than the inner toe. While the outer toe is more spread, it is not as much so as in the track of the avocet (D), Plate 137. The trail is illustrated in (E).

American Woodcock (*Philohela minor*). The woodcock frequents the wooded and swamp areas. Since it feeds upon earthworms, it is usually found where the earth is soft enough to probe with its long, sensitive bill. The holes it makes are called "borings" and these are usually found in groups, certain evidence that the woodcock is in the neighborhood (A), Plate 138.

The woodcock's toes are long and slender, the hind and outer toe in line with each other. The joints of the middle and inner toes are enlarged (B), Plate 138. The feet are placed diagonally ahead of each other, forming a sort of zigzag trail (C). The narrow, stiff primary wing feathers of the woodcock produce a high whistling music, which is delightful to the ear, especially during its sky dancing at mating time.

Wilson's Snipe (*Capella gallinago delicata*). The Wilson's snipe is another wing musician. Especially on moonlit nights, its wing music, as it darts downward like a dive bomber, is most unique and beautiful. When disturbed it takes off in a zigzag flight. It

Plate 137

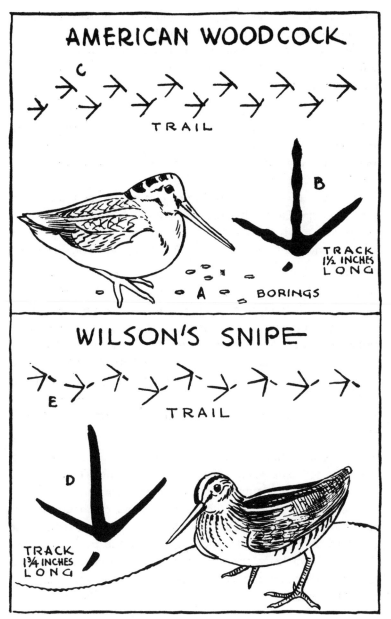

AMERICAN WOODCOCK

C

TRAIL

B

A

TRACK
1½ INCHES
LONG

BORINGS

WILSON'S SNIPE

E

TRAIL

D

TRACK
1¾ INCHES
LONG

Plate 138

chooses open places such as wet meadows and marshy areas, for it must have soft earth in which to probe for food.

The snipe track resembles the woodcock's, the toes being slender and the rear toe in line with the outer toe (D), Plate 138. The tracks in the trail show alternate prints (E).

Dowitcher (*Limnodromus griseus*). Although similar in proportion to the Wilson's snipe, the dowitcher is found on beaches and flats, an area seldom used as a hunting ground by the snipe. It migrates in very compact flocks, and at times its numbers may cover an entire sandbar when resting.

The track of the dowitcher resembles somewhat that of the Wilson's snipe except that the toes are more widely spread and the middle toe is shorter in proportion to the other toes. The toes, too, make a heavier imprint (A), Plate 139. The dowitcher trail is shown in (B).

Stilt Sandpiper (*Micropalama himantopus*). The stilt sandpiper often hunts in deeper water than do most shore birds. It usually migrates west of the Mississippi River and is less common along the East Coast. Its track looks like a smaller edition of the dowitcher's track. However, the toes are more slender at their tips but gradually thicken as they join at the base (C), Plate 139. The hind toe barely registers. Since the bird has long legs, the footprints are more widely spaced in the trail (D).

Knot (*Calidris canutus rufus*). The knot travels mostly along the Atlantic Coast. Only a few are seen inland. They hunt on the beaches and sometimes probe in the mud for their food. Like the dowitchers, they often "bunch" in compact flocks, making easy marks for gunners. The knot's track toes-in more than either the dowitcher or the stilt sandpiper. While the track is smaller than the dowitcher's, the toes of the track are about the same thickness. Only the three foretoes register in the track (A), Plate 140. The trail shows the characteristic toeing-in (B)

DOWITCHER

B

TRAIL

TRACK
1½ INCHES
LONG

A

STILT SANDPIPER

D

TRAIL

C

TRACK
1¼ INCHES
LONG

Plate 139

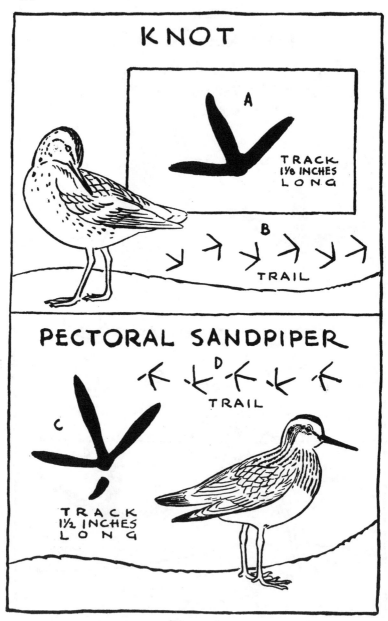

KNOT

A

TRACK
1⅛ INCHES
LONG

B

TRAIL

PECTORAL SANDPIPER

D

TRAIL

C

TRACK
1½ INCHES
LONG

Plate 140

Pectoral Sandpiper (*Erolia melanotos*). The pectoral sandpiper is often found on wet meadows instead of beaches. Because of this habit it is sometimes called "grass snipe." The three front toes of its track thicken toward the middle of the toes and are slender at the tips and base. The hind toe registers much more clearly than do the hind toes of the dowitcher or stilt sandpiper (C), Plate 140. The pectoral sandpiper toes-in almost as much as the knot, as shown by its trail (D).

White-Rumped Sandpiper (*Erolia fuscicollis*). The white-rumped sandpiper is rightly named, for it is the only small, streaked sandpiper with a white rump. It is found along the beaches on the Atlantic Coast and around inland pools. The tracks show very slender toes with just a small indication of the hind toe in line with the outer toe (A), Plate 141. Like many of its family, it toes-in as it walks (B).

Least Sandpiper (*Erolia minutilla*). The least sandpiper is about sparrow-size, the smallest of all the family. While it is found on the beaches, it is also seen in grassy meadows. Only the three very slender front toes register in the track (C), Plate 141. The foot itself toes-in slightly (D).

Red-Backed Sandpiper (*Erolia alpina pacifica*). The red-backed sandpiper is rusty red above and is the only sandpiper that has a black belly. It likes the company of its fellows and flies and feeds in flocks. It is unafraid and rather stupid. When the bird is walking, only the foreparts of the three front toes register in the track (A), Plate 142. It does not toe-in but points its middle toe straight ahead (B).

Semipalmated Sandpiper (*Ereunetes pusillus*). This is the commonest of the smaller sandpipers in the East. Because of their partially webbed toes they are called "semipalmated." This partial webbing shows in the track between the middle and outer toe. The toe marks in the track are exceedingly slender. The hind

Plate 141

toe registers slightly (C), Plate 142. When walking, it toes-in somewhat (D).

Western Sandpiper (*Ereunetes mauri*). The western sandpiper migrates along the Atlantic Coast and is commonly found wintering along the southern seacoast. In the tracks of this sandpiper, the toes thicken in the middle, tapering at the tips and bases, where they join at the heel. A slight mark is made by the hind toe (A), Plate 143. The western sandpiper toes-in a little more than does the semipalmated variety (B).

Sanderling (*Crocethia alba*). The sanderling, a small, plump sandpiper with a white stripe down the wing, frequents the eastern seashores. It is the only one of the snipes or sandpipers that has but three toes. While its track is just a bit smaller than the western sandpiper's, the toes register much heavier in the track because of a webbing bordering the toes. The middle toe seems to be closer to the inner toe than to the outer one, which adds to the toeing-in effect (C), Plate 143.

Marbled Godwit (*Limosa fedoa*). Godwits are larger shore birds of a buff-brown coloring, common on the western prairies, rare on the eastern coast. The track shows long toes partly webbed with the hind toe showing slightly (A), Plate 144. The godwit points its toes straight ahead as it walks (B).

Greater Yellow-Legs (*Totanus melanoleucus*). The greater yellow-legs is a large slim, gray-and-white sandpiper with bright yellow legs. The toes are widely spread, the outer closer to the middle toe. There is a slight webbing between the middle and outer toes. The hind toe registers slightly (C), Plate 144. In walking, the middle toe is placed straight ahead (D).

Lesser Yellow-Legs (*Totanus flavipes*). The lesser yellow-legs looks like its larger relative, but it is smaller in size. It migrates throughout eastern North America. While the track is smaller than that of the preceding member of the family, the toes seem

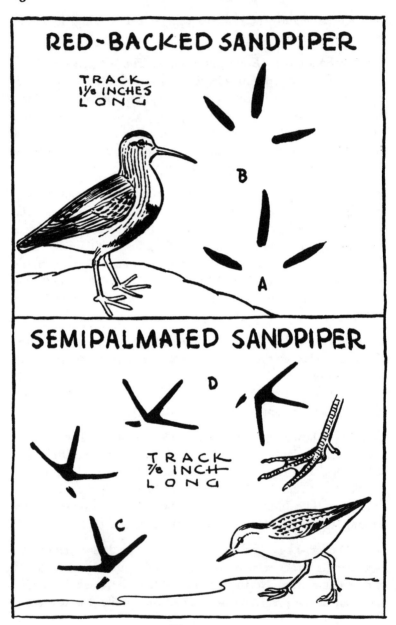

RED-BACKED SANDPIPER

TRACK
1⅛ INCHES
LONG

B

A

SEMIPALMATED SANDPIPER

D

TRACK
⅞ INCH
LONG

C

Plate 142

Plate 143

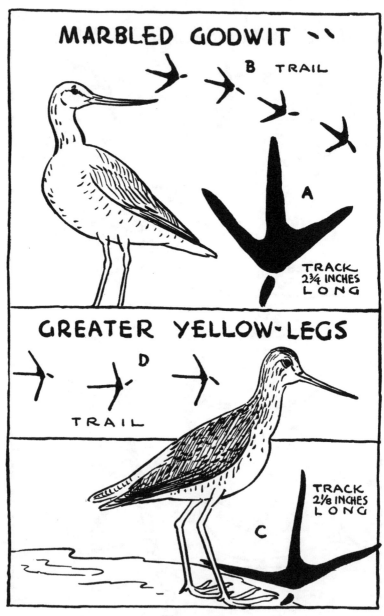

MARBLED GODWIT

B TRAIL

A

TRACK
2¾ INCHES
LONG

GREATER YELLOW-LEGS

D

TRAIL

TRACK
2⅛ INCHES
LONG

C

Plate 144

to be about the same thickness. Only the three front toes register. Like the greater yellow-legs, this member has a slight webbing between the middle and outer toe (A), Plate 145. It, too, points its feet straight ahead (B), as the trail shows.

Solitary Sandpiper (*Tringa solitaria solitaria*). Like the yellow-legs, the solitary sandpiper nods when walking, and is about the size of the lesser variety. It is a dark bird, dark above and whitish below with a white eye-ring and dark legs. This sandpiper is found near woodland ponds, lakes and streams. The solitary sandpiper makes a very slender-toed track. A very slight webbing extends from the middle to the outer toe, and there is an almost infinitesimal webbing between the middle and inner toe. Just a dot indicates the hind toe (C), Plate 145. This bird toes-in slightly (D).

Willet (*Catoptrophorus semipalmatus*). The willet is a gray-and-white shore bird, larger than the yellow-legs, with black-and-white wings and bluish legs. The eastern species is found along the Atlantic Coast. The toes are slightly webbed at their bases, and this webbing sometimes shows in the track. Only a slight indication of the hind toe is seen in the track (A), Plate 146. In walking, the willet toes-in slightly (B).

Western Willet (*Catoptrophorus semipalmatus inornatus*). The western willet is slightly larger, and breeds in the interior. Its track resembles that of the greater yellow-legs both in size and construction, except that the toes seem to be thicker. Like its eastern relative the toes are slightly webbed (C), Plate 146. The tracks toe-in very slightly in the trail of this bird (D).

Spotted Sandpiper (*Actitis macularia*). This is the common sandpiper whose tracks are found in the mud of the margins of most lakes and streams throughout the country. As it runs, it teeters up and down (A), Plate 147. Its breast is covered with large round spots during the breeding period. This is the only sandpiper that has definite spots. Its track resembles that of the

Plate 145

WILLET

TRAIL B

A

TRACK
2⅛ INCHES
LONG

WESTERN WILLET

D

TRAIL

C

TRACK
2¼ INCHES
LONG

Plate 146

SPOTTED SANDPIPER

C

TRAIL

A

B

TRACK
1¼ INCHES
LONG

LONG·BILLED CURLEW

E

TRAIL

D

TRACK
2⅛ INCHES
LONG

Plate 147

solitary's in size and appearance, except that the hind toe registers more clearly. The marks of the toes are most delicate, and there is a web between the outer and middle toe (B), Plate 147. As it walks or runs, it makes tracks that toe-in slightly more than the solitary's track (C).

Long-Billed Curlew (*Numenius americanus*). The long-billed curlew is well named, for its extremely long bill is nearly twice as long as that of the Hudsonian curlew. As it flies, the bright cinnamon color of the underwings is its surest identification. This bird is common along the Texas coast. The track is a little more than 2 inches in length and all four toes usually register, as well as the webbing between the toes. There is a greater development of the web between the outer and middle toes than between the inner toes. The hind toe shows slightly (D), Plate 147. In walking, the foot is pointed straight ahead (E).

Hudsonian Curlew (*Numenius phaeopus hudsonicus*). The curlews have long, sicklelike bills that curve downward. They are large brown shore birds that often fly in a wedge formation with their curved bills extended and their legs trailing (A), Plate 148. They migrate chiefly along the coast. In this instance, the track shows only the forepart of the toes, the webs and "heel" of the track not being visible. Only a bit of the hind toe has left its mark (B), Plate 148. This curlew also seems to toe-in somewhat (C).

Golden Plover (*Pluvialis dominica dominica*). The plovers resemble the snipes somewhat, but their short bills and stocky proportions afford a striking contrast. The golden plover likes marshes, fields, sand flats and burnt-over areas. On the ground they run lightly and rapidly. They migrate north in the spring through the Mississippi Valley, and off the Atlantic coast in the fall. The golden plover has only three toes, the hind toe being absent. The middle and outer toes seem closer together, the inner toe being at a complete right angle to the middle toe. While there

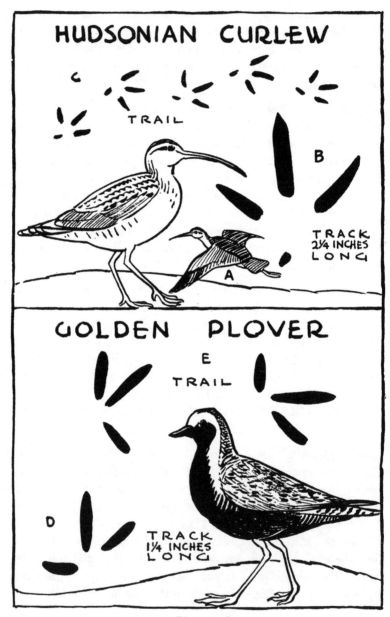

Plate 148

are webs between the base of the toes, these seldom register in the track (D), Plate 148. This plover toes-in slightly (E).

Killdeer (*Charadrius vociferus vociferus*). The killdeer is the common plover of fields and pastures. Because of its loud, noisy "Killdee," it is rightly named *vociferus*. The hind toe often does not register in the track. The middle toe is longer than either the outer or inner toe and makes a heavier track. The outer toe is closer to the middle toe than is the inner one (A), Plate 149. The killdeer is quite "pigeon-toed" in its walk (B).

Semipalmated Plover (*Charadrius hiaticula semipalmatus*). This plover is half the size of the killdeer and chooses sandy beaches, flats and marshes for its feeding grounds. When feeding, it runs about independently of the others, but when in flight these birds travel in small compact groups, all seemingly imbued with the same idea. The semipalmated plover's track is unique, being similar to the letter Y in appearance. The outer and middle toe are close together and, since this bird toes-in very much indeed, it gives Y appearance to the track (C), Plate 149. The trail is shown in the drawing (D).

Piping Plover (*Charadrius melodus*). Often found on the beaches, its color is much like the sun-dried sand of its hunting grounds. Because of this camouflage, it is difficult to see and melts into the background the minute it stands still. The Y track of the piping plover resembles somewhat that of its semipalmated relative. However, the middle toe is separated to a greater degree from the outer toe. The toes of the track, too, are heavier and the inner toe is shorter than the others. Like the semipalmated plover, this bird toes-in to quite a degree (A), Plate 150. Its trail is pictured in (B).

GALLINACEOUS BIRDS (GALLINAE)

Bobwhite or Quail (*Colinus virginianus*). The bobwhite clearly calls its name when it gives its characteristic whistle. In colora-

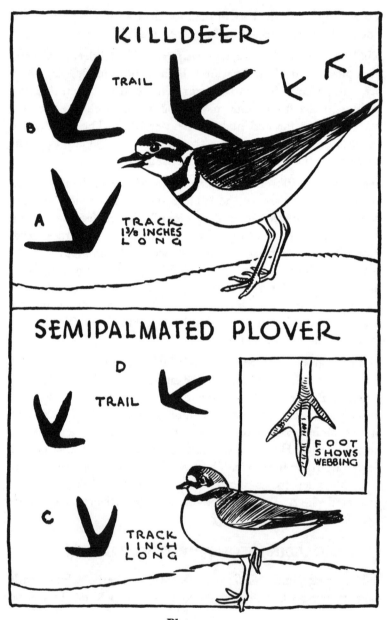

Plate 149

Plate 150

tion it resembles the dead leaves on the ground, and it relies upon this camouflage to escape detection. It roosts upon the ground, forming a circle with its fellows, tail to tail, with heads outward, and the circle literally explodes in all directions when disturbed. The track of the bobwhite may show all four toes, the inner and outer toes being sometimes widely spread. The outer toe is about the same length as the middle toe and the hind toe is small (C), Plate 150. Like many walking birds, the quail toes-in as it walks (D).

Ruffed Grouse (*Bonasa umbellus*). The ruffed grouse are brown, chickenlike birds found in thick woodlands. If they take to wing when disturbed, they make a most startling noise with their wings. The male at mating time selects a fallen tree trunk upon which he "drums" his famous rhythms, sounding like a distant "flivver."

In the summer track of the ruffed grouse, the toes are slender in comparison to the winter track. All four toes register in each season, the hind toe, however, showing very little in the track (A), Plate 151. In winter, a fringe, looking much like short, yellow hemlock needles, grows upon the foretoes (B). This growth acts as snowshoes and enables the grouse to walk upon the surface of the snow. This seasonal growth, of course, makes the tracks of the toes look much wider than in summer. The trail of the ruffed grouse shows that it, too, toes-in a bit (C), Plate 151. It also takes the shortest stride of all the grouse family. During extremely cold weather the grouse sometimes "holes in" under the snow (D).

Spruce Grouse (*Canachites canadensis*). The spruce grouse is slate colored and lives in the evergreen forests of the North. It is unsuspicious and unafraid of human beings, allowing them to approach close enough to kill it with a stick. Because of this, it is often called "fool hen." The tracks of most of the grouse are much alike, and it is difficult to distinguish one from the other.

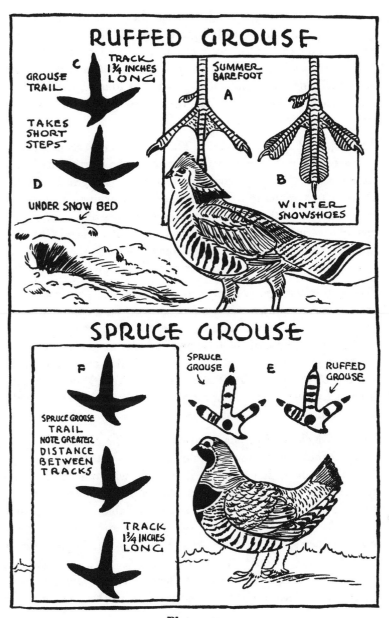

RUFFED GROUSE

C GROUSE TRAIL

TRACK 1¾ INCHES LONG

SUMMER BAREFOOT

A

TAKES SHORT STEPS

D

UNDER SNOW BED

B

WINTER SNOWSHOES

SPRUCE GROUSE

F

SPRUCE GROUSE TRAIL NOTE GREATER DISTANCE BETWEEN TRACKS

SPRUCE GROUSE

E

RUFFED GROUSE

TRACK 1¾ INCHES LONG

Plate 151

Nevertheless, some trackers say that they can distinguish the spruce grouse from the ruffed grouse by the number of nodules on the middle toe that might register under perfect tracking conditions. They say that the spruce grouse has two such nodules on the middle toe while the ruffed grouse has four (E), Plate 151. The spruce grouse toes-in like the ruffed grouse but takes a longer step as it walks (F).

Ptarmigan (*Lagopus lagopus*). The ptarmigans are small Arctic grouse found in the bleak, barren wastes of the North. Like many creatures of the snow country, this bird changes its brown plumage of summer to a white camouflage in winter. At the same time it grows feather moccasins and snowshoes on its feet, completely covering them with this growth (A), Plate 152. While the summer track of the ptarmigan may resemble the grouse, in winter these feather snowshoes transform the tracks entirely (B).

Sharp-tailed Grouse (*Pedioecetes phasianellus*). This is a prairie grouse with a pointed tail. Its feet seem to be a combination of the ptarmigan and the ruffed grouse, for they are covered with feathers to the base of the toes, and the toes themselves have the fringe of growth, like that which the ruffed grouse develops in the fall of the year (C), Plate 152. The track shows both the fringed toes and the feathering about their base (D). Like the other grouse, it toes-in as it walks (E).

Prairie Chicken (*Tympanuchus cupido*). The prairie chicken is a large henlike bird, brown in color, that lives in the open prairies. It is noted for its dance, which it executes with other males on a special dance ground during the courtship period. It also makes a display of its feathers, giving a three-syllable call at the same time. The track (A), Plate 153, is about the size of a small domestic hen's, but the toes widen at the base, giving the track a different aspect from that of the domestic fowl. All four toes register, the hind toe, however, the least of all. It does not spread its toes as widely as the other grouse, and neither does it toe-in

Plate 152

PRAIRIE CHICKEN

B

A

FOOT IN WINTER

C

TRACK 2¼" INCHES LONG

TURKEY

E

TRAIL

WING DRAG

D

TRACK 5" INCHES LONG

Plate 153

as the others do. The trail is shown in (B). A drawing of a foot is shown in (C).

Turkey (*Meleagris gallopavo silvestris*). The tail feathers of the domestic turkey have white tips while the eastern wild turkey has chestnut tips. The characteristic "gobble" is given by both. The wild turkey usually feeds in small flocks of six to twelve and returns to the same roosting ground each night in wooded bottom lands. The three rather thick front toes and the tip of the hind toe off to one side register in the track. The middle toe is slightly curved inward, which adds to the toeing-in effect of the track (D), Plate 153. The size of the turkey track is most distinctive since it is our largest game bird. When the bird is strutting, the stiff wing feathers often make marks on each side of the trail (E).

Ring-Necked Pheasant (*Phasianus colchicus torquatus*). The ring-necked pheasant is a large, showy, gamecocklike bird with a long pointed tail. The male is gayly colored, but the female is brownish, resembling a grouse somewhat. This is a bird introduced from China. When disturbed, it quickly runs to any scanty cover it can find, and it is surprising how quickly it disappears. The pheasant is difficult to flush, preferring the safety offered by tall grass and undergrowth. All four toes register in the track. Of the three front toes, the middle toe is longest, the inner toe shortest. The pheasant prefers a straight and narrow trail. There is no toeing-in, the middle toe making almost a straight line (A), Plate 154. The drawing (B) shows the trail of this bird.

PIGEONS AND DOVES (COLUMBAE)

Mourning Dove (*Zenaidura macroura*). The mourning dove is a small brown pigeonlike bird with a pointed tail. In flight this dove makes a whistling sound with its wings. It is usually seen in pairs. Unlike some birds, this dove can drink without raising its head. The young are fed with "pigeon milk," a predigested food regurgitated from the crop of the parent. The track of the mourn-

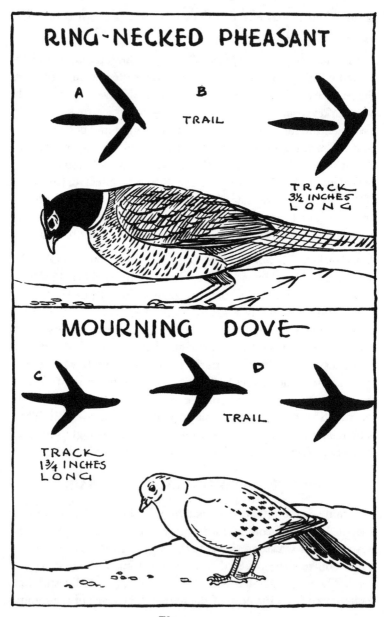

Plate 154

mg dove shows all four toes. The middle toe is longer; the outer and inner toe, equally spaced, are about the same length. The hind toe also registers (C), Plate 154. It toes-in slightly as it walks (D), placing one foot ahead of the other.

BIRDS OF PREY (RAPTORES)

Red-Tailed Hawk (*Buteo jamaicensis*). In spite of common opinion, most hawks are a great benefit to the farmer, for they consume myriads of rodents. The red-tailed hawk is especially destructive to rats and mice. Hawks strike their prey with their feet, and while they are seldom found upon the ground, occasionally a track may be discovered. Like perching birds, hawks have three toes in front and one at the back of the foot, with strong, curved talons (A), Plate 155. Consequently, if this track is found, it shows these characteristics (B), and they are so marked that in soft mud or wet sand the tracks look like grotesque dancing will-o'-the-wisps made by the dragging of the sharp talons.

Barn Owl (*Tyto alba pratincola*). This is a light-colored owl with a heart-shaped face (C), Plate 155, commonly found in attics, towers and steeples. It is an extremely valuable bird, for it feeds mostly upon mice, rats and other destructive creatures. The foot of this owl (D), Plate 155, is interesting, for the middle claw has comblike teeth (E) and the inner toe is as long as the middle toe, which is unlike most owls, whose inner toes are shorter. This characteristic, of course, is present in the track (F).

Great Horned Owl (*Bubo virginianus*). The great horned owl is a large owl with "horns" or feathered tufts on its head. It frequents wooded areas, and its deep toned "hoo, hoo-hoo, hoo, hoo" may sound somewhat like the faraway barking of a dog. At times it gives a blood curdling scream. The feet of the horned owl are covered with feathers up to the long, sharp talons (A), Plate 156. Unlike that of the barn owl, the inner toe is shorter than the middle toe. Often, in the snow around the blood-stained

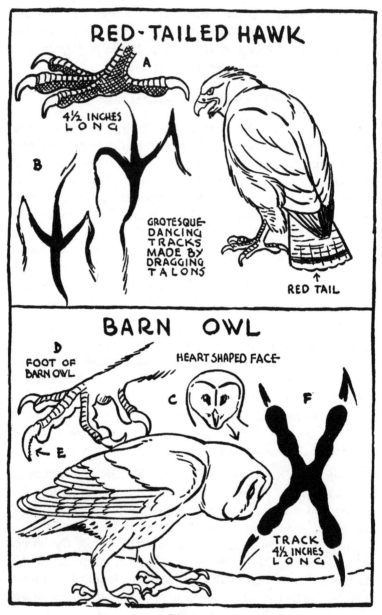

RED-TAILED HAWK

A

4½ INCHES
LONG

B

GROTESQUE-
DANCING
TRACKS
MADE BY
DRAGGING
TALONS

RED TAIL

BARN OWL

D
FOOT OF
BARN OWL

HEART SHAPED FACE

C

E

F

TRACK
4½ INCHES
LONG

Plate 155

Plate 156

remnant of a rabbit, its "X"-like tracks may be found (B). In other words, X marks the spot.

Screech Owl (*Otus asio*). The screech owl, a common, small owl, has two color phases, a reddish brown and a gray phase. It has a mournful quavering cry that runs down the scale and can be approximated on a musical saw. It elongates itself or puffs out its feathers until it looks twice its size (C), Plate 156. It may be found in dwellings, but prefers a hollow tree for its home. Like the great horned owl, the track of the screech owl is "X"-shaped with a short inner toe (D), Plate 156. It can walk or run rather awkwardly upon the ground, making a trail similar to (E).

Burrowing Owl (*Speotyto cunicularia*). This is a small brown owl about the size of the screech owl, but without ear tufts, and it lives in burrows in the ground. It has long legs without any leg feathering, and, unlike the screech owl, is most active during the day. It is found in the open areas of southern Florida where it is very abundant. The western variety is found all over western United States and Canada. Like all owls, it can see by day or night, having most adaptable pupils that enlarge, nearly filling the entire eye, or contract, according to the amount of light. It walks and runs upon the ground as well as it flies, making the typical X-shaped mark of the owl family (A), Plate 157. Its trail is like the drawing (B).

WOODPECKERS (PICI)

Hairy Woodpecker (*Dendrocopus villosus*). The hairy woodpecker, like the downy, is a white-backed woodpecker. Both are almost alike in color and pattern, but the hairy is larger in size. Its "square holes" have been touched upon on page 221. The feet of this woodpecker have two toes in front and two behind, which aids it in clinging to tree trunks (C), Plate 157. Its track, like those of all the four-toed woodpeckers, is paired and looks like two K's facing each other (D).

Plate 157

Downy Woodpecker (*Dendrocopus pubescens*). The downy woodpecker, the most familiar of our woodpeckers, is commonly found with nuthatches and chickadees in winter. It excavates the smallest of the "round woodpecker holes" as described on page 221. The downy's foot has two toes in front and two behind, making the characteristic K tracks of the one section of the woodpecker family (A), Plate 158.

Redheaded Woodpecker (*Melanerpes erythrocephalus*). The redheaded woodpecker is easily identified by its all-over red head and black-and-white body. The redhead excavates "the middle size round hole" as shown on page 223. It can catch its food on the wing, and will also eat nuts and fruits. Like the above-mentioned woodpeckers, it has two toes in front and two in the back of its foot, making the same type of track (B), Plate 158, except for size. The foot of the redheaded woodpecker is shown in (C).

Flicker (*Colaptes auratus*). The flicker is a large brown woodpecker with a white rump visible when the bird flies. This is perhaps the best field mark. Like most of the woodpeckers, its flight is undulating (A), Plate 159. It makes the largest of the round woodpecker holes. See page 223. Unlike the woodpeckers, the flicker often hunts upon the ground, frequenting anthills, where it hops about making its double-K track (B), Plate 159. Its feet, like others of its family, have two foretoes and two hind toes (C).

Yellow-Bellied Sapsucker (*Sphyrapicus varius varius*). The yellow-bellied sapsucker is our only woodpecker with a red forehead patch. Unlike others of this family, the sapsucker's tongue has developed through specialization into a brush (D), Plate 159, for this bird feeds largely upon the sap of trees. It goes round and round a tree or branch, punching small holes, carefully spaced as if it had used a tape measure for accuracy (E). See page 224.

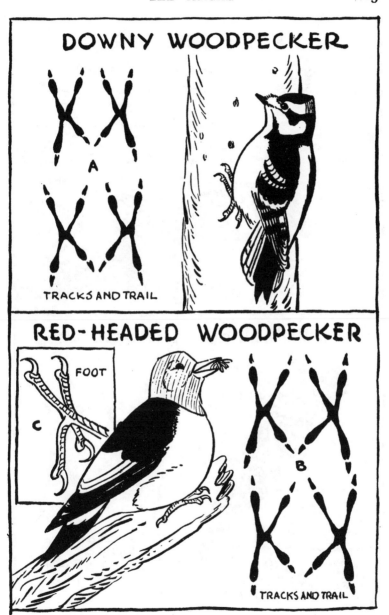

DOWNY WOODPECKER

A

TRACKS AND TRAIL

RED-HEADED WOODPECKER

FOOT

C

B

TRACKS AND TRAIL

Plate 158

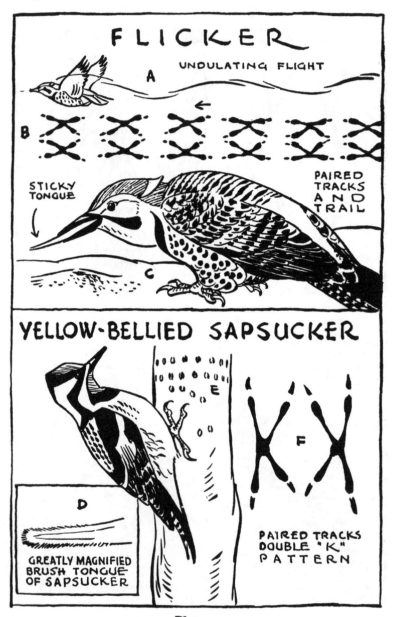

FLICKER

UNDULATING FLIGHT

A

B

STICKY TONGUE

PAIRED TRACKS AND TRAIL

C

YELLOW-BELLIED SAPSUCKER

E

F

D

GREATLY MAGNIFIED BRUSH TONGUE OF SAPSUCKER

PAIRED TRACKS DOUBLE "K" PATTERN

Plate 159

Its feet have two fore and two hind toes, making the typical double-K track of most of the woodpeckers (F), Plate 159.

Pileated Woodpecker (*Hylatomus pileatus*). The pileated woodpecker is large, almost the size of a crow, with a very showy, raised red crest. Its body is black and white. Its large, oblong excavations tell of its presence. See page 223. Its flight differs from that of most woodpeckers, since it usually is in a straight line instead of undulating (A), Plate 160. It, too, has the characteristic toe formation of most woodpeckers, that of two toes in front and two behind (B).

Arctic Three-Toed Woodpecker (*Picoides arcticus*).

American Three-Toed Woodpecker (*Picoides tridactylus bacatus*). Both of the three-toed woodpeckers have yellow caps on the forepart of their heads. However, the Arctic three-toed has a solid black back, while the American three-toed has a black-and-white ladder back. Both live in the evergreen forests of the North where their presence is made known by large patches on dead tree trunks that have been scaled of their outer bark (see page 223). Both of the three-toed woodpeckers have only three toes on each foot, two in the front and one behind (C), Plate 160, making a Y track with each foot (D). The tracks are always paired. The flight of the Arctic three-toed is deeply undulating (E).

California Woodpecker (*Balanosphyra formicivora bairdi*). This woodpecker ranges over most of the Pacific coastland in southern Texas and Arizona. It feeds upon insects, but about half of its food consists of acorns. Some of the insects are caught while flying. However, its storing of acorns is its most characteristic habit. It digs small holes in the bark of trunks and branches and then wedges an acorn into each hole so tightly it is difficult to remove it. The trees are literally studded with acorns when the crop is good (A), Plate 161. The California woodpecker has four toes, two in the front and two behind, and should it alight upon the ground, its paired feet make the typical double-K track of the woodpecker family (B).

PERCHING BIRDS (PASSERES)

Horned Lark (*Eremophila alpestris*). This terrestrial bird of streaked brown with two small black-feathered horns is somewhat larger than the English sparrow. It has a black collar below a yellow throat. The horned lark is a winter visitor and is usually seen in numbers, running or walking over snow-covered fields. It never hops. It has three toes in front and one in back. The nail of the hind toe is greatly elongated, being almost as long as the middle toe (C), Plate 161. This long claw usually drags in the trail, exaggerating the length of the hind toe in the track. The trail shows the footprints alternate, the hind toe dragging as the bird walks (D).

Prairie Horned Lark (*Eremophila alpestris praticola*). The prairie horned lark is lighter in color, the throat whitish instead of bright yellow. Once this bird was found only on the prairies and open barren lands, but now it has made its appearance in the East where there is open country. It is strictly a ground bird, running about, never hopping. Its track is similar to the horned lark's (A), Plate 162, an alternating, walking track with a dragging of the hind toe (B).

Meadowlark (*Sturnella magna*). The meadowlark is common in our fields, a rather large bird with a white patch on each side of a short, wide tail, and a yellow breast with a black gorget upon it. It has large feet with three toes in front and one behind. It does not hop, but walks, making an alternating trail as in (C), Plate 162. The individual track is shown in (D).

PILEATED WOODPECKER

STRAIGHT FLIGHT

A

B

PAIRED TRACK

ARCTIC THREE-TOED WOODPECKER

C

3 TOED FOOT

UNDULATING FLIGHT

E

D

PAIRED 3 TOED TRACK

Plate 160

CALIFORNIA WOODPECKER

A

INLAYS
ACORNS

B

PAIRED
TRACKS
HOPS

HORNED LARK

C

LONG CLAW
ON HIND
TOE

D

ALTERNATE
TRACKS
SHOW
LONG
HIND
CLAW

1½ INCHES
LONG

Plate 161

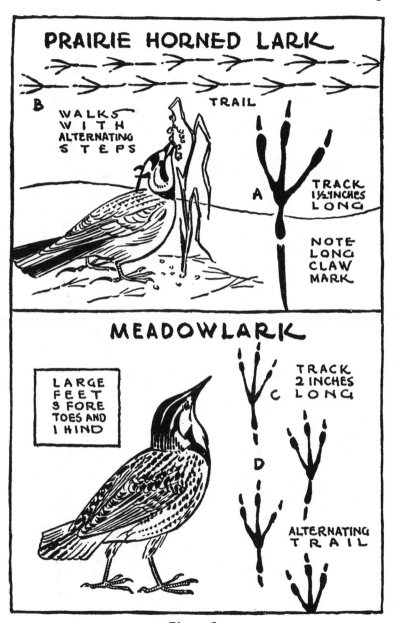

Plate 162

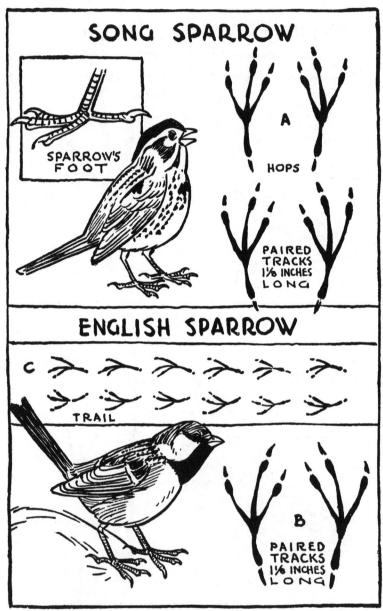

Plate 163

Plate 164

Song Sparrow (*Melospiza melodia*). The song sparrow is a common bird of rich brown with the breast streaked with black and rufous brown and a large dark splash in the center. It pumps its rounded tail as it flies. Like other sparrows, it hops, making a track much like the English sparrow, its paired feet toeing-in somewhat (A), Plate 163.

English Sparrow (*Passer domesticus domesticus*). The English sparrow, not a sparrow, but a European weaver finch, was brought to this country in 1851. Today it is found through the length and breadth of the land, and its paired tracks are found in our back yards everywhere (B), Plate 163. It hops, making a trail similar to that of the song sparrow (C).

Wood Thrush (*Hylocichla mustelina*). The wood thrush is slightly smaller than the robin. It has a bright reddish brown head and numerous large round spots on the breast. The flutelike songs of the thrushes in the woods, especially at eventide, are exquisitely beautiful. Its feet are much like the robin's, sometimes walking and sometimes hopping (A), Plate 164.

AMPHIBIAN AND REPTILE

TRACKS

13

Long before the tracks of birds or mammals appeared upon the earth, the footprints of amphibious creatures and the later arrivals, the reptiles, were scattered everywhere. From the oozy depths of Paleozoic swamps 300 million years ago these early amphibians first crawled forth upon the land, and then in later ages, scaly reptiles appeared, adding their autobiographic trails to the earlier track signatures of the amphibian first born. Thus, in the fossil files of ancient rock strata are recorded the trail beginnings of our present-day frogs, toads, salamanders, snakes, turtles and lizards, creatures beloved by small boys but viewed with alarm by their mothers.

Just as the tracks of these early creatures were left in Carboniferous and Permian mud flats, so today are found tracks and trails of our contemporary amphibians and reptiles. Many of their trails are seldom seen because the creatures are small, leaving only faint traces. However, to the observant person, signs of their presence may often be found both in dust and mud.

AMPHIBIA

FROGS AND TOADS (SALIENTIA)

Common Toad (*Bufo americanus*). Often, on the wet sands of our beaches and in the moist earth of gardens, the rounded

293

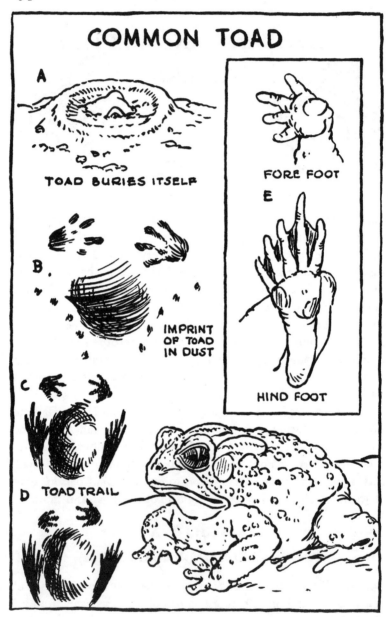

COMMON TOAD

A

TOAD BURIES ITSELF

B.

IMPRINT OF TOAD IN DUST

C

D TOAD TRAIL

FORE FOOT

E

HIND FOOT

Plate 165

mound of an almost buried toad may be discovered, only its protruding eyes and nose showing above the earth (A), Plate 165. The toad buries itself to keep its skin moist, for without moisture it would die.

Sometimes, if the dust or mud is of the right consistency, the imprint of the four feet and the fat little tummy of the toad will register perfectly (B) and (C). Ordinarily the toad takes only short hops of 2 or 3 inches, but larger toads in a hurry may take longer jumps. They keep a surprisingly straight course (D). The forefoot of the toad has only four well developed toes, while the hind foot has five toes joined together by webbing. There are little horny plates on the hind feet which aid it in its digging (E), Plate 165. When burying itself, the toad seems to shuffle backward into the soft earth, making the little mounds pictured in (A).

Spadefoot Toad (*Scaphiopus holbrooki*). While all toads are excellent excavators, the spadefoot toad is the most expert. It has larger horny plates on its hind feet with which it digs into the earth and literally sinks out of sight as if by magic (A), Plate 166. Figure (B) pictures this toad and its specialized hind feet. The eye of this toad is peculiar, resembling that of a cat, hence the name "cat's-eye toad," on occasion (C). The skin, too, is less warty, more like the skin of a frog. While all toads bury themselves in the earth during cold weather, the spadefoot toad remains underground all year except for a few rollicking days during the mating season. Figure (D) shows the hopping trail of a spadefoot.

The Olympic broad-jumping records of our human athletes are mere amateurish efforts in contrast to the frog's jumping ability. Any ordinary small frog can easily jump twenty times its length (E), Plate 166, while man's feeble jump, at best, is not more than four times his length (F). Examination of a frog reveals the reason for this extraordinary leaping ability. One

Plate 166

look at the highly developed muscular springs the frog has for legs, and we know whence this power comes.

Leopard Frog (*Rana pipiens*). The leopard frog is a particularly outstanding jumper and is often seen in the grass some distance from water. There are two color phases in this frog, a green and a bronze coloration. It is covered with large spots, hence the name "leopard." Taking long leaps, it is soon lost in the maze of tall grasses (A), Plate 167.

Wood Frog (*Rana sylvatica*). Another land frog with astonishing jumping ability is the wood frog. Its mask and the golden tan tones of its skin make it one of the most beautiful of our frogs. The wood frog has an unusual trick of turning at some time during its leap, so that it faces the intruder when it touches the ground (B), Plate 167. Because of this habit, its course is anything but straight. In fact, its jumps will take it in every direction of the compass, and it is so bewildering that it is difficult to keep it in sight after a few leaps. The tracks of the leopard and wood frogs are seldom seen unless the frogs accidentally land in the dust or in mud of the right consistency to make a good print.

Spring Peeper (*Hyla crucifer*). Birdlike peeping heard in the spring or fall is often made by a small tree frog commonly known as the "Spring peeper." Having adhesive toes (A), Plate 168, it spends much of its life on the bark and twigs of trees, but in the spring it does its courting in pools and ponds. It is then that you may accidentally find the tiny imprint of its track on the shore mud (B). Although not much larger than your thumbnail, the peeper is a good Scotchman, for it wears a St. Andrew's cross upon its back (C).

Bullfrog (*Rana catesbeiana*). The bullfrog is the largest of our North American frogs, and its cellolike tones are common sounds in the swamps and marshes. The bullfrog's legs have long been a table delicacy, since they are large and muscular, providing a

LEOPARD AND WOOD FROGS

LEOPARD FROG

WOOD FROG

TURNS AERIAL SOMERSAULTS

B

A

WOOD FROG'S ERRATIC TRAIL

STRAIGHT TRAIL

Plate 167

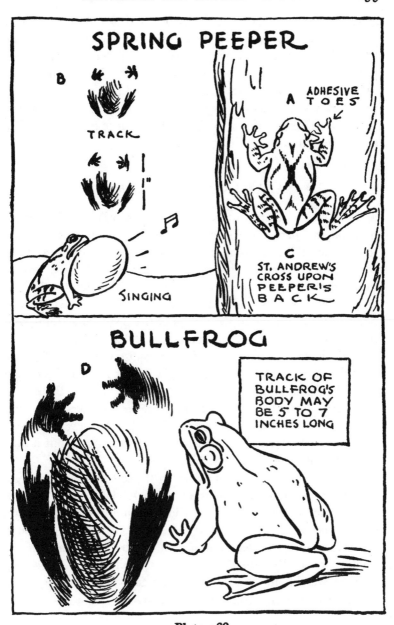

Plate 168

generous amount of meat. In color, it is a dusky olive-green with irregular dark blotches upon its smooth skin. Spending most of its life in the water or upon water vegetation, it is only by accident that its track may be found on the shore mud. Like most amphibians, the bullfrog has four toes on the forefeet and five on the hind which are fully webbed. The track of the bullfrog's body its the largest of our toads and frogs, since it sometimes has a body length of from 6 to 9 inches (D), Plate 168.

SALAMANDERS (CAUDATA)

Spotted Newt (*Triturus viridescens viridescens*). Unlike that of most salamanders, the skin of the spotted newt seems dry to the touch when this newt is on land, yet it needs moisture just as the rest of its relatives do. Salamanders all have smooth skins, usually moist, some even slimy. Some lay their eggs on land, others in water where they spend their babyhood. The spotted newt is hatched from the egg in the waters of the ponds or streams, and it has gills during this amphibious stage. Later it becomes terrestrial, however, and stays ashore in moist woodlands for two or three years. At that stage it is bright orange in color with small vermilion spots outlined in black (A), Plate 169. At the end of its sojourn on land, it changes its color to an olive-green, and its tail looks somewhat like a tadpole's (B). However, the vermilion spots remain. It then goes back to water again but it does not regain its gills of infancy.

Its tracks are seldom seen except in the soft mud as it emerges or returns to the water. The drawing (C), Plate 169, was made from a photograph by William Wild, a naturalist of East Aurora, N. Y., who came upon the newt as it was making its way through the soft mud. It is very reminiscent of the fossil trails of the ancient world. Perhaps the mud was too soft and the newt too light in weight, for the details of the four-toed front feet and five-toed hind were lost, or never registered.

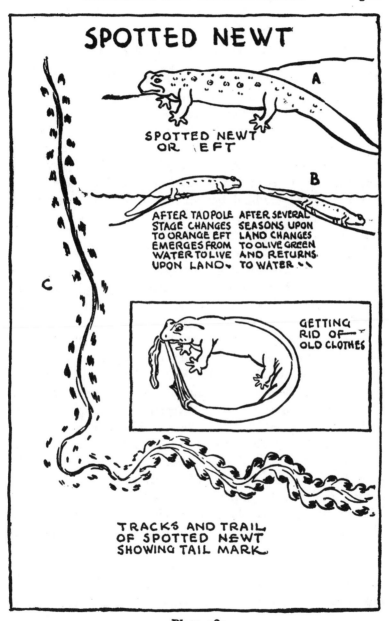

SPOTTED NEWT

A

SPOTTED NEWT
OR EFT

B

AFTER TADPOLE   AFTER SEVERAL
STAGE CHANGES   SEASONS UPON
TO ORANGE EFT   LAND CHANGES
EMERGES FROM   TO OLIVE GREEN
WATER TO LIVE   AND RETURNS.
UPON LAND.   TO WATER

C

GETTING
RID OF
OLD CLOTHES

TRACKS AND TRAIL
OF SPOTTED NEWT
SHOWING TAIL MARK.

Plate 169

REPTILIA

ALLIGATORS (CROCODILIA)

Alligator (*Alligator mississippiensis*). The alligator, found in swamps, streams and lakes of southern United States, looks like a leftover from a prehistoric world. It has enormous jaws armed with fierce teeth and sometimes may grow from 15 to 18 feet in length. It has a long powerful tail and short legs. The toes of the feet are widely spread and are joined together by webbing, which aids in water and mud travel. The forefoot has five toes and so, too, does the hind, but the fifth toe on the posterior foot is small and hardly discernible. The toes are equipped with well developed claws (A) and (B), Plate 170.

The alligator trail is readily identified by the imprints of the clawed feet and the groove of the dragging tail between (C). The trails often found leading from the swamps and sloughs in various directions are narrow, deeply rutted, winding paths, similar to cattle trails in damp pasture lands.

The trails usually lead to the "hole" in which the alligator lives. The hole is often a small, deep, water-filled depression surrounded by a dense growth of vegetation (D), Plate 170. In fact, the location of the hole is often plainly visible because of the more vivid green and greater growth of vegetation surrounding it, due perhaps to dung deposits of the alligator. The holes may be made or deepened by the alligator digging out the earth and roots with its feet and mouth and then sweeping it to one side with its powerful tail. Under the bank of this water-filled hole, the alligator also digs its den, a burrow or chamber 10 to 15 feet deep. The chamber may not be entirely filled with water. Here the alligator retires during the cold months from October through March.

If a female lives in this place, her nest may be found on the bank not far away. The nest is easily seen, for it is a mass of brown rotting vegetation which stands out against the green of

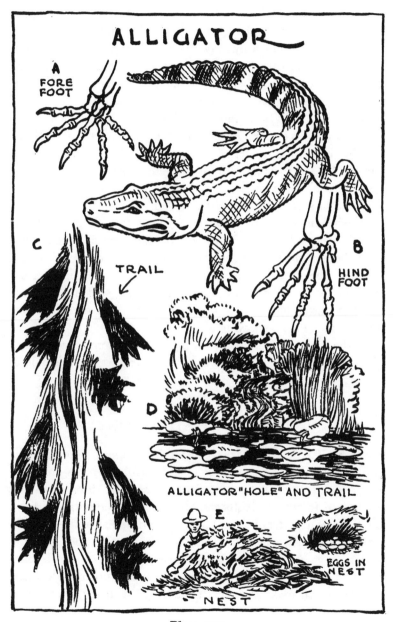

ALLIGATOR

A
FORE
FOOT

C

TRAIL

B
HIND
FOOT

D

ALLIGATOR "HOLE" AND TRAIL

E

NEST

EGGS IN
NEST

Plate 170

surrounding vegetation (E), Plate 170. The female alligator bites and tears masses of vegetation and piles it into conical heaps, often mashing it down by crawling over it with her heavy body. As the vegetation rots it becomes even more compact. After this mass has decayed sufficiently, the female scrapes a hole into the moist top and lays her eggs there, covering them with more rotted vegetation. The eggs are no doubt incubated by the heat of the sun and the decomposition of the vegetation of the nest. If the weather is too dry, the female alligator will often water it several times a day with secretions from her body, since the eggs absorb a great deal of moisture.

Alligator scent trails are often made by this creature at mating time when it gives off musk from glands located in the lower jaw. It gives off a quantity of sweetsmelling musk which scents both the air and the surface of the water and lingers for several hours in the vicinity. The female often gives off a musk from glands located in the cloaca during the rutting season. The musk is a brownish yellow, waxy mass which seems to ooze from the glands. There is no spraying of it.

In the dark, alligator eyes glow brilliant red from reflected light if it is an old bull, and greenish or bluish yellow in the female or young.

TURTLES (TESTUDINATA)

Snapping Turtle (*Chelydra serpentina serpentina*). The snapping turtle is a vicious and most aggressive member of this group. It has evidently long been a resident in the East, for its remains have been found as Pleistocene fossils tens of thousands of years old. Today it prefers ponds, lakes, streams and swamps—usually slow or sluggish water. It has a roughly serrated shell and tail and a large vicious head with hooked jaws. The rough back of this turtle is often covered with algae and other underwater growth which make a perfect camouflage with the slimy rocks.

SNAPPING TURTLE

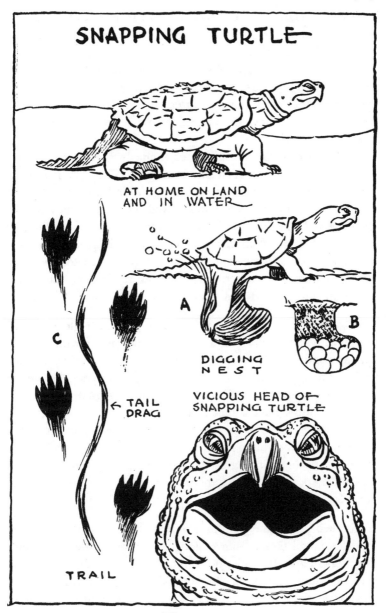

AT HOME ON LAND
AND IN WATER

A

C

DIGGING
NEST

B

← TAIL
DRAG

VICIOUS HEAD OF
SNAPPING TURTLE

TRAIL

Plate 171

It has an extremely long neck and can strike with its powerful jaws and inflict a bad wound. Once it secures a hold, it hangs on with bulldog tenacity.

The nest is dug in fairly open areas where the sun can incubate the eggs. The hind legs are used in excavating, and the eggs are deposited and covered over with earth. The drawings (A) and (B), Plate 171, show the operation and a cross section of the completed nest.

The trail is an undulating track made by the long tail, with alternate footprints on each side of it (C), Plate 171. The snapping turtle seems to be more at home on land than the average run of turtles, for its shell is raised well off the ground and, because of the smaller size of the plastron, or undershell, the legs have a greater freedom of movement. While its gait seems awkward, it is not slow on land. It can often be seen too, walking on the bottom underwater. The snapping turtle often hibernates in groups in the mud and sometimes even in muskrat holes.

Painted Turtle (*Chrysemys bellii*). The painted turtle is a small turtle with light yellow and red markings underneath. It frequents ponds and lakes where aquatic vegetation grows abundantly, and it is found sunning in groups upon logs or other debris just above water level. During the mating season, it is often found on land some distance from the water.

The nest is bottle-shaped and dug by the female in much the same way as the snapping turtle's. The trail is less undulating than that of the snapping turtle's (A), Plate 172, and the rather straight mark of the tail is flanked on each side by the alternating tracks of the feet.

Loggerhead Turtle (*Caretta caretta*). The loggerhead, a sea turtle, is found in abundance along the shores of the Gulf States and north along the Atlantic to North Carolina. Its Pleistocene remains found in Florida also show that it established residence there tens of thousands of years ago. It is a large turtle sometimes

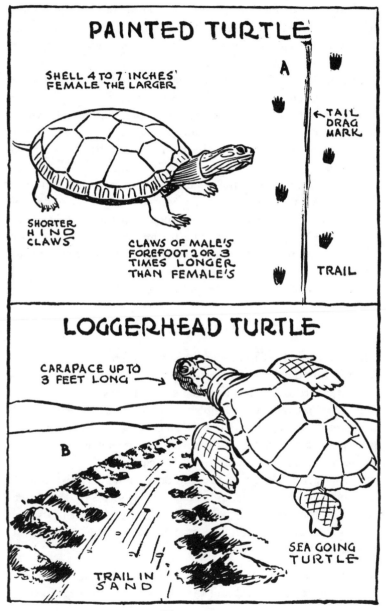

PAINTED TURTLE

SHELL 4 TO 7 INCHES
FEMALE THE LARGER

A

←TAIL
DRAG
MARK

SHORTER
HIND
CLAWS

CLAWS OF MALE'S
FOREFOOT 2 OR 3
TIMES LONGER
THAN FEMALE'S

TRAIL

LOGGERHEAD TURTLE

CARAPACE UP TO
3 FEET LONG →

B

SEA GOING
TURTLE

TRAIL IN
SAND

Plate 172

weighing 450 pounds, and there are records of even larger ones being taken in the past. The tail of the male turtle is longer than that of the female. Being a sea turtle, it has limbs which are flipper-shaped, and each has two claws.

The tracks of the female are often found on southern beaches, and the trail shown in the sketch was made in South Carolina. The trails often lead to and from the nests. The double row of flipper prints are dug into the sand as the turtle drags itself over the surface. There seems to be no mark left by the tail (B), Plate 172.

The nest is dug above the tide mark in the sand and is crescent shaped, excavated by the two hind flippers. In the center a hole is dug into which the eggs are dropped. They are then covered, the sand being packed from time to time about the eggs. After the hole and crescent trench is nearly covered, the turtle throws sand over it in all directions to conceal it. Although the tracks lead to and from the nest, the eggs are often difficult to find.

LIZARDS (SAURIA)

Collared Lizard (*Crotaphytus collaris collaris*). The collared lizard is found in rocky desert areas throughout the Southwest to central Oregon. It has a large head, a rather thin neck and a long, rounded tail. The double black collar easily identifies it. It is sometimes a straw-yellow or green tinged with orange, the underparts being cream with an orange or yellow throat. It is pugnacious and will attempt to bite its captor.

The surprising habit of running on its hind legs like a small dinosaur also identifies it (A), Plate 173. It seems to dance away quickly in this way when pursued, lifting the forepart of its body entirely off the ground. The tracks (B) look like little fairy imprints in the fine desert dust.

Gila Monster (*Heloderma suspectum*). The gila (Heel-ah) monster or beaded lizard and the Mexican beaded lizard are the

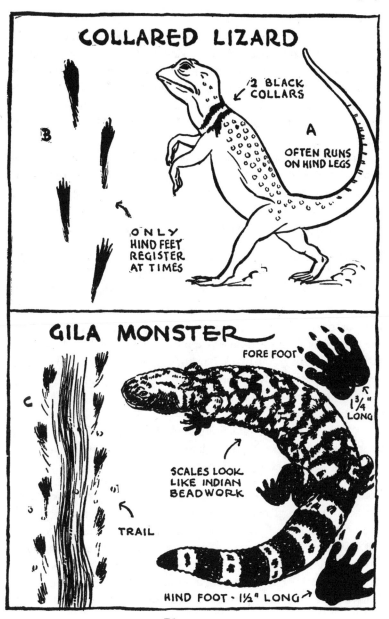

COLLARED LIZARD

2 BLACK COLLARS

B

A

OFTEN RUNS ON HIND LEGS

ONLY HIND FEET REGISTER AT TIMES

GILA MONSTER

FORE FOOT

C

1¾" LONG

SCALES LOOK LIKE INDIAN BEADWORK

TRAIL

HIND FOOT · 1½" LONG

Plate 173

only poisonous lizards in the New World. The poison is a nerve poison, but there is some controversy as to its deadliness. In the sunlight this lizard becomes very vicious, but when in the shade for some time, it is docile. Although it seems slow, it can strike with remarkable quickness. Its large thick tail serves as a storage pantry for food. In times of good hunting the tail becomes quite swollen. The black and salmon Indian beadlike scales easily identify this creature.

Its somewhat undulating trail is made by the dragging of its heavy body and tail (C), Plate 173. Like many of the desert dwellers it stays out of the rays of the sun, coming out at dusk or at night. Although a desert lizard, it likes water and often digs a hole on a sunny stream bank as a nest for its eggs.

Northern Earless Sand Lizard (*Holbrookia maculata maculata*). This sand lizard is found from southern South Dakota to northeastern New Mexico in dry, sandy areas as its name would indicate. This lizard has no ear opening. With a ground color of light gray or gray-brown on its back, it has a broad gray line along the backbone with dark brown spots on each side. On the underside are two diagonal black bars at the sides of the belly. Long before sunset, it beds in some burrow or hole, seldom choosing sleeping quarters under rocks. Often found in pairs, it has a well developed curiosity.

Its trail shows alternate footprints. The mark of the tail may or may not be present (A), Plate 174. When running it seems to lift its tail off the ground and there is no imprint of it.

Coachella Uma (*Uma inornata*). This fringe-footed sand lizard has a prominent growth of scale fringes on the toes of both the fore and hind feet. Found in California in the Coachella Valley, it is a striking lizard having a network of black lines surrounding little round spots of light gray or white arranged in rows. The spots, especially on the back, have small black spots in the centers. It lives in sections where there is loose sand. Sometimes it buries

NORTHERN EARLESS SAND LIZARD

A

TRAIL

WHEN RUNNING
TAIL MARK
IS ABSENT

LIZARDS CAN
GROW NEW TAILS

FRINGE FOOTED SAND LIZARD

B

FORE

C

NOTE FRINGED
TOES

TRAIL MAY OR
MAY NOT SHOW
FORE FEET
WHEN SPEEDING

HIND

FRINGED TOES AID
IN "SWIMMING"
THROUGH SAND

Plate 174

itself in the loose sand, only the head being exposed. It may leave behind a small blind burrow with an oval, depressed mouth. When frightened it runs over the edge of a sand hill and runs and slides down the side to the shelter of some hole or vegetation.

The toe fringes (B), Plate 174, are used not so much as sand snowshoes as for "sand swimming." In burrowing into the loose sand the head and forepart of the body make sidewise movements, while the hind legs do the propelling. The forelegs are held close to the body at that time. The toe fringes are spread when the feet push backward and are folded back along the toes when the feet are brought forward. In the tracks (C), Plate 174, on the surface, the forefeet seldom register except when walking. This lizard runs on its toes, the palm or sole prints being absent in the track.

SNAKES (SERPENTES)

Snake Locomotion. Lacking legs or appendages, snakes are wholly dependent upon the movement of their bodies and the cross scales of the undersides of their bodies to move from place to place. One of the commonest modes of progression is an undulating movement of the body from side to side (A), Plate 175. The entire length of the snake is flat upon the ground, while it moves its body in a rhythmic, wavy movement alternating from side to side. All of the body follows the track of the head end. If this undulating crawl is done in sand, a series of slightly curved hillocks of sand is left at the base of each curve. These hillocks are used by the snake to push its body forward. Without some brace such as this, the snake could not make progress.

Sometimes, however, in dusty roads a trail is found that looks as if a heavy hawser has been pulled through the dust in a straight line. These are rattlesnake trails and are made by a snake that is unhurried. The underside of snakes is composed of narrow scales that are placed crosswise on the body. The ends of these cross scales are fastened to the ends of the ribs. The belly muscles are arranged to move these plates so that a wavelike motion results, beginning at the neck and moving backward. One wavelike movement follows another, the free end of the cross scales pushing against the earth. This results in a sort of caterpillar movement which pushes the snake's body forward in a straight line (B), Plate 175.

Another type of movement, used especially by desert snakes to overcome the difficulty of travel in loose sand, is a looping of the body in such a way that it seems to be flowing along sidewise. This is called "sidewinding" (C), Plate 175.

Lesser Cerastes Viper (*Cerastes vipera*). In the hot sands of South Africa sometimes are seen rhythmic scrolls in the sand as if some one had been drawing beautiful curvilinear designs. These are the curls and scrolls of cerastes, the sand viper. It is well to walk with care to avoid treading upon this sand painting, for directly beneath this intriguing sand design is the living viper itself. Being cold blooded, this reptile cannot stand extremes of either heat or cold, and to protect itself from the deadly rays of the desert sun, it digs straight down into the sand. With wavelike movements of its body, the sand viper literally sinks into the sand, heaping the grains over its body in graceful design, for it is really a sand painting of the snake itself that warns the traveler : "Don't tread on me !" (D), Plate 175.

Diamond-Back Rattlesnake (*Crotalus adamanteus*). Another poisonous snake, in fact, the largest poisonous snake in the United States and the most dangerous, is the diamond-back rattlesnake. It is a stout, heavy reptile sometimes 8½ feet in length, and is found in the southeastern coastal regions. An olive or gray-green snake, the characteristic diamond-shaped markings of dark greenish black cover its back. Each diamond has a narrow edging of yellow. Like all members of the rattlesnake family, it has the characteristic rattle on the tail (A), Plate 176, and the two

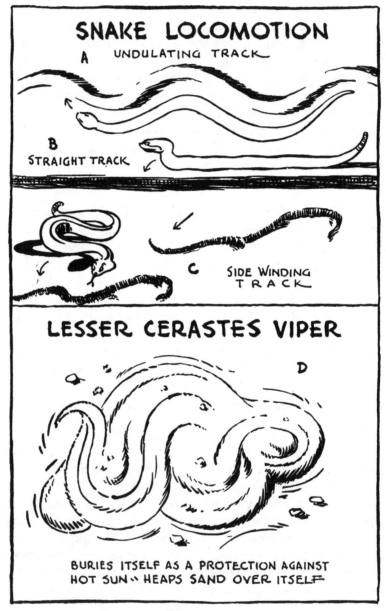

SNAKE LOCOMOTION

A UNDULATING TRACK

B STRAIGHT TRACK

C SIDE WINDING TRACK

LESSER CERASTES VIPER

D

BURIES ITSELF AS A PROTECTION AGAINST HOT SUN ~ HEAPS SAND OVER ITSELF

Plate 175

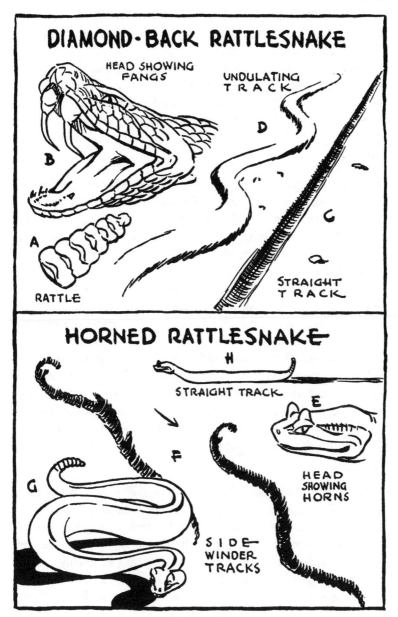

DIAMOND-BACK RATTLESNAKE

HEAD SHOWING
FANGS

UNDULATING
TRACK

D

B

A

RATTLE

C

STRAIGHT
TRACK

HORNED RATTLESNAKE

H

STRAIGHT TRACK

E

F

G

HEAD
SHOWING
HORNS

SIDE-
WINDER
TRACKS

Plate 176

hypodermiclike fangs in the upper jaw, the fangs being sometimes an inch long (B). While many snakes lay eggs, the young
of the rattlesnakes are born alive.

Rattlesnakes, when not in a hurry, make a perfectly straight
trail, a single furrow as direct as an arrow (C), Plate 176. This
trail is often seen in the dust and sand of roads in the South.
However, when disturbed and in a hurry, they resort to the
undulating wavy movement and make the common snake
trail (D).

Horned Rattlesnake (*Crotalus cerastes*). The horned rattlesnake
or sidewinder is a small rattlesnake found in the desert areas of
the Southwest. The characteristic hornlike projections above the
eyes make it easily recognizable (E), Plate 176. It is a sandy
brown color with dull rounded blotches on the back.

The sidewinder makes a very distinctive "S" shaped track
when disturbed (F). It seems to roll at an angle, throwing a
loop of its body forward, then making a sidewise jump. It keeps
all but two parts of its body off the ground, and each of these
parts registers in the sand. In other words, the sidewinder seems
to make a "spiral of its body of less than two turns and then rolls
it." The drawing (G) shows the position of the body when sidewinding; one loop follows another with alternate symmetry. The
vipers of the African deserts have developed similar locomotion.
Ordinarily, when unhurried, it glides forward in a straight line
with its head slightly raised like other rattlesnakes (H), Plate
176.

Puff Adder (*Heterodon contortrix*). The puff adder or hog-nosed
snake is the outstanding actor of the snake family. Sometimes it
frightens its enemies by coiling its body, flattening and expanding
the head and neck, and giving off loud hisses (A), Plate 177.
Should this ferocious play-acting fail to scare its enemy, it then
tries an act at playing dead (B). Its death writhings and con-
tortions are most realistic and convincing. Then with a final con-

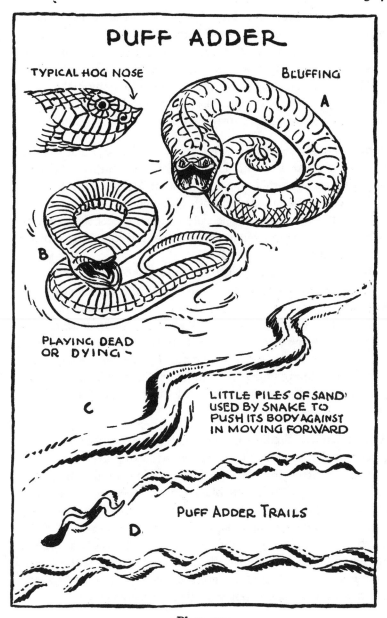

PUFF ADDER

TYPICAL HOG NOSE

BLUFFING

A

B

PLAYING DEAD OR DYING—

C

LITTLE PILES OF SAND USED BY SNAKE TO PUSH ITS BODY AGAINST IN MOVING FORWARD

PUFF ADDER TRAILS

D

Plate 177

vulsive quiver, it becomes limp, lying upon its back. However, if placed upon its belly, it immediately rolls over upon its back again. After a time, if it thinks its enemy has gone, it slowly raises its head and crawls away. In traveling, the puff adder employs the undulating movement common to many snakes (C). In the sand, the track shows the characteristic hillocks used by the snake in pushing itself forward (D).

Banded Burrowing Snake (*Chilomeniscus cinctus*). The banded burrowing snake is found in the deserts of southern Arizona, southeastern California and northwestern Mexico. In color, it is a deep orange or orange-red with black bands (A), Plate 178. The head of this snake is especially adapted for its characteristic burrowing in the sand, having a wedge-shaped snout that projects well beyond the lower jaw (B).

It spends a great deal of its time beneath the surface, its wedge-head easily pushing through the soft sand, the body quickly disappearing beneath the surface. When moving close to the surface, it produces waves in the sand as it would in water. It can really swim beneath the surface, sometimes traveling quite rapidly. The drawing (C) shows the tracks made by the burrowing snake actually swimming under the sand. The characteristic tracks are more often seen than the snake itself, since it is nocturnal in its habits.

Ringed Ground Snake (*Sonora occipitalis*). Another nocturnal desert snake that swims in the sands is the ringed ground snake or sharp-snouted ground snake. Its coloration is milk-white, pale yellow or pink with narrow black stripes. There is also a black crescent at the back of the head. Like the burrowing snake, this species also has a wedge-shaped head that enables it to swim under as well as over the sand (D), Plate 178. Its tracks are the best evidence of its presence. Being nocturnal, it is seldom seen. The undulating tracks of the ground snake (E) show the snake as a small reptile usually not more than 12 inches long.

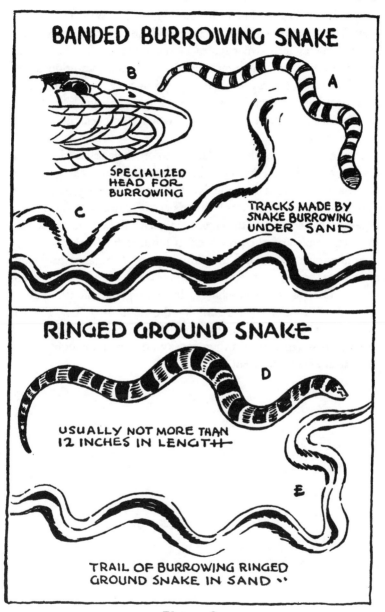

BANDED BURROWING SNAKE

B

A

SPECIALIZED
HEAD FOR
BURROWING

C

TRACKS MADE BY
SNAKE BURROWING
UNDER SAND

RINGED GROUND SNAKE

D

USUALLY NOT MORE THAN
12 INCHES IN LENGTH

E

TRAIL OF BURROWING RINGED
GROUND SNAKE IN SAND

Plate 178

Snake Scent Trails. Snakes follow food trails. With the help of their feelers or forked tongues they evidently convey microscopic scent particles into two cavities in the front of the roof of the mouth, known as "Jacobson's organ." This is an addition to the smelling area of the nose. The nose, however, is an important sensory organ. A small ground snake with its eyes blindfolded readily followed the trail of another which had been rubbed on a smooth surface.

In mating, snakes depend largely upon their sense of smell in detecting the female by odor. It is thought that scent glands of the snake are particularly active during the mating season and that the reptiles follow each other's scent trails. The Jacobson's organ, in connection with the tongue, seems to be used to identify the scent trails and the prey itself in hunting for food.

Snakes give off various individual odors. The garter and common water snake both emit most obnoxious secretions when annoyed. The fox snake discharges from its glands at the base of the tail a secretion that resembles the odor of a fox. The rat snakes, too, are noted for their scent, and the king snake and the queen snake emit a strong musky odor when caught. Probably all snakes make scent trails.

CRUSTACEAN, MOLLUSK
AND INSECT TRACKS
14

Every living thing leaves some evidence of its presence. If we have eyes keen enough to see, we can often find tracks, trails and other signs of myriad creatures both large and small. Often we fail to realize that such creatures as crustaceans, mollusks and insects leave as well defined trails as do the larger animals. Often we pass up trails and signs, even though we see them, because we are unacquainted with the trail makers themselves. Some, of course, are very minute, such as the tracks made by insects. Others are most peculiar because of the strange construction of the legs or bodies, such as the crustaceans and mollusks.

CRUSTACEANS (CRUSTACEA)

Crayfish (*Cambarus bartoni*). The crayfish is perhaps one of the commonest members of the crustacean family and is found in fresh water, especially muddy pools or streams. As we wander along some shallow creek, we often see something dart under a flat rock amid a smoke screen of mud. This is a common sign of the crayfish who uses its fan-shaped tail as a catapult to shoot backward into a muddy hiding place. The disturbed, muddy bottom successfully screens its further movements (A), Plate 179.

321

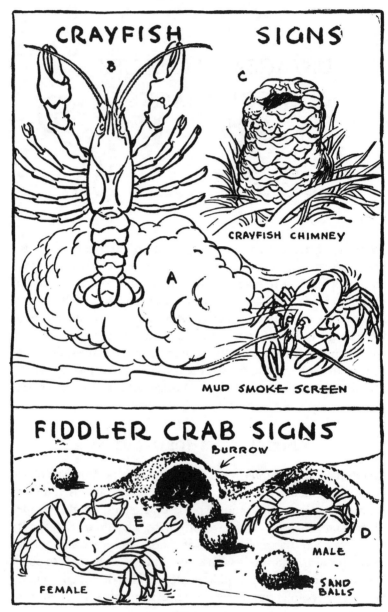

CRAYFISH   SIGNS

CRAYFISH CHIMNEY

MUD SMOKE SCREEN

FIDDLER CRAB SIGNS

BURROW

MALE

SAND BALLS

FEMALE

Plate 179

The crayfish looks somewhat like a lobster in miniature and has two prominent front claws with which it grasps its prey. It has stalked eyes and two pairs of antennae, and with these it explores its surroundings. The body is jointed, and a number of swim-merets are on the underside, used in swimming (B), Plate 179. The crayfish often burrows into the earth near the water, and a "chimney" of mud pellets is sometimes placed around the opening of the burrow (C), Plate 179.

Fiddler Crab (*Uca minax*). Most crabs spend their entire lives under water, but the fiddler crab prefers to live on land. It occurs in great numbers on the Atlantic coast and burrows in the area between the tide marks. The male fiddler crab has a great claw held in the front like a large bass viol (D), Plate 179. The female's claws, however, are small and equal in size (E). The ovenlike entrances to their burrows and the balls of excavated sand are common signs of the fiddler crab's presence on the beach (F), Plate 179.

Ghost Crab (*Ocypoda arenaria*). The ghost crab is well named, for it is a white apparition with eight flashing legs. Its sidling, zigzag gait is as swift as a hare's. Walking on tip-toe, it makes a most curious trail about 4 inches in width. The sharp pointed feet dig into the sand like knife points, and each footprint looks as if a pocket-knife blade had been thrust into the sand and then pulled backward (A), Plate 180. Sometimes, when hiding, only its black stalked eyes are visible above the sand (B).

XIPHOSURIDAE

King Crab or Horseshoe Crab (*Limulus polyphemus*). The horseshoe crab is not a crustacean but an arachnid, a relative of the scorpions, mites and spiders. It can trace its unbroken descent from the trilobites of 300 million years ago. This is the only species found on our coast and is a resident of the ocean from

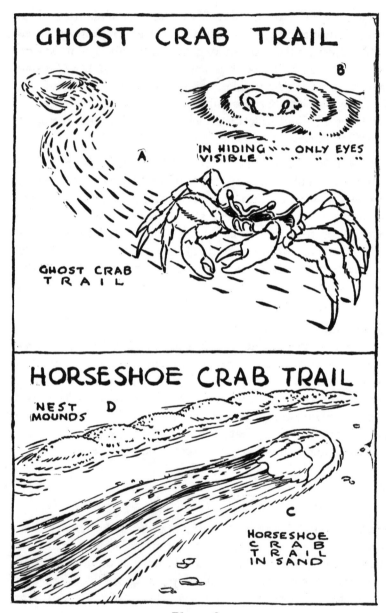

Plate 180

Maine to Florida. While it is an underwater creature, it can spend some time ashore when it deposits its numerous eggs in shallow holes in the tide area. On shore it makes a ribbonlike trail about a foot wide as it drags itself through the wet sand, its many-footed tracks breaking into the smooth band of the trail (C), Plate 180. The series of nesting mounds made by the female when depositing its eggs in the sand is shown in (D).

MOLLUSKS (MOLLUSCA)

Garden Snail (*Polygyra thyroides*). The common snail's silvery trail is often seen on the walks of our gardens. Unlike our roadways and pavements, that of the snail is sticky and slimy and is discharged from a slime duct just below its mouth (A), Plate 181. Over this broad band of mucous the snail slides forward upon its one and only foot.

If you look closely at the trail after the snail has gone by, you will see a number of wavy ridges left by the undulating movements of the lone foot. The slime trail not only smooths the way for the snail, but it also enables him to stick to the trail whether he is right side up or upside down. Snails sometimes make other trails, narrow pathways through green algae often found growing on trees. They eat their way, making blazed trails through the minute green growth (B), Plate 181.

Common Slug (*Philomicus caroliniensis*). Slugs are relatives to the snails but do not carry the portable shell cottage. Like snails, however, slugs make slime trails wherever they go. Sometimes they go a step farther and use the mucous secretion to make ropes with which they can descend or ascend from vegetation to ground.

When they descend they go head first. They grip the mucous with the sides of the foot (C), Plate 181. They can also climb up again, but the ascent is slower and more laborious. In climbing, the head is uppermost. They seem to bring the head and

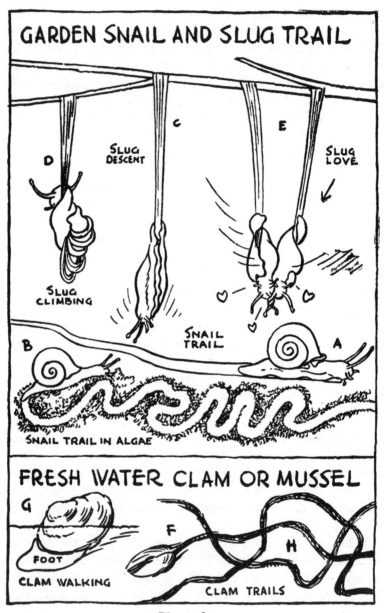

Plate 181

tail together, gathering the accumulated mucous thread near the tail (D). This rope trick is sometimes practiced by water snails, who make mucous threads to aid in climbing to the surface.

In spite of the fact that slugs have combined male and female characteristics, they sometimes fall in love with another slug, and then a strange courtship takes place. Like human lovers they sometimes like to "spoon" in a swing. This they make, each lowering itself on its thread of mucous and then cuddling in loving embrace, while they swing back and forth in mid-air. But unlike human lovers, they swing with their heads toward the earth like two trapeze performers (E), Plate 181.

Fresh Water Clam or Mussel (*Sphaerium transversum*). The yellow, black and slough sand shell mussels are the most active trail makers of this family, but the rabbit's foot (*Quadrula cylindrica*), especially the younger, are also active.

The mussel frequently moves along the bottom, leaving a distinct trail behind it (F), Plate 181. It moves about by thrusting its muscular foot forward into the bottom, expanding the outer end and then contracting special muscles so as to draw the shell and body toward the foot (G). At times the bottoms of fresh water ponds are crossed and criss-crossed with the trails of traveling mollusks (H), Plate 181. This form of travel, however, does not take them too far. Their greatest traveling is done in infancy, when they become parasites and attach themselves to fish. After a time, they leave their finny hosts and go on their own for the rest of their lives.

INSECTS (HEXAPODA)

The name "Hexapoda" is made up from two Greek words, "hex" meaning six and "pous" foot. In other words, insects are creatures having six legs. Many have wings as well.

Insect tracks and trails are delicate, often only visible in soft mud or dust. In fact, a good place to study insect tracks is on sand dunes or beaches. There, numerous autobiographies can be discovered in a radius of a few hundred yards, fascinating tiny trails that sometimes remain intact for millions of years.

Insect Scent Trails. Like mammals, many insects have scent which is used to inform other members of the family of their presence. But unlike higher animals, who depend upon their noses, the insects' sense of smell seems to be located in their antennae. Here are located tiny olfactory pits or knobs which seem to give them smell power (A), Plate 182. Some insects seem to have their smelling tuned like a radio, receiving only their own group of odors. Ants, like bees, seem to have distinguishing odors, individuals seemingly recognized by their scent.

Ants blaze trails with scent. As they run along a path, they touch the ground with the tips of their abdomens (B), Plate 182. Scientists have blazed artificial ant trails with a weak solution of formic acid and the ants followed it as readily as the scent trails of their own making.

Other insects have scent trails carried by the air currents. The female Cecropia, Polyphemus and Luna moths have a perfume that is wafted by the breezes as they flit about (C), Plate 182. In a short time, scores of moth gallants will follow the lady's trail. The males of most of our larger moths have larger and more elaborate antennae (the plumelike projections from their heads) than do the females.

The male of the monarch butterfly, on the other hand, has the scent, a small black spot on each lower wing which are scent scales that leave a delicate trail of perfume as the butterfly flits about (D), Plate 182.

The mountain silver-spot butterfly (*Argynnis atlantis*) male gives off a decided odor of sandalwood. Likewise the male pipe-vine swallow-tail gives off a scent.

Butterfly Migration Trails. We usually think of the butterfly as a very fragile creature, yet several kinds travel thousands of miles

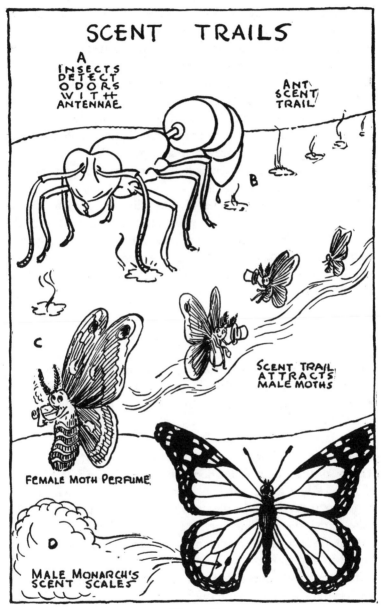

Plate 182

each year, buffeted by the elements. One is the common monarch butterfly. Large numbers gather and often travel together in the autumn, but their flight North in the spring seems to be made individually. Their travel northward is governed largely by the sprouting of the milkweed, upon which their caterpillars feed.

One of the migration mysteries is how the new generation finds its way back to the South in the fall, for none are among the company who flew North in the spring. During September and October great numbers are often seen going South. They have many resting places on the way, and often trees play host to hundreds of resting monarchs.

Some 250 different species of butterflies make such long or short sky-trail flights. One famous traveling butterfly is the painted lady. On occasion, vast hordes of these butterflies get the wanderlust and travel together in one huge company. Certain sulphur butterflies, too, travel in yellow clouds, crossing hundreds of miles of open sea.

NEUROPTERA

Ant Lion (*Myrmeleon imaculatus*). It is the larva or baby stage of this insect that is the fierce predator. The adult is a delicate, gauzy-winged creature, often attracted by bright lights (A), Plate 183.

The larva is usually found in sandy areas and sometimes makes complicated winding trails in the sand or dust. Miss Heather Thorpe of the Junior Education Division of the Buffalo Museum of Science had a pet ant lion larva called "Petey" who kindly made the trails shown in the drawing (B), Plate 183. In making these paths, the ant lion travels backwards. It travels this way until it finds a suitable spot in which to dig its characteristic funnel-shaped pitfalls.

This trap is about 2 or 3 inches across and an inch deep. Burying itself in the middle with only its head showing, it lies in wait

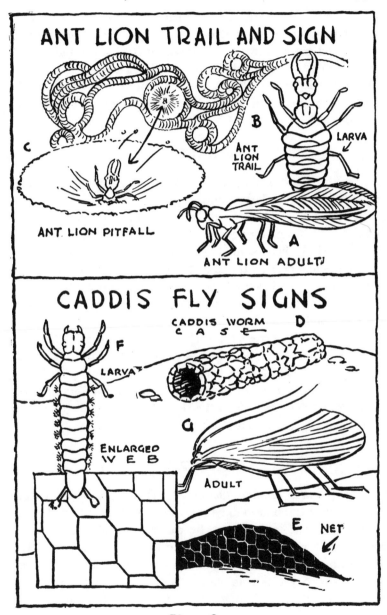

ANT LION TRAIL AND SIGN

C

B
ANT
LION
TRAIL

LARVA

ANT LION PITFALL

A
ANT LION ADULT

CADDIS FLY SIGNS

CADDIS WORM D
CASE

F

LARVA

G

ENLARGED
WEB

ADULT

E NET

Plate 183

for its prey (C), Plate 183. Suddenly an ant will heedlessly approach the rim. When it arrives at the edge, the ant lion begins to hurl sand grains. Although the volley is haphazard, the grains being thrown by the mandibles, soon a tiny avalanche is created around the victim, tumbling it into the waiting jaws of this baby ogre. After it has eaten its fill it flings the remains of its victim from the pit.

TRICHOPTERA

Caddis Fly (*Hydropsyche analis*). While the adult caddis flies are air-minded, the larvae and pupae are aquatic. All of the larvae of this insect seem to be vegetarians except that of *Hydropsyche*. Common signs of the caddis worms' presence are the cylindrical shelters made of various materials, and their amazing fishing nets. In the case of *Hydropsyche*, the hut is made of tiny pebbles and debris firmly fastened together (D), Plate 183. The net is close to the habitation, so attached as to catch anything coming down stream (E).

The larva (F), Plate 183, anchors itself with a silken thread fastened to its dwelling so that, when emerging from its stone cottage, it can pull itself back should the current sweep it along. When ready to change to adulthood, it is said, the pupa leaves its childhood home, swims to the surface, and the winged adult (G), Plate 183, shoots out of the pupa skin and flies away.

ORTHOPTERA

Cricket (*Gryllus assimilis luctuosus*). This large, black patent leather fellow is found in our back yards, chirping fast or slowly, according to the temperature, by rubbing the file on its wing covers together. In fact, some observers say you can ascertain the temperature by the number of cricket chirps per minute. All you have to do to get this animated thermometer to tell you the temperature Fahrenheit is to count its chirps per minute, subtract 40, divide this result by 4 and add 50. Since this cricket is relatively tame, its tracks and trail can be readily obtained in sand or dust. The trail (A), Plate 184, shows where the cricket landed after a jump (B), its legs spread out, and its trail as it leisurely walked away. Its body made a furrow (C) and its legs made tiny indentations in the sand on each side (D).

The Gay Winged Locusts (*Dissosteira carolina*). This track is somewhat similar to that of the cricket, but the footprints are not so deeply indented, and the furrow of the body is entirely absent or shows only slightly in the sand, since the locust's legs are longer, carrying the body free of the ground.

Tree Cricket (*Oecanthus niveus*). The tree cricket is a delicate greenish white musician who belongs to a symphonic orchestra, for its chirpings are in perfect timing with the rest of its fellows. Its egg trail (E), Plate 184, is found upon the twigs of raspberry, currant and apple where it pushes its eggs into the bark.

HOMOPTERA

Cicada (*Tibicina septendecim*). This is the seventeen-year locust. For sixteen years in the North, the young suck at the roots of plants in the earth. In the spring of the seventeenth year the nymph digs to the surface of the ground, making a smooth, firm tunnel (F), Plate 184. The tunnel opening is a little larger than that of an earthworm's. If the ground is moist, it may also construct a wall or "chimney" around the exit hole. The nymph climbs and hangs onto the rough bark of a tree trunk and shortly the nymphal skin cracks and the moist adult crawls out.

The adult life of the cicada is short, lasting only a week or so. However, in that short span, it leaves its egg trails upon the twigs (G), Plate 184. The twig is split and the eggs inserted. The "hot weather" song of the cicada is a common sound in summer. The "singer" is the male who makes the music by vibrating mem-

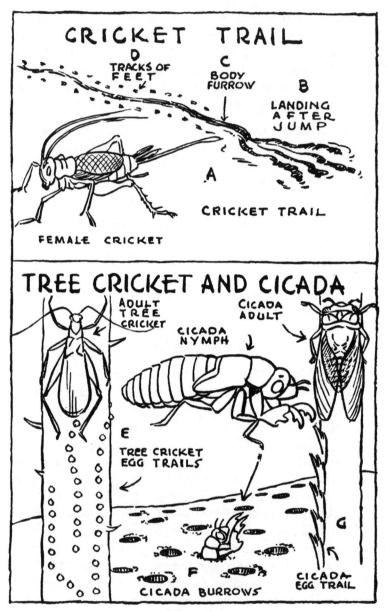

CRICKET TRAIL

D
TRACKS OF FEET

C
BODY FURROW

B
LANDING AFTER JUMP

A

CRICKET TRAIL

FEMALE CRICKET

TREE CRICKET AND CICADA

ADULT TREE CRICKET

CICADA ADULT

CICADA NYMPH

E
TREE CRICKET EGG TRAILS

F
CICADA BURROWS

G
CICADA EGG TRAIL

Plate 184

branes stretched across small openings on each side of its abdomen.

Frog Hopper or Spittle Insect (*Lepyronia quadrangularis*). The young of the frog hoppers make the bubble blazes on grass stems that are commonly found in fields and meadows (A), Plate 185. On close examination, it looks as if a tiny elf had been blowing minute bubbles. And so he is, for if you brush away the froth, you will discover a little green fellow busily blowing bubbles in which to house himself from the weather and his neighbors. He sucks the sap from the grass stems and then expels a sticky fluid from his body, blowing it into a froth about him.

Buffalo Tree Hopper (*Ceresa bubalus*). This strange green brownie is rightly named, for it can hop in a most vigorous fashion when disturbed. The tree hoppers vary in shape and are amusing to look at. This particular hopper is called the buffalo tree hopper because of its bisonlike hump (B), Plate 185. It is injurious to young orchard trees since it scars the bark in laying its eggs. At each place it makes two slits in the bark. The characteristic egg scars are shown in (C).

LEPIDOPTERA

Signs of a creature's presence need not be confined to its footprints or trails. Often, evidences of its work or the home or shelter it creates tell the woods-wise who is about in the area. The cocoons of our large silkworm moths tell of their having been in the neighborhood as readily as if they had written their names.

Cecropia Moth (*Samia cecropia*). The large cocoon of this moth is fastened along one entire side to the twig (D), Plate 185. This attachment to the twig is characteristic of the cecropia cocoon.

Cynthia Moth (*Philosamia cynthia*). This is an Asiatic moth that was brought to America in the sixties. The cocoon is spun

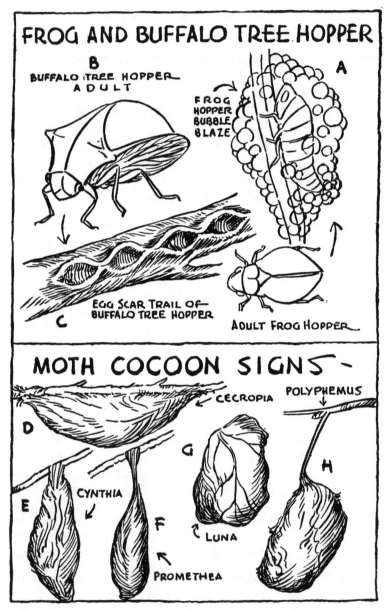

Plate 185

upon a leaf which has been fastened to the twig with silk by the caterpillar. The drawing (E), Plate 185, shows the characteristic cynthia cocoon.

Promethea Moth (*Callosamia promethea*). The cocoon of this moth resembles the cynthia's somewhat, but is darker in color and slimmer. It is less likely to have silken strands over the leaf which forms part of the cocoon (F), Plate 185.

Luna Moth (*Actias luna*). The cocoon of this beautiful jade green moth is very thin and looks like a small bundle wrapped in dried brown leaves upon the ground (G), Plate 185.

Polyphemus Moth (*Telea polyphemus*). This cocoon is rotund in shape, like the Luna's, but is more solidly made (H), Plate 185. Although the cocoon may fall to the ground, this is not always the case. It is made of a long, easily unwound silken thread, which would be valuable commercially.

Tent Caterpillar (*Malacosoma americana*). The characteristic silken community tent of these caterpillars is a common sign, especially upon wild cherry trees (A), Plate 186, but its trail blazing is perhaps more interesting. When the caterpillars leave the tent on their various expeditions, they blaze their trails with silken threads spun as they wander along (B), so that they can find their way home.

Bag Worms (*Thyridopteryx ephemeraeformis*). In the fall, small silken bags are seen in which small bits of leaves and evergreen needles are interwoven. These are the portable tents of the bag worms (C), Plate 186, and are carried about all summer by the caterpillar. In the Southern States the bag worm (*Oiketicus abboti*) makes a portable log cabin instead of a camouflaged tent (D), Plate 186. The caterpillar cuts the tiny twig logs with its jaws as neatly as if it had a miniature ax. Instead of fastening the logs with pegs or spikes, it binds them with silk.

The adult of the bag worm is a moth, but only the male has

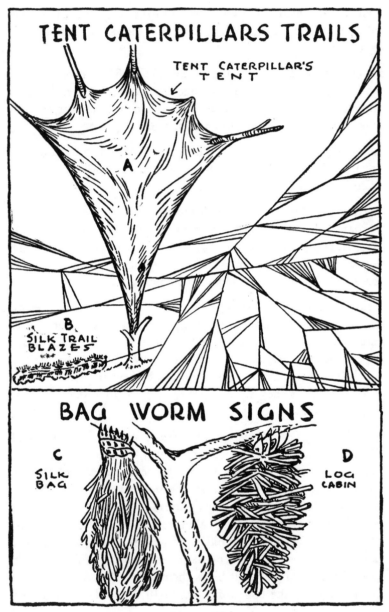

TENT CATERPILLARS TRAILS

TENT CATERPILLAR'S TENT

A

B
SILK TRAIL BLAZES

BAG WORM SIGNS

C
SILK BAG

D
LOG CABIN

Plate 186

wings. The female never leaves the bag, and is a footless, wingless creature, dying after the eggs are laid.

LEAF MINERS

Leaf Miners are the larvae of moths, beetles, flies and saw flies, and although the adults differ entirely, the larvae are very similar. They are among the smallest of plant-eating animals and find both food and shelter within the space between the upper and lower epidermis of a leaf.

The leaf miner trails are plainly in view for all to see. Almost any oak, hornbeam, apple, jewelweed, white snakeroot or goldenrod and many other plants will show the various trails of leaf miners.

For instance, on the leaves of jewelweed, the mining trails of a small fly (*Agromyza borealis*) are found starting as a tiny larva, the trail growing larger and larger as the larva increases in size (A), Plate 187. On the broad-leaved plantain, you may find the characteristic and involved trail of a small beetle larva (*Dibolia borealis*) (B), Plate 187.

Winding miner trails may also be found upon the water shield leaves made by the larvae of a greenish midge (*Chironomus braseniae*) (C), Plate 187. Apples sometimes have winding mine trails on the skin of the fruit. This is the trail of *Marmora pomonella* (D), Plate 187. On the leaves of lamb's quarters, the serpentine trails of *Chrysopora larvae* are often present. (E), Plate 187, shows two examples of this leaf miner's trails.

COLEOPTERA

Leaf Roller Beetle (*Attelabus rhois*). Signs of this beetle may often be found on hazel and alder bushes, neat little rolled-up leaf packets, some fresh and green, others dried and brown (A), Plate 188. Their purpose is to house the eggs of this beetle. In

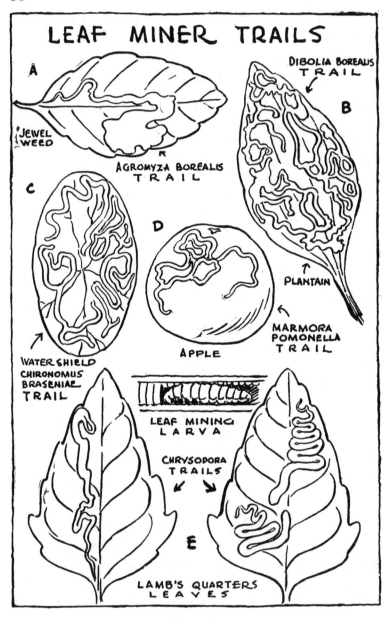

Plate 187

Plate 188

making the leaf rolls, the female bites through the leaf to the mid-vein close to the stem and nearly through the midrib. The sun soon wilts the leaf, making it easier to roll. The beetle then folds it along the midrib and rolls it with its tiny legs, enclosing an egg before it is entirely rolled (B). When the job is completed, a loosely cut edge is turned to overlap the last fold. This holds the roll together. When dry it soon falls to the ground (C).

Shot Hole Borer (*Scolytus rugulosus*). Certain parts of the bark of trees often appear to have been penetrated by a load of bird shot. These are the signs left by the shot hole borer (D), Plate 188, an adult which has emerged from each little round hole.

After its "coming-out party," the young female burrows and gnaws a tunnel between the bark and the sapwood (E). Along the sides of this excavation it makes small pockets into which an egg is placed. The larvae, emerging from the egg, dig trails of their own at right angles to the parent's burrow and then pupate at the end of their tunnel (F). On reaching adulthood, they bore straight out, each one making a tiny "shot" hole (D).

Flat-headed Borer (*Chrysobothris femorata*). Strange Maorilike designs may sometimes be found on the branches of various trees such as the apple, pear, peach, plum, cherry, maple, hickory, beech, chestnut and numerous others. This is the work of the larvae of the flat-headed borer beetle. The young larvae create these shallow engravings in the sapwood, making most interesting designs (A), Plate 189. Later they burrow into the heartwood. Here they spend the winter and emerge as adult beetles in the spring (B).

HYMENOPTERA

Common Ant (*Cremastogaster lineolata*). In the crotches of dog-woods and other shrubs, a strange plastering or daubing is some-times found. These are the "stables" made by ants to protect

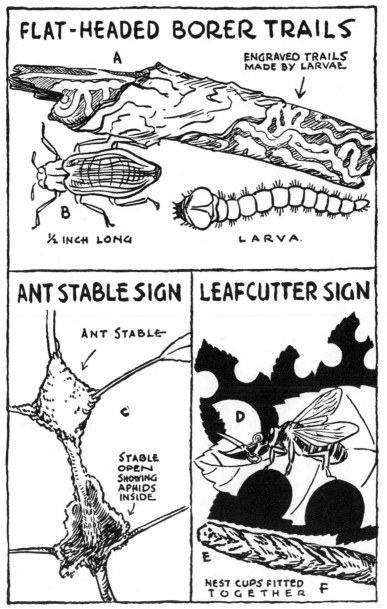

Plate 189

their "cows" (aphids). Built of a mortar compounded of mud and some vegetable material known to them, the stables advertise the ants' dairy farms wherever they are found (C), Plate 189.

Leaf-Cutter Bee (*Megachile brevis*). The leaf-cutter bee announces its presence by the circular cuttings on leaves and flowers. It is the female who makes these characteristic cuttings with its scissorlike jaws. Standing on the leaf, the bee clips from the edge, pivoting as it cuts, thus making the curves so typical of the leaf cutter (D), Plate 189.

The circular pieces are fitted and glued into thimble-shaped cells (E), and these are placed into holes in branches or in the ground. Sometimes a number of these cups are arranged one ahead of the other in the tunnel (F). In each cell, the leaf cutter bee leaves a bit of food made from pollen and honey, together with a tiny egg. The cells are then sealed. Both the cells and the circular leaf cuttings are positive signs of the leaf cutter bee, excellent clues to its presence.

Potter Wasp (*Eumenes fraternus*). The tiny mud pots sometimes found on plants or twigs look as if they had been fashioned by Indian Elves (A), Plate 190. They are the nurseries of the potter wasp, for each contains the egg or grub of this wasp, together with paralyzed larvae of harmful moths or beetles upon which the wasp baby feeds. Thus, while the wasp may not be seen, its tiny mud pots reveal its presence in the neighborhood.

Mud Dauber Wasp (*Sceliphron cementarium*). You may have some uninvited guests in your house whom, perhaps, you have never met. You may, however, find evidences of their visit on the rafters of your attic, clay modelings that make you wonder whence they came.

These are the mud nurseries of the mud dauber. The female collects tiny mud pellets at some near-by puddle (B), Plate 190, and flies with them to the place where it is building its cradles. Here the wasp pats them into place, smoothing each pellet into

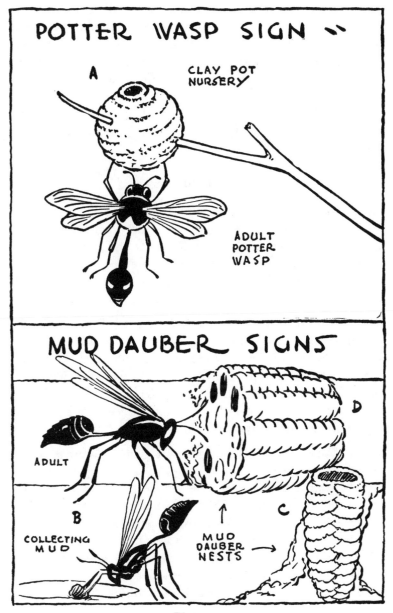

Plate 190

a thin band that reaches halfway around the cell. The clay pellet is placed first on one side and then on the other, gradually forming a strange herringbone receptacle (C). A number of these mud cells are placed side by side or again in a mass, the whole being eventually covered with a coating of mud. As each cell is finished, the mother wasp fills it with paralyzed spiders which it has stung, and then lays an egg upon them, eventually sealing the opening with mud (D). These "adobes" are sure clues of the mud dauber.

GALL SIGNS

Gall Markers. Often, on plants and trees, on their stems and on their leaves, we find strange distortions that serve notice of the comings and goings of certain tiny insects and other creatures. Some are moths; some are flies; others are saw flies, mites and aphids. The galls are really the distorted growth of plant cells influenced by some chemical stimulus given off by the larvae.

Goldenrod Galls. There are several different galls found on the goldenrod, but two of the best known are the spherical type made by the larvae of a fly (*Eurosta solidaginis*) (A), Plate 191, and the elongated spindle-shaped one by the caterpillar of a moth (*Gnorimoschema gallae solidaginis*), (B). If a small hole has been made in the gall (C), the inmate has left. If no such opening is found, the larvae is still at home.

Willow Cone Gall. This strange silver conelike growth on the tips of willow twigs is the gall sign of a little gnat's nursery (*Rhabdophaga strobiloides*). The female gnat lays its egg in a willow bud, and as soon as the grub hatches and starts to eat, the growth of the bud is changed into a strange, abnormal cone, each leaf in the bud turning to a scale (D), Plate 191. Within this gall the grub feeds and rests all winter, emerging in the spring, a tiny gnat whose seldom-seen presence in the neighborhood will be announced by the growth of other willow cone galls.

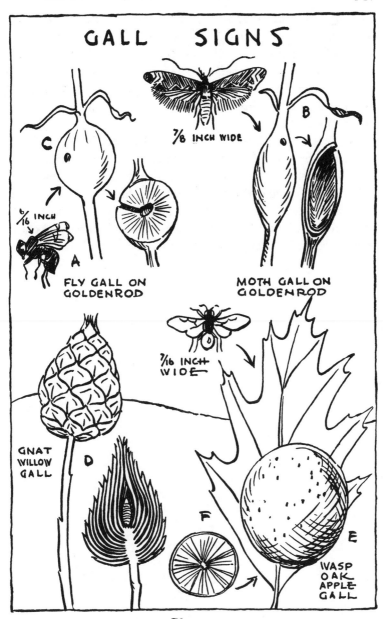

GALL SIGNS

⅞ INCH WIDE

C

⁶⁄₁₆ INCH

A

FLY GALL ON
GOLDENROD

B

MOTH GALL ON
GOLDENROD

⁷⁄₁₆ INCH
WIDE

GNAT
WILLOW
GALL

D

F

E

WASP
OAK
APPLE
GALL

Plate 191

Oak Apple Galls. While "bear trees" tell of the presence of bears and "beaver mud pies" of beavers, the light green or tan oak apples sometimes found growing on oak leaves inform you that a tiny wasp (*Amphibolips inanis*) has visited these oak leaves and has left its mark (E), Plate 191. The oak apples are as sure a sign of this insect's visit as if it had left a 12-inch track in the mud.

The female wasp lays an egg upon an oak leaf. When the larva hatches, it begins to eat its way into one of the leaf veins. As it feeds, it gives off some chemical which changes the growth of the leaf tissues, forming the thin-skinned globular gall filled with radiating fibers, in the center of which the grub develops (F), Plate 191. At long last, it changes into an adult wasp about a quarter of an inch long, and leaves its oak apple home forever.

REPRODUCING
TRACKS
15

For millions of years Nature has preserved the tracks of many of her earth dwellers in the fossil pages of rock strata. After the creature made the tracks, silt or dust covered them over, and with each successive layer buried them deeper, until the pressure and weight of the numerous layers gradually changed those buried deeply into stone.

Mud Casts. We, too, can take a hint from Nature in reproducing tracks. If a track impression is found in dried mud, a reproduction of mud can be made in the following way (A), Plate 192. Take some clay and mix it with water into a creamy "slip" (B). Build a wall of clay around the track about 1½ inches high (C) and (D). Then pour a thin coating of bacon grease or oil into the track, followed by the clay slip. Let it dry and become hard, after which the dried mud cast can be removed (E).

Tracking Album. An interesting record of your wild neighbors can be secured every day by making a "Tracking Album." Select a flat open space in some quiet place near your home or camp. Place a low flat stone or board in the middle (F), Plate 192, and sprinkle a covering of fine ashes, dust or sand in a broad area around the center stone (G). Place seeds, grains or

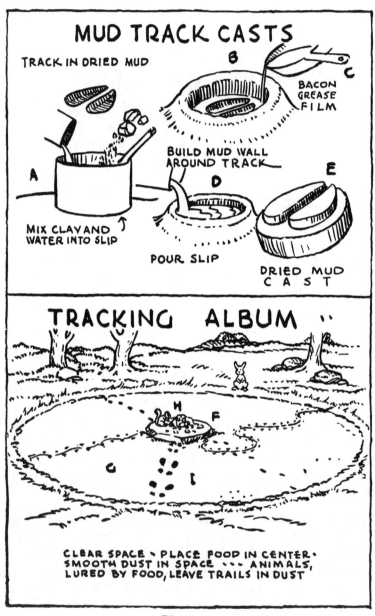

Plate 192

other food upon the rock (H) and carefully rake the ashes or dust smooth so that any creatures walking over it will leave a clear, well defined trail (I). In this way a variety of tracks may be secured from which drawings or photographs may be made.

Track Silhouettes. The same materials are needed as are used in making other types of silouettes—that is, mainly a number of cards about 6 by 9 inches, some black paper, scissors and some paste. Sketch the track upon the black paper (A), Plate 193, and then cut it out (B) and paste it upon a white card (C). In this way, an interesting collection of tracks may be made, their success depending upon the care and skill displayed.

Plaster Casts of Tracks. Plaster casts of tracks in mud or wet sand may be made with little equipment. All the materials needed are strips of cardboard about 12 to 15 inches long, paper clips, two tin cans (one for water and one for mixing), dental plaster and a mixing stick that can be picked up anywhere.

Find a clear track and remove all sticks or straws (D), Plate 193. Clip a cardboard strip into a circle large enough to surround the track and press it into the earth around the track (E), thus making a wall around it.

Then pour enough water into a can to cover the track by more than an inch (F), Plate 193, and gently sift the plaster into the water, making a mixture as thick as warm molasses or pancake batter (G). Thump the container from time to time to make the air bubbles rise (H) and then pour the mixture into the track (I). Allow the plaster to run into the deeper parts, never pour directly into it. If the cast is large in area, place a few cross sticks in the wet plaster to reinforce it (J). Allow the plaster to harden, and then tear away the cardboard strip. Wash mud or earth from the cast (K), which can be colored later if desired by dipping into some pigment.

Candle Wax Track Casts. Track casts may also be made in this way by pouring melted candle wax or paraffin into the track

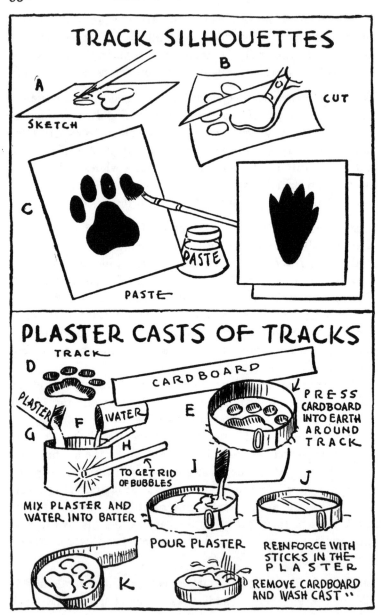

Plate 193

CANDLE WAX TRACK CASTS

A — MELT WAX

CARDBOARD WALL

B — POUR WAX

C — WASH CAST

PLASTER TRACK CASTS IN SNOW

D — SPRAY WATER ON TRACK

ICE COATING FORMS ON TRACK — E

F — MIX SNOW WITH PLASTER AND WATER TO LOWER TEMPERATURE OF MIXTURE

PLASTER — WATER — SNOW

G — PLACE CARDBOARD WALL AROUND TRACK AND POUR PLASTER INTO TRACK

Plate 194

instead of plaster. Candles or paraffin may be melted in a tin can over a small fire (A), Plate 194, and then poured into the track (B). When the wax hardens, wash away the adhering earth or mud (C). Care should be taken not to expose the wax casts to heat, since they may be distorted or even destroyed by the hot sun or fire.

Latex Track Casts. Liquid latex used in making molds, etc., may be substituted for plaster or wax and poured into the track. This will make a faithful cast which cannot be broken. Enlargements can be made from the original cast by merely making a number of molds and casts in succession; each will be a little larger than the former one. In this way enlarged reproductions can be made of a small track.

Plaster Track Casts in Snow. If the snow is not too powdery, spray the track with a fine spray of water from an atomizer or spray gun. Do this carefully so as not to melt the snow (D), Plate 194. After spraying several times, a coating of ice will form inside the track (E). When the ice coating is thick enough, make the pancake batter mixture of plaster, adding snow (F) with the water and plaster to reduce the temperature to that of the surroundings. Pour it into the track and allow the plaster to harden (G). Remove the cast from the track.

Plaster Track Cast in Dust. While the cast of a track in the dust will not compare with one made in mud or wet sand, nevertheless, a fair reproduction can be made. Carefully sprinkle the track from a distance above it with fine table salt from a salt shaker (A), Plate 195. Then mix the plaster (B) and pour it to one side of the track, letting it flow into the track just before it begins to set (C). It is a good thing to remember that salt added to plaster of paris hastens the hardening, while vinegar delays it.

Tracks in Garden Stepping Stones. Plaster or paraffin casts of tracks may be pressed into soft concrete stepping stones. When

PLASTER TRACK CAST IN DUST

A

MIX PLASTER
POUR AT ONE
SIDE JUST BEFORE
PLASTER SETS

PLASTER B

SPRINKLE
SALT
INTO
TRACK
IN DUST

C

SALT *HASTENS*
SETTING OF PLASTER
VINEGAR *DELAYS IT*

FINISHED
CAST

TRACKS IN GARDEN STEPPING STONES

PATH

D

CEMENT
3" THICK

SMALL → STONES

LARGE → STONES

15"

G

E

F

WAX CAST PRESSED
INTO WET CEMENT

Plate 195

making the stepping stones, irregular holes about 15 inches deep
may be dug (D), Plate 195, where the pathway is wanted. A
layer of large stones is first placed in each hole, and then a layer
of gravel. The concrete mixture is then filled in to the surface
of the ground. While the concrete is still wet, the casts are pressed
into it (E), leaving an impression as if the animal had walked
over it (F). If a number of track casts are used, an interesting
and permanent display will result (G).

Track Ceramic Decorations. Impressions of small tracks may be
made in the wet clay of various ceramic objects which will become permanent when the object is fired. The casts of tracks for
such use, of course, cannot be too deeply impressed into the pottery. Tracks of birds and other small creatures are most suitable
(A), Plate 196. Track pendants, earings, buttons and other pottery objects can also be made (B), Plate 196. In fact, impressions of the track casts can be made in uniform circles or squares
of clay and then fired to make them more permanent if a collection is being made.

Tracking Blocks. Taking a suggestion from the Indians of Mexico
mentioned on page 13, Chapter 2, who make tracking sandals
for their children, we can make tracking blocks for trailing and
tracking games.

Get some blocks of soft wood about 2 inches thick and in proportion to the size of the track desired (A), Plate 197. Trace the
outline of the track of the animal upon it (B) and then with a
pocket knife or gouge, cut around the track (C) so that it will
leave a lifelike impression of the animal's foot when pressed into
soft earth (D). Two holes are bored into the block (E), Plate
197, and cord is threaded through the holes (F). This is used to
bind the blocks to the soles of the feet (G). When the wearer
walks across soft earth, he will make a track as shown in (H).

Tracking Irons. Ernest Thompson Seton in his "Book of Wood-
craft" shows how tracking irons are made from metal strips,

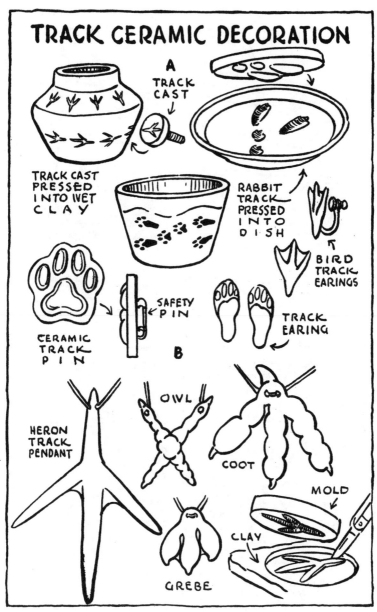

TRACK CERAMIC DECORATION

A
TRACK CAST

TRACK CAST PRESSED INTO WET CLAY

RABBIT TRACK PRESSED INTO DISH

BIRD TRACK EARINGS

CERAMIC TRACK PIN

SAFETY PIN

TRACK EARING

B

HERON TRACK PENDANT

OWL

COOT

MOLD

CLAY

GREBE

Plate 196

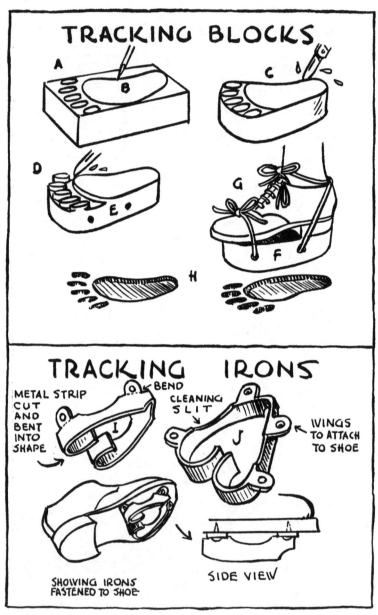

TRACKING BLOCKS

A

B

C

D

E

F

G

H

TRACKING IRONS

METAL STRIP CUT AND BENT INTO SHAPE

BEND

CLEANING SLIT

WINGS TO ATTACH TO SHOE

I

J

SHOWING IRONS FASTENED TO SHOE

SIDE VIEW

Plate 197

(I), Plate 197, with wings attached by which they are nailed or screwed to the soles of shoes. His tracking irons resemble those pictured in (J). They are made of metal strips easily bent and shaped to resemble the track desired. Anyone who can follow the tracks of these irons can follow the tracks of a living animal. Thus it is good training for tracking and trailing to make the trails and follow them.

TRACKING GAMES

16

Tracking games are fun and at the same time develop the senses that must be used in real tracking and trailing. Good eyesight and a well developed sense of observation are fundamental requisites of a good tracker, and these qualities are often greatly improved by play.

Trail Makers. There are a number of methods of making trails. Of course, snow, soft ground or sand offer excellent opportunities for trail making (A), Plate 198. However, when the ground is not favorable, some sort of "trail maker" is necessary. On city sidewalks, chalk marks are sufficient (B). In the woods, fields and meadows, some sort of blaze or broken and disturbed vegetation (C) may be used to mark a trail. (See page 22, Chapter 2.) At times "trail markers" of various kinds are used.

Kernels of corn or other grain may be dropped from time to time to mark a trail (D), Plate 198. Again, small pieces of colored cardboard may be stuck into the bark of trees or bright colored chalk marks may be made upon tree trunks at eye level (E). One type of trail marker is made from a section of a small log, studded with small spikes. A staple is driven into one end to

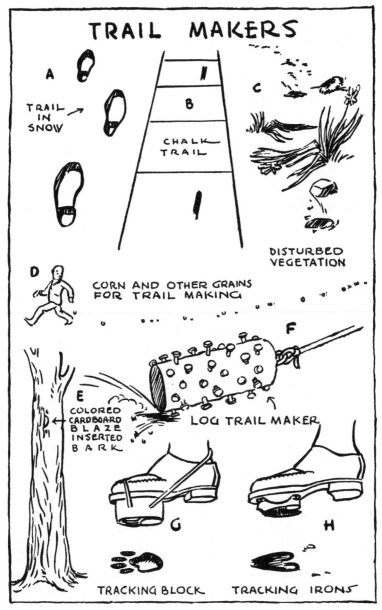

Plate 198

which a rope is attached (F). As a runner drags this along the ground, the log leaps, scrapes and hops about in an amazing manner, making a very erratic trail.

If the ground is soft, "tracking blocks" as shown in Chapter 15, page 358, can be made and bound to the feet. When the wearer walks, he leaves the lifelike tracks of the animal whose footprints have been carved into the blocks (G), Plate 198.

Another type of trail marker is the "tracking irons" illustrated on page 358 of the preceding chapter. These fastened to the sole of the shoe, (H), Plate 198, and will cut into the ground more deeply than the wood block tracks.

Tracking Games. A well known common trailing game is "Hare and Hounds." This has been played on the city streets for generations.

The "hare" has a piece of chalk and is given a three-minute start. As he runs, he makes a chalk mark from time to time on the sidewalks (A), Plate 199. The "hounds" follow the chalk marks and each "hound" must place his mark across the "hare's" blazes as he speeds away (B). The chase may cover a dozen blocks. If the hare succeeds in getting back to his starting point without being caught by the hounds, he is the winner. Hounds may bag the hare by catching up with him and touching him. Each hound should carry a distinctive color in chalk so that a check can be made as to his faithfulness in marking each blaze he passed.

City Tracking. This is a game where each contestant makes a record of the different tracks that he can find in a city block. These tracks may be made by any living creature—bird, mammal, insect, man, woman or child, etc. The one finding the greatest number of tracks is the winner.

City Trail Blazes. In this game, a group will hike a mile or two along city streets to see how many modern city blazes each one can find. A blaze may be a street car or bus stop, stop lights,

Plate 199

safety zones, traffic markers, police and fire boxes, direction point-
ers, one-way street markers, etc. The person who collects the
greatest number is the winner. (See illustration on Plate 199.) A
blaze is a simple sign conveying information without words. City
blazes are the descendants of those used by the wilderness savages,
and in some instances the mark is the very same used in an earlier
time.

Modern Road Blazes. On your next auto ride into the country,
see how many road signs your party can identify. This is a good
way to learn the modern road signs used in your "auto driver's
manual." For instance, identify and know the meaning of broken
lines, solid lines, double solid lines, three-lane road, stop sign,
stop-and-go, slow, railroad crossings, "S" curves, crossroad, side
road, the meaning of diamond, octagonal, round and square road
signs. Use your state driver's manual for information. (See Plate
200.)

Early Trail Blazers. Your neighborhood offers an interesting
evening's discussion. Have each member of the group try to track
down early trail blazers of your community and give the stories
of their exploration. Also try to find the early trails and travel
routes which some of your modern streets and roads may follow.
Your historical museum and libraries can be of help.

Treasure Hunts. In the park, by using various blazes with stones,
long grass, twigs and tree blazes, a hunt can be made quite excit-
ing, especially if there is a worth-while treasure at the end of
the trail. See Chapter 2, page 22, for trail blazing suggestions.
Instead of chopping blazes into the bark of trees, stick a small,
round piece of white cardboard into the bark. The first one to
unravel the trail will find the treasure. Any number can partici-
pate. The trail is laid out in advance and all begin at a starting
point and follow the trail blazes. The various types of blazes
should be scattered along the trail so that the individual's observation will be well taxed. (See Plate 200.)

TRACKING GAMES
MODERN ROAD BLAZES

- - - - - - - - - - - -
BROKEN LINE
DEFINES TRAFFIC LANE.
CROSS ONLY WHEN SAFE.

————————
SOLID LINE
TO BE CROSSED ONLY
WHEN NO OTHER CAR
IS IN SIGHT

- - - - - - - - - - - -
————————
SOLID AND BROKEN LINE
DO NOT CROSS SOLID LINE
BROKEN LINE MAY BE CROSSED
ONLY WHEN SAFE " "

————————
————————
DOUBLE SOLID LINE
NO CROSSING ALLOWED
FROM EITHER SIDE

OCTAGONAL
SIGN MEANS
STOP

ROUND
SIGN
R.R. CROSSING

DIAMOND   SIGNS
REDUCE   SPEED
WINDING   CURVE
ROAD

SQUARE SIGNS
CAUTION
SIDE   CROSS
ROAD   ROAD

STOP   PROCEED   GO
CAUTIOUSLY

TREASURE HUNT

VARIOUS BLAZES POINT DIRECTION

Plate 200

Trail Stories in Snow. Take a winter hike to a near-by woods or park and have your hikers follow an individual animal's trail, making notes and rough sketches of all that the trail tells. At the end of the hike, gather together in the evening, perhaps around the fireplace and have each one relate his findings. The person who has the most detailed and interesting story is the winner.

Indian War Trail. Each participant in this game makes an Indian scalp of a round piece of leather or felt about 3½ inches in diameter, with long strands of horsehair, string, yarn, thread or raffia threaded through the middle. A loop for fastening the scalp is attached to the leather or felt. This is the individual's scalp (A), Plate 201, which he may lose if he is not careful on the war trail.

The "hostiles" make a fairly obvious trail by disturbing vegetation, turning over stones, bending twigs, uprooting small bits of moss, making footprints in the soft earth or mud, etc. (B). Each clue is worth a certain per cent of the whole. Players keep records of each clue they find in sequence, so that it can be compared with the master record. The one who spots the greatest number of clues and discovers the "hostiles" is the winner and collects their scalps. If the trackers fail to discover the hostiles, they lose their scalps to the enemy.

Snow-Trailing the Bear. The "bear" wears a hood with round ears sewed to it, (A), Plate 202, carries a 3-foot club made of burlap stuffed with straw (B), and has a balloon fastened securely to his back (C). The hunters wear caps (D), and carry large handkerchiefs with a knot tied at one end (E).

The bear is given a 10-minute start and the hunters follow his trail in the snow. The first one to come upon the bear tries to kill him by breaking the balloon with the knotted handkerchief. The bear, in turn, can put the hunter out of the game by knocking the hunter's cap off with the straw club. The fight and hunt continue until the bear is bagged or all the hunters are "killed."

Plate 201

Plate 202

In making the trail, the bear can use all the ingenuity and strategy at his command, making use of side stepping, backtracking, ambush, etc.

Seton's Trailing Game. Ernest Thompson Seton used to play a trailing game in camp. One of the campers, who was chosen as the deer, wore a pair of tracking irons and was given one hundred beans, thirty slices of potato and a 10-minute start. He made his trail as crooked as he pleased, dropping a bean every 3 or 4 yards, a slice of potato every 20 yards. After a 10-minute run, the deer hid in the brush. The trackers following him picked up the beans and potato slices. Each bean counts one point and each slice of potato two. The one who discovers the deer, scores ten.

Track Quizz. Make a number of black and white drawings of common tracks on cardboard squares large enough to be seen at a distance. Arrange the players in two files facing each other, and run the program like a spelling bee. Start at the head of the lines. If the person in the first line fails to recognize the track, the one on the opposite side is given a chance to identify it. The person who fails to identify a track is dropped from the group. The game is played until only one player remains.

Trail Detectives. A party is divided into two groups. The first group, given scissors and white paper, select the tracks of several animals and cut the footprints out of paper, enough to make trails that will tell of some incident. This group will then proceed to lay out the various trails upon the floor, and the other group will try to identify the animal's footprints and interpret the story. If the group succeeds, they are given an opportunity to cut the tracks and lay the paper trails.

The drawing Plate 202, shows a typical trail story. A mother bear (E) and her cub (F) were walking along through the woods (G), when the mother bear saw a man (H) coming along in the opposite direction (I). She stopped (J) and hurried

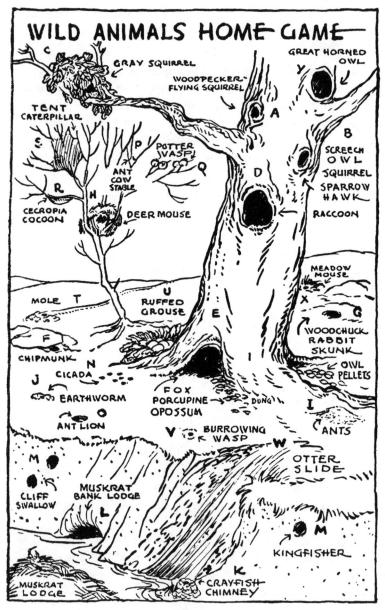

Plate 203

her cub up a near-by tree (K). She then rose on her hind legs and made for the man (L), who turned and ran away (M). Incidents such as this can be easily told in tracks.

Wild Animals Home Game. Have a group scatter through a small woodland. Each has a notebook and pencil and each one keeps a record of all the signs of animal homes that he finds in the area. The one who spots the greatest number is the winner. The drawing Plate 203, shows a number of such apartments that might be seen. (A) shows a typical woodpecker hole, (B) a screech owl's, squirrel's or sparrow hawk's pent house, (C) a leaf tree house of the gray squirrel, (D) a raccoon tree home, (E) the hollow tree den of porcupine, gray fox or possum, (F) a chipmunk's burrow, (G) a woodchuck, rabbit or skunk hole, (H) a remodeled deer mouse nest, (I) an ant nest, (J) earthworm's burrow, (K) a crayfish chimney home, (L) a muskrat bank burrow and a muskrat cattail house in the swamp, (M) a kingfisher's or cliff swallow's burrow, (N) cicada tunnels, (O) ant lion's funnel, (P) ant cow's stable, (Q) potter wasp nest, (R) cecropia cocoon, (S) tent caterpillar nest, (T) mole burrow, (U) ruffed grouse nest, (V) burrowing wasp, (W) otter slide, (X) meadow mouse, (Y) great horned owl. These are just a few home signs of the wild folks. There are, of course, many more that tell of an animal's presence as surely as do his tracks. Hunting for these sharpens your eyes and develops your observation, so important in tracking and trailing.

Tracking Suggestions:

Keep a track notebook
See how many autobiographies you can find after each snow-
    fall
Make tracking irons of metal
Make a trail marker
Make plaster casts
Look for old remains of Indian trail blazing

Try to find trail routes of early explorers in your neighborhood

Make various types of track casts

Make a dust autograph album

If you know of a tracking game, please send it to the writer
and you will be given credit for it.

And with the ending of this chapter, we bring "Tracks and
Trailcraft" to a close. However, this is by no means the end of
the trail for this vast subject of tracking. There are thousands of
tracks, trails and signs that have not been included within the
pages of this book, thousands of footprints, and other evidences
of the presence of men and animals upon this earth. There is
still a vast network of trails for those interested to follow, trails
into the unknown, unexplored, unrecorded. However, if you follow these unknown trails, be sure to blaze the way as you go,
for it is the sign of a good woodsman to be able to find his way
back.

INDEX

373